THE BAKE SHOP

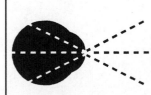

This Large Print Book carries the
Seal of Approval of N.A.V.H.

AN AMISH MARKETPLACE NOVEL

THE BAKE SHOP

AMY CLIPSTON

THORNDIKE PRESS
A part of Gale, a Cengage Company

LIBRARY OF CONGRESS CIP DATA ON FILE.
CATALOGUING IN PUBLICATION FOR THIS BOOK
IS AVAILABLE FROM THE LIBRARY OF CONGRESS

ISBN-13: 978-1-4328-7174-1 (hardcover alk. paper)

Published in 2019 by arrangement with The Zondervan Corporation, a subsidiary of HarperCollins Christian Publishing, Inc.

Printed in Mexico
1 2 3 4 5 6 7 23 22 21 20 19

With love and appreciation for
Eric Goebelbecker,
the coolest big brother on the planet

GLOSSARY

ach: oh
aenti: aunt
appeditlich: delicious
Ausbund: Amish hymnal
bedauerlich: sad
boppli: baby
bopplin: babies
brot: bread
bruder: brother
bruderskind: niece/nephew
bruderskinner: nieces/nephews
bu: boy
buwe: boys
daadi: granddad
daed: father
danki: thank you
dat: dad
Dietsch: Pennsylvania Dutch, the Amish
  language (a German dialect)
dochder: daughter
dochdern: daughters

7

Dummle!: Hurry!
Englisher: a non-Amish person
faul: lazy
faulenzer: lazy person
fraa: wife
freind: friend
freinden: friends
froh: happy
gegisch: silly
gern gschehne: you're welcome
grossdaadi: grandfather
grossdochder: granddaughter
grossdochdern: granddaughters
grossmammi: grandmother
gross-sohn: grandson
Gude mariye: Good morning
gut: good
Gut nacht: Good night
haus: house
Hoi!: Get back here!
Ich liebe dich: I love you
kaffi: coffee
kapp: prayer covering or cap
kichli: cookie
kichlin: cookies
kind: child
kinner: children
krank: sick
kuche: cake
kuchen: cakes

kumm: come
liewe: love, a term of endearment
maed: young women, girls
maedel: young woman
mamm: mom
mammi: grandma
mei: my
Meiding: shunning
mutter: mother
naerfich: nervous
narrisch: crazy
onkel: uncle
Ordnung: the oral tradition of practices required and forbidden in the Amish faith
schee: pretty
schmaert: smart
schtupp: family room
schweschder: sister
schweschdere: sisters
sohn: son
Was iss letz?: What's wrong?
Wie geht's: How do you do? or Good day!
willkumm: welcome
wunderbaar: wonderful
ya: yes
zwillingbopplin: twins

THE AMISH MARKETPLACE SERIES FAMILY TREES

GRANDPARENTS

Erma m. Sylvan Gingerich
|
Lynn m. Freeman Kurtz
Mary m. Lamar Petersheim
Walter m. Rachelle
Harvey m. Darlene

SECOND GENERATION PARENTS AND CHILDREN

Lynn m. Freeman Kurtz
Christiana ⊥ Phoebe

Mary m. Lamar Petersheim
Cornelius (Neil) ⊥ Salina

Darlene m. Harvey Gingerich
Bethany ⊥ Anthony

Rachelle m. Walter Gingerich
|
Leanna m. Marlin Wengerd

Leanna m. Marlin Wengerd (deceased)
|
Chester

Joyce m. Merle Stoltzfus
Jeffrey ⊥ Nicholas

A NOTE TO THE READER

While this novel is set against the real backdrop of Lancaster County, Pennsylvania, the characters are fictional. There is no intended resemblance between the characters in this book and any real members of the Amish and Mennonite communities. As with any work of fiction, I've taken license in some areas of research as a means of creating the necessary circumstances for my characters. My research was thorough; however, it would be impossible to be completely accurate in details and description, since each and every community differs. Therefore, any inaccuracies in the Amish and Mennonite lifestyles portrayed in this book are completely due to fictional license.

PROLOGUE

Christiana Kurtz watched as a car pulled up to her bake stand near the road in front of the large, white farmhouse where she'd been born and raised. The warm early May breeze tickled her nose, and the scent of moist earth and flowers mingled with the sweet aroma of her homemade baked goods.

She quickly straightened the rows of pies, cookies, and cakes on the shelves on either side of her and then pushed the ties from her prayer covering behind her shoulders.

The dark sedan's doors opened, and two middle-aged women stepped out, dressed in T-shirts and shorts.

"Good morning." Christiana stood straighter and smiled. "How may I help you?"

"We heard you had the best cookies and pies in Lancaster County. Is that true?" one of the women asked.

"Oh . . . well . . ." Christiana's cheeks

heated. "I do have quite a few regular customers."

"What are your most popular items?" the other woman asked.

"Most people seem to enjoy my whoopie pies." Christiana gestured toward the shelves to her right and left. "But the shoofly pies and chocolate chip cookies are popular too. What would you like?"

"Hmm." The first woman pursed her lips. "I think the whoopie pies — one of each flavor."

"Yeah, that sounds good," the second woman said. "I'll take one of each too."

Two more cars pulled up as Christiana filled bags with whoopie pies. When she took the women's money, she glanced at the four women now waiting behind them. A couple of them seemed impatient. Unfortunately, she'd grown used to that.

"Here you go, and thank you for stopping by," Christiana said as she gave the women their change and then their bags. Then she turned her attention to the next customers. She wasn't sure which of them had stepped up to the stand first, so she said, "I can help who's next."

"Do you sell pumpkin whoopie pies?"

"Do you have any carrot cake?"

The two women she'd sensed were unhappy waiting had spoken at the same time, and now they turned to stare at each other. Christiana took a deep breath. She wouldn't allow these pushy women to get under her skin.

"Yes, we do have carrot cake." Phoebe, her younger sister, appeared behind Christiana, fresh from the house, her smile as bright as if she were talking to a dear friend instead of an outspoken customer. "It looks like we have one left. Let me get that for you."

"*Danki,* Phoebe," Christiana said under her breath. Then to the woman who had asked for them, she said, "How many pumpkin whoopie pies would you like? I have a dozen here."

"Don't you have more?" she snapped. "I need at least two dozen."

"Yes, I have more. Let me get these down for you, and then I'll go get the rest."

As Phoebe stretched for the carrot cake and Christiana leaned toward the pumpkin whoopie pies, the sisters collided. Christiana stumbled forward, sending her cash box crashing to the ground. At the same time, Phoebe dropped the carrot cake.

Christiana heard the customers gasp, and she gritted her teeth as she picked up the cash box and took in the demolished cake.

"Was that your last carrot cake?" the woman who'd wanted one asked, her eyes narrowing. "It's my husband's birthday, and I promised him a carrot cake from Amish Country. I really need that cake for his party tonight."

Christiana swallowed against her dry throat and squared her shoulders. "I'm not sure if I have any more in the house —"

"Well, can you check? I told you. I need one today." The woman tapped her fingers on the counter.

Christiana turned to Phoebe, and when she saw that her face had twisted into a frown, she decided she'd better send her to the house instead of going herself. "Will you see if there's another carrot cake in the refrigerator, please, and —"

"Get another dozen pumpkin whoopie pies too!"

Christiana avoided looking back at the woman so intent on getting enough pies.

Now Phoebe's eyes flashed with what Christiana knew was annoyance, but she nodded. "Yes. I'll check."

A third woman spoke up for the first time. "And, uh, could you please see if you have some cherry turnovers? I don't see any on your shelves. I'm sorry, but we're in kind of a hurry." At least this woman wasn't rude, and the fourth woman had been looking at her phone the whole time.

And at least no one was traipsing up to the house when they found the bake stand closed. She couldn't believe how often that happened.

Christiana plastered a smile on her face and focused on the two women who'd been so demanding. "My sister will be right back. In the meantime, would you like to look at my other selections?"

Later that afternoon, Christiana and Phoebe packed the few remaining baked goods into a cooler, and then they took it, the cash box, and the unused bags to the house.

After loading the leftovers into the refrigerator, Christiana plopped into her father's favorite easy chair in the living room and rested her feet on his footstool.

"Busy day at the bake stand?" *Mamm* asked as she came into the room.

"The busiest."

Christiana blew a loose strand of her fiery red hair out of her face as she thought about the truth of the matter. Managing rude customers and being extra busy was one thing, but she wished she didn't feel so isolated at the bake stand. Phoebe was responsible for helping their mother with most of the household chores when the bake stand was open, though, and Christiana couldn't expect her help nor her company.

She sighed. Unless her business became so successful that she could afford to hire a helper — and that was unlikely — she'd just have to get on with it alone. Selling her baked goods was too important to her to give up.

1

"Christiana!"

Christiana's cousin Bethany Gingerich smiled brightly as she sat at a high-top walnut table on a matching ladder-back chair in her Coffee Corner booth at the Bird-in-Hand market. Sitting on either side of Bethany were Christiana's two other favorite cousins, Leanna Wengerd and Salina Petersheim.

"Gude mariye." Christiana greeted them all and set her purse and tote bag on the floor beside the empty stool at the table. She inhaled the rich aroma of Bethany's delicious coffee. The smell made her taste buds dance with delight. It was no wonder her cousin's booth was so successful. "How are you all?"

"We're great," Bethany said. The other two nodded as they sipped their coffee. "We were just catching up before the market officially opens." Bethany smoothed her hands down her black apron, and her light-blue eyes seemed to sparkle under the fluorescent lights glowing above them. Although she was twenty-two, Bethany always reminded Christiana of a happy kitten with her unfailing energy and constant smile. "How are you doing this lovely Thursday morning?"

"I'm fine," Christiana said. "I had to run an early errand for *mei mamm* before opening my bake stand, so I thought I'd drop in. The greeter at the door remembered I'm your cousin and let me in."

"Sit with us." Leanna patted the empty stool. At thirty-four, she was both their oldest cousin and the shortest, standing at only five foot three. Christiana considered her to be the bravest and most resilient. She'd lost her husband in an accident three years ago, but she persevered, raising her son on her own.

"I do have a little time." Christiana hopped up on the stool and then glanced over her shoulder at the counter where the coffee and donuts were beckoning her.

"*Kaffi?*" Bethany asked, as if reading Christiana's mind. "Cinnamon is the special today."

"*Ya,* that would be perfect." Christiana pulled a bill from her pocket and handed it to Bethany. "*Danki.*"

"Gern gschehne," Bethany sang out as she slid from her stool and headed toward the counter.

"How are things at the bake stand?" Salina picked up her cup and took a sip.

"It's *gut.* Busy." Christiana shook her head. "I can hardly keep up with the demand. I have to come back to the *haus* more than once to replenish my inventory, and if I close the stand early because I've run out of baked goods, sometimes customers knock on our door asking for pies, *kichlin . . .* everything. Sometimes they've come even after hours!"

Salina and Leanna locked eyes.

"What?" Christiana leaned forward as if to catch their unspoken thoughts.

"Here you go." Bethany set a cup of coffee and a donut on the table. Then she divided a look between Salina and Leanna. "Did I miss something juicy?"

"Christiana was just saying her bake stand is so busy that she can't keep up with the demand . . . and she has a few other challenges too," Leanna said.

"*Ya.* Customers come to her door even if the bake stand is closed." Salina made a sweeping gesture toward the back of the market. "What were we just discussing, Bethany?"

At twenty-four, Salina was just two years older than Bethany, but Christiana had always considered Bethany and Salina to be opposites. While Bethany was a bubbly chatterbox, Salina was quiet and thoughtful, with dark-brown hair framing her blue eyes.

"Oh!" Bethany's eyes rounded as she picked up her cup of coffee. "You mean the empty booth."

"There's an empty booth?" Christiana took a bite of the chocolate donut and savored the taste. The best, just like Bethany's coffee!

Leanna nodded. "*Ya,* there is. The knickknack boutique closed down. I heard the owner decided to find a storefront. A bakery is just what we need here at the market. Besides the gift shops, we have a deli, a candy shop, and then my Jam and Jelly Nook and Salina's Farm Stand, but I think customers would love to see baked goods."

"You should snatch up that booth before someone else gets it," Salina said.

"Then the four of us will have Thursdays, Fridays, and Saturdays together every week." Bethany beamed. "Wouldn't that be fun?"

"I don't know." Christiana shook her head. "I may be twenty-five, but you know how strict *mei dat* can still be. He's always

24

leery of anything that, as he says, might allow either of his *dochdern* to spend too much time in the *English* world. Plus, I can't leave all the chores for Phoebe and *Mamm*."

"But we're here only three days a week." Salina held up three fingers.

"*Ya.* Don't you step away from chores to run the bake stand six days a week now?" Leanna shrugged. "You'd have more time to help with chores at home if you sold your baked goods only the three days you're here. And I'm sure you'd make just as much money. Maybe more."

"Exactly!" Bethany snapped her fingers.

"That does make sense." Christiana let their reasoning roll around in her mind as she sipped her coffee. "It would be nice to not have to deal with customers at the *haus* all the time. I could put a sign out by the road inviting them to come here to buy their baked goods instead."

"Right." Salina nodded.

Christiana flattened her lips and then asked, "But how much is the booth rent?"

"It's not too bad. I'm sure you could make your rent quickly," Leanna said.

"*Ya,* that's true," Salina chimed in.

"But you both have regular customers, and I don't know if mine would really come

25

here." Christiana nodded at Salina. "You have customers who come every week for your produce." She turned to Leanna. "And you have regulars for your jams and jellies." Then she looked at Bethany. "I don't even need to discuss how popular this booth is. It's always busy when I stop by to see you. You never have to worry about making booth rent and a profit."

"Now, now. Let's not be *gegisch*. You have plenty of regulars, too, and I do think they'd come here for your baked goods." Bethany looked over her shoulder, and her eyes lit up. *"Gude mariye,* Jeff. *Wie geht's?"*

Christiana looked up as the young Amish man Bethany addressed walked toward them. She took in his solemn expression as he murmured a response to Bethany and followed her to the counter. He looked to be in his mid to late twenties, and she guessed he was a few inches taller than her five-foot-seven height. He was clean shaven, which meant he was single, and dark eyes matched hair that was both wavy and curly. One thick curl was falling over his forehead. He was attractive, but his sad expression was what tugged at her heartstrings.

Turning on the stool, Christiana looked back at the counter as Bethany slipped behind it.

"Do you want your usual?" Bethany asked him. Then she tilted her head. "The special today is cinnamon. Maybe you want to try something new."

"I'll just take the regular roast. *Danki.*" He pulled his wallet from his trousers pocket.

Bethany poured his cup of coffee. "It's warm out there, isn't it? It feels more like July than mid-May. I think it's going to be a hot summer."

Christiana turned back to Salina and Leanna and tried to put this Jeff's sad expression out of her mind. Instead, she concentrated on the booth opportunity at the market. "I'll talk to my parents about this. Maybe it would be a *gut* idea to close down the bake stand and just concentrate on running my business from here." *And I wouldn't be so isolated!*

"I think you'll be *froh* you did," Leanna said. "I appreciate that I can go home and leave my booth behind."

"Me too." Salina folded her arms over her chest.

"I'll see what *mei dat* says." Christiana sipped her coffee and then set the cup down on the table. She pushed herself off the stool. "I need more creamer."

"Wait!" Leanna called. "Christiana!"

As Christiana pivoted, she slammed into

27

Jeff, sloshing his hot coffee onto his dark-blue shirt and knocking his donut to the floor.

Christiana gasped as she looked up at him. His face had twisted with a deep scowl.

"Uh-oh!" Bethany called from behind the counter. "I'll grab a towel."

"Let me get napkins." Salina popped down from her stool and grabbed a handful from the counter.

"Oh no. I-I'm so sorry," Christiana said as Jeff set his empty cup on the table. She thought her cheeks might combust with embarrassment. "I-I didn't see you, and I —"

"Forget it." Jeff took the towel from Bethany and began to mop his shirt.

"Let me help." Christiana grabbed the napkins from Salina and started to wipe at his soaked sleeve.

"Please don't." He stepped away from her, and her cheeks flared hotter.

"Let me buy you another cup of *kaffi* and donut," Christiana said, offering what she could.

"Don't worry about it," he muttered. "I guess nothing is going to go right today." He looked over at Bethany. "I'll see you tomorrow."

"Wait, Jeff." Bethany rushed over to the

28

counter. "Let me give you another cup of *kaffi* and another donut. I insist."

"I'm so sorry," Christiana repeated as she handed him more napkins. "I should have looked behind me before I got up."

"It's fine." He swallowed, and when his gaze met Christiana's, his grimace warmed slightly. "After the morning I've had, nothing surprises me."

"Here you go." Bethany sidled up to him and held out another cup of coffee and donut.

"Let me pay for these." Christiana pulled her wallet from her apron pocket.

Bethany waved her off. "Accidents happen."

"*Danki.*" Jeff cleared his throat and then started toward the exit.

"I hope your day gets better," Christiana called after him, but he didn't look back at her.

Salina began to wipe up the lake of coffee at Christiana's feet, and Bethany picked up the damaged donut and threw it away.

"Let me clean that," Christiana said, insisting. "I caused the mess."

"It was an accident," Leanna said as she wiped up the table. "It's like I tell Chester all the time. Accidents happen. Just clean it up and move on."

29

"*Ya,* but his shirt might be ruined." Christiana heard the hint of a whine in her voice. "He got soaked, and that *kaffi* was hot too."

"He'll be fine." Bethany smiled. "Stop beating yourself up."

"Who is he? Jeff who?" Christiana asked.

"Jeff Stoltzfus," Salina said. "He runs a leather and wood booth."

"Leather and wood?"

"*Ya,* you know." Bethany deposited a pile of wet napkins into a trash can. "He makes personalized leather bracelets and belts and those wooden letters people use to spell out names, like on signs. He also makes little trains made from wood letters that spell out little kids' names and key chains with names on them. The *Englishers* love that stuff."

"Oh." Christiana cupped her hand to her forehead. "I can't believe I bumped into him. I feel so stupid."

Leanna rubbed her arm. "You're too hard on yourself. It was just a mistake."

Christiana helped finish cleaning up the coffee spill. "I'm really sorry for the hassle," she told Bethany.

"It was no trouble at all. And at least we know Jeff will never forget you." Bethany grinned.

"Stop." Christiana swatted her arm. "I should get going."

Bethany squeezed Christiana's hand. "See you soon."

"I need to get back to my booth. The market just opened." Leanna gave Christiana a quick hug. "Let me know what your parents say."

"I will."

"Why don't I show you the empty booth on your way out?" Salina said. "It's across from mine. They're both on corners where two aisles intersect — mine and a main one."

"Okay." Christiana walked through the aisles with Salina, passing both *English* and Amish customers just coming in to visit the variety of booths. She'd always liked exploring the one with used books.

When they reached the far end of the market, they approached Salina's booth, the Farm Stand.

"Here's the empty booth." Salina pointed across the aisle and then led Christiana inside. "I think it's perfect. The last vendor left all the shelving." She gestured around. "You could organize it with pies over here and maybe cookies here." She pointed to the back. "There's electricity, as you know, so you could even use a small refrigerator to —"

"Oh no." Christiana shook her head. "*Mei*

31

dat would never allow me to use electricity. You know how he feels about worldly things."

"No electricity? Really?" Salina spun toward her, and then she lowered her head and nodded. "*Ya,* I should've known that. *Onkel* Freeman is strict." She pointed to the back of the booth again. "But you'd have plenty of room for supplies."

"I would need a propane oven to keep up with the baking since I couldn't just run home to get more. I do think this could work, though. But will *mei dat* allow me to come here?"

"I think he will." Salina looped her arm around Christiana's shoulders. "Just be sure to tell him that you'll have more time to help with chores at home earlier in the week."

"Right. At least when I'm not baking." Christiana wound her finger around one of the ties from her prayer covering as she scanned the large booth. It did have more shelves and storage than her bake stand. She could sell more goods and decorate it with a theme for each season. She felt her lips turn up in a smile as she imagined adding pumpkins and leaves to the shelves in the fall and then a poinsettia and greenery at Christmastime. This would be *her* store, her place to do what she loved — sell her baked goods.

"From the grin on your face, I get the feeling you like this idea." Salina bumped Christiana with her shoulder.

"*Ya*, I do." Christiana turned toward her cousin. "And seeing you, Leanna, and Bethany is the best part."

"*Ya*, it is."

Christiana's grin widened. How she adored her favorite cousins! And because they shared their deepest secrets, they often felt like sisters.

"I need to get to my booth." Salina pointed to where the colorful, fresh produce from her garden was already on display for customers to inspect and buy.

"Have a *gut* day." As Salina left, Christiana stepped out of the empty booth and turned the opposite direction from where they'd come. The booth next door boasted the sign Unique Leather and Wood Gifts. She stopped when she spotted personalized bracelets, key chains, and belts inside. A shelf beside those items displayed wooden signs, blocks, and letters. Beyond the shelves and a counter were a workbench, a table, a couple of stools, and tools.

And Jeff Stoltzfus.

When her gaze collided with his, her

stomach seemed to drop. Standing, he was wiping a paper towel over the large, dark stain on the front of his shirt.

He offered her a curt nod, which she returned before spinning on her heel and hurrying out of the market.

"I stopped by the market this morning," Christiana said as she set two sheets of peanut butter cookies in the oven late that afternoon.

"Oh *ya?*" *Mamm* was mixing the ingredients for a batch of chocolate chip cookies.

"If you had told me you were going, I would have gone with you." Phoebe frowned as she pulled together ingredients for lemon bars. "You know I like to see our cousins too." She stuck her lip out, and Christiana bit back a laugh at her cute expression. At eighteen, Phoebe was seven years younger than her, but unlike her, Phoebe was the spitting image of their mother with her light-brown hair and blue eyes.

Christiana had always believed Phoebe looked like she belonged to their parents more than she did. With her red hair and blue-green eyes, Christiana thought she looked like a stranger in her own family, but her parents had shared that her great-uncle Harvey, whom she never knew, also had red hair and green eyes.

"I promise I'll take you next time." Christiana moved to the counter and began putting cooled butter cookies into boxes.

"How are the *maed*?" *Mamm* asked.

"They're *gut.*" Christiana looked at her over her shoulder. "There's an empty booth available across from Salina's, and I'm wondering if I should move my business there."

"What?" *Mamm* spun to face her. "You want to close down your stand here?"

"I think it would be a *gut* idea." Christiana explained all the reasons she and her cousins had come up with. "It would make *gut* business sense, protect our home from unwanted customers, and give me more time to help you and Phoebe here."

"Hmm." *Mamm* tapped her chin. "We'll have to discuss it with your *dat.*"

Christiana nodded. "I know. I think he'll agree to it since my cousins are there, and other Amish have booths there too. I wouldn't have any more interaction with the *English* at the market than I do here." She turned back to the counter as her thoughts turned to Jeff Stoltzfus. He'd been rather rude when she apologized to him and tried to help him clean up the mess. After all, the spill had been an accident, and she'd

35

expected him to be a little more forgiving. Amish were taught to forgive others from a young age.

And maybe he could have been a little warmer, especially when she saw him in his booth. Of course, he was still trying to get the coffee stain out of his shirt.

Still, she couldn't get his sad eyes out of her mind. Nor could she forget her embarrassment. How would she face him if she did take the booth next to his?

"Did you hear what I said, Christiana?"

"I'm sorry." Christiana pivoted to face her mother. "What did you say?"

Mamm tilted her head. "I said Phoebe has something to ask your *dat* too. But why are you so lost in thought?"

"Oh, it's nothing, really." Christiana waved off the comment as she packaged more cookies. "Something just happened at the market this morning. It was — well, it was embarrassing."

"What happened?" Phoebe was at her side in a flash.

Christiana frowned. Why had she even brought up the subject of her clumsiness in the Coffee Corner?

"Tell me." Phoebe's eyes were wide.

Christiana sighed. "I had *kaffi* with the *maed* this morning, and one of the vendors came in. I wasn't paying attention when I got up from the stool to get more creamer, and I bumped into him. I dumped his *kaffi* all over his shirt and made him drop his donut."

Phoebe gasped, and then she cupped her hand over her mouth to muffle a giggle.

"It's not funny," Christiana deadpanned. "It was humiliating."

"*Ach* no." *Mamm* shook her head. "Did you apologize?"

"Of course I did." Christiana leaned back against the counter. "I also tried to help him clean up, but he told me to stop. He wasn't very nice. But he made a comment about how he was already having a bad day, so I guess I just made it worse."

"Accidents happen," *Mamm* said.

"I know, but there's more to the story." Christiana gestured widely. "His booth is next to the one I want to rent. That means I'll have to see him every day I'm at the market. It's going to be awkward."

"What does he sell?" Phoebe asked.

"He makes wooden and leather gifts." Christiana shook her head. "I don't know how I'll face him again."

"You said he wasn't nice to you, but was he rude?" *Mamm* asked.

"*Ya,* he was." Christiana tapped her finger

37

to her chin. "But he also seemed *bedauer-lich.*" Those eyes! She couldn't get them out of her mind.

"Is he Amish?" Phoebe asked.

Christiana nodded.

"He probably *was* just having a bad day," *Mamm* said. "We all have those. Say a prayer for him."

"I will." Christiana turned back to the counter. "I need to get this baking done before it's time to start supper. *Danki* for your help — both of you."

"You're welcome." Phoebe shook a finger at Christiana. "But you do need to take me to the market when you go again."

Christiana smiled. "I promise."

Later that evening, Christiana scooped a pile of green beans onto her plate and then passed the bowl to her sister.

"Christiana had an interesting day," *Mamm* began from her seat at one end of the table, surprising Christiana. Her mother was taking the lead? She hadn't expected that. "She visited the Bird-in-Hand market and saw her cousins, and she also found out there's an open booth. She'd like to move her business there."

"Why would she do that?" *Dat*'s eyes widened as he looked at *Mamm* and then at

38

Christiana.

Christiana's stomach tightened. "You know how busy my stand has been and how it's been hard for me to keep up. I keep having to come back to the *haus* to get more of my baked goods. If I move to the market, I'll have more room. And I would be selling my baked goods only Thursday through Saturday. That means I could help *Mamm* and Phoebe with chores Monday through Wednesday when I'm not baking."

Dat pointed to the table. "But you wouldn't be *here* those three days to help as much as you do now."

"I can handle all the chores on those days," Phoebe said, chiming in.

Christiana smiled at her across the table.

"Isn't the market owned by an *Englisher*? Don't they have electricity there?" *Dat* asked.

Christiana nodded. "*Ya,* they do."

Dat shook his head. "I don't think it's a *gut* idea. You know using electricity is against our beliefs, and it's better if you're home and away from the *Englisher* world."

"I won't use the electricity," Christiana said. "Salina and Leanna don't use it. I can put my baked goods in a cooler like I do now. And I'd set up a little propane oven so

I could bake *kichlin* during the day to keep up."

Dat shook his head. "No, it's best if you stay here. You see your cousins at church and at family gatherings."

Christiana's shoulders slumped. She stared down at her pork chop, disappointment plaguing her. Her vision of talking to her cousins at the Coffee Corner before the market opened and maybe at times throughout the day evaporated. How could she convince her conservative father that selling her baked goods at the market wouldn't weaken her loyalty to the Amish church and its beliefs?

Christiana felt a sharp kick on her shin, and she sucked in a breath as she looked up at Phoebe. Phoebe lifted her eyebrows as if to offer encouragement. How Christiana adored her baby sister! With their seven-year age difference, Christiana often felt like her second mother.

Phoebe suddenly sat up straight and folded her hands on the table. "I spoke to Suzanna today. Her parents have given her permission to go to Mexico with a group of young people from the community this fall. They're going to build a *haus,* and she asked me if I'm going too." She bit her lip and exchanged a look with *Mamm.*

Christiana set her fork on her plate and watched her father.

Dat kept his eyes focused on his plate. "You already know my answer, Phoebe. We've discussed this."

"I thought maybe you'd change your mind if you knew one of *mei freinden* is going. We won't be gone very long — not even a week. That means I won't leave *Mamm* and Christiana with chores for long, and I also —"

"No." *Dat*'s response was clipped as he frowned at Phoebe. "There's no *gut* reason for you to go to Mexico."

Her sister winced as if *Dat* had slapped her.

"But it's a mission trip. We're going to help people just like the Bible tells us to." Phoebe's pleading voice tugged at Christiana's heartstrings.

"The answer is no," *Dat* said. "There's no more discussion."

"But you always said we need to live a life of service, and —"

"Phoebe Kate!" *Dat* bellowed. "The answer is no. Now, please drop it."

A heavy silence fell over the kitchen, utensils scraping the dishes creating the only sound.

Christiana met Phoebe's gaze and gave her an encouraging smile. Phoebe nodded

41

and then looked down at her meal.

"Did you have a *gut* day, Freeman?" *Mamm*'s voice was cheerful.

"*Ya,* we worked on that *haus* over in Strasburg. We almost have the foundation done."

"How exciting. How big is that *haus* again?"

A knock on the back door sounded, halting her father's response.

"Are you expecting company?" *Mamm* asked *Dat.*

"No." *Dat* shook his head as he wiped his graying light-brown beard with a paper napkin.

"May I answer the door?" Phoebe asked.

Dat nodded.

Phoebe popped up from her chair and rushed through the mudroom to the back door. Voices sounded before Phoebe reappeared in the doorway.

"An *English* woman is here," Phoebe told Christiana. "She wants to know if you have any apple and shoofly pies. She'd like one of each."

Christiana saw Phoebe's lips twitch. Why did she find this funny? Then it hit her — this interruption was demonstrating one of her points, the one their father might find the most important.

Perfect timing!

"I do have them." Christiana glanced at her mother, who seemed to be suppressing a smile. "I'll take them out to her." She retrieved the pies from the refrigerator and hurried to the back door. A young woman clad in jeans and a denim jacket stood on the porch. "Hello. My sister said you want to buy some pies?"

"Yes, I do!" She rubbed her hands together. "I'm going to my boyfriend's parents' house for supper tomorrow, and my mother suggested I take something special for dessert. She said you sell the best pies in Lancaster County."

"Tell her I said thank you." Christiana told her the price, took the money, and then handed her the pies. "Have a nice evening."

"You too!" The woman smiled, and then Christiana watched as she headed to her small car.

Christiana closed the back door and then dropped the money into her apron pocket as she returned to the kitchen. When she slipped into her chair, she forked a piece of her pork chop and put it in her mouth as silence once again fell over the kitchen.

"You know, Freeman," *Mamm* said, "if Christiana moved her business to the market, our supper wouldn't be interrupted by

43

eager customers."

Christiana's gaze snapped to her mother's as she held her breath. *Please agree with her,* Dat. *Please let me move to the market!*

"That's true." *Dat* lifted his glass of water as his blue eyes focused on her before turning to *Mamm.* "But, Lynn, the market is owned by an *Englisher —*"

"And you build for *Englishers.*" Christiana wanted to take back the words as soon as they escaped her mouth. She'd never been so bold toward her father before. She chewed her lower lip, awaiting his explosion.

Instead, *Dat* nodded. "You're right. I do." He took another bite and was obviously mulling that thought over as he chewed. Then he looked up and said, "Christiana, if I allow you to rent a booth at the market, you must promise me that you'll keep our Plain ways."

She sat up taller. "Of course I will."

"Then I will allow it — but on a trial basis. If I see you're not keeping our Plain ways, you'll move your business back to the bake stand here."

"Danki, Dat." Christiana smiled. "May I go to the market tomorrow to talk to the manager?"

"Ya." He gave her a curt nod.

44

"I want to go with you," Phoebe said. Her tone held a note of insistence.

"Okay," Christiana told her.

"Once you confirm that the booth is yours, I'll take down your stand so customers will stop knocking on our door," *Dat* said. "I'll put up a sign asking them to visit you at the market instead."

"Danki." Christiana looked at her mother, who smiled openly this time. "This is going to be *wunderbaar.*"

2

Jeff stood at his kitchen sink and scrubbed his shirt with such force that he thought the dark-blue material might shred. He gritted his teeth and silently willed the coffee stain to disappear.

When the screen door clicked shut from the mudroom behind him, he peered over his shoulder just in time to see his mother appear in the doorway.

"Hi, *Mamm.*" He did his best to sound bright and sunny despite his foul mood.

"What are you doing?" She crossed the kitchen and took the soiled shirt from his hand. "Are you trying to destroy this shirt?" She turned it over. "What is this stain?"

"*Kaffi.*" He did his best not to roll his eyes as he remembered the stares his shirt had caused at the market. All day long, his customers had seemed more interested in his stain than his items for sale.

Mamm's dark eyebrows rose above her

equally dark eyes. "How did you manage to spill *kaffi* all over this shirt?"

"It's a long story." He sighed as the pretty redhead's shocked face filled his mind. What had Leanna Wengerd called her? Christine? Christina? No, it was Christiana.

Mamm shook her head as she examined the stain. "The secret to getting rid of a *kaffi* stain is applying warm water, dishwashing liquid, and white vinegar for fifteen minutes. I'll take care of it." She met his gaze again. "Now tell me this long story of yours."

"It's not that interesting." Jeff folded his arms over his chest, ignoring his damp hands. "I went to the Coffee Corner to buy my usual cup of *kaffi* and a donut. As I was leaving, a *maedel* bumped into me, and my entire cup of coffee spilled. Not just on my shirt, but all over the floor. I dropped my donut too. Anyway, I spent the rest of the day trying to ignore customers' stares. It was pretty embarrassing. I suppose I should keep a change of clothes in the booth in case of future emergencies. It was just a terrible day from the start."

"Did you say a *maedel* bumped into you?" A smile spread across her lips. "Who was the *maedel*? Is she *schee*? Is she single?"

Jeff swallowed a groan. He wasn't in the mood for one of his mother's lectures about

47

how he wasn't getting any younger and needed to get over his heartache and move on before it was too late. "Was that all you heard me say, *Mamm?* Did you not hear that I had a really bad day?"

"I'm sorry." She folded the shirt and slung it over her arm. "Why did you have a bad day?"

"I had to stop for supplies on my way to the market, and Ella and her husband were at the hardware store."

Mamm waited a beat before responding. "Oh. Well, what did Ella have to say?"

He looked down at the off-white linoleum and kicked at a scuff with his shoe. His mother would always remember what happened; he knew that. But he didn't want her to see the whole truth in his eyes. He didn't want her to know how fiercely he still seethed at the mere sight of Ella and the man she'd married.

"She didn't say anything. I had already made my purchases, so I just slipped out the door before they could see me. I don't care to talk to either one of them." He shook his head. "It just kind of set the tone for my day, though. Then I went to get *kaffi* and the *maedel* dumped it on me. I sold just four wooden signs all day long." He looked up into his mother's warm eyes, and guilt

48

rolled over him. Did he have any right to complain when he had a family who cared for him?

He reached for his shirt. "I can wash my shirt. Just tell me how much dishwashing detergent and vinegar to use."

"That's not necessary." *Mamm* pulled the shirt away from him. "I'll do it since you don't have anyone to do your laundry."

Jeff felt his lips press into a thin line. Not only had he run into his ex-fiancée today, but his mother also had to remind him that he was alone in the house he'd built for her.

Could this day get any worse?

"Are you coming for supper?" *Mamm* gestured toward the back door. "I made your favorite — steak."

"Ya." Jeff raked his fingers through his thick waves and curls. *"Danki."*

He followed his mother through the small mudroom, out the back door, down the porch steps, and up the path that led from his three-bedroom house to the large, four-bedroom, whitewashed house where he'd been born and raised. He glanced around the lush, green pastures of the dairy farm he and his younger brother helped their father run.

As he and *Mamm* approached her back porch, he looked over his shoulder at the

49

white house he'd built for Ella. Had his father's farm and the house he'd built not been good enough for her? What did John Lantz have that Jeff didn't?

These questions had haunted him ever since Ella had broken his heart more than a year ago.

"Jeffrey?"

"Ya?" Jeff turned toward his mother's gentle smile.

"Do you want to talk about what's bothering you?"

Jeff bit back a sardonic smile. Hadn't she heard anything he'd said earlier?

"I'm fine, but *danki.*" He rubbed his hands together. "I'm ready for some of your fantastic steak."

Jeff entered the kitchen behind his mother and waved a hello to his father and younger brother, Nick, as they sat down at the table. The delicious aroma of steak, potatoes, and freshly baked rolls wafted over him, causing his stomach to gurgle with delight.

"We were wondering if you were going to join us." Nick grinned as he sat across from Jeff. At twenty-four, Nick was four years younger than Jeff, and he'd inherited the same dark hair and eyes from *Mamm* as Jeff had. Jeff thought again about how he secretly envied Nick's straight hair that didn't

50

seem to protest attempts to brush and comb it into submission.

"Jeff was busy trying to get a *kaffi* stain out of his shirt." *Mamm* set the shirt on the counter and then took her seat across from *Dat*. "A *maedel* bumped into him at the market and spilled his entire cup of *kaffi*, most of it on him."

"Oh really?" Nick's smile transformed into a smirk. "Who was the *maedel*?"

Jeff closed his eyes. Why had he shared the coffee story with *Mamm*?

"Let's pray," *Dat* announced.

They all bowed their heads in silent prayer. When every head had lifted, they filled their plates with the delicious food.

"So who was the *maedel*?" Nick asked again as he passed the basket of rolls. "Was she *schee*?"

Ya. She was.

Jeff shoved the thought away as he swiped a roll. "I don't know who she was. She was talking to Bethany Gingerich and Bethany's cousins when I went into the Coffee Corner."

"What did you say to provoke her?" Nick chuckled.

"I didn't say anything to her. It was just an accident. But I had to deal with strange looks from customers all day."

51

Nick guffawed, and Jeff fought the smile that threatened to overtake his lips. He had to admit it was kind of funny.

"So was she *schee*?" Nick asked again.

Jeff shrugged. "I don't know. I don't even know her." He cut his steak and racked his brain for a way to change the subject.

"You don't need to know a *maedel* to decide if she's attractive," Nick said. "You should have found out her name."

"I know her name." The response leapt from Jeff's lips without any forethought.

"What is it?" Nick asked.

Jeff hesitated. If he said her name aloud, Nick would nag him relentlessly until Jeff found out more about her or even asked her out on a date. He didn't need to be harangued about finding someone to replace Ella. He wasn't ready to move on or trust anyone else with his heart.

"That's enough, Nicholas," *Dat* said, and Jeff swallowed a sigh of relief. "Did you sell a lot of items today?"

"Only a few." Jeff shook his head. "But there's always tomorrow."

"That's right." *Dat* smiled and pointed his fork at him.

Jeff always appreciated his parents' upbeat attitude no matter what troubles they encountered. It was their optimism that had prompted Jeff to open the booth at the market after Ella had broken their engagement. They had encouraged him to move forward and try something new as a way to repair his heart. Although he enjoyed his new business venture, his heart was still in shambles. This hobby was his solace, and he was grateful his grandfather had taught him how to create wood and leather crafts when he was younger, but sales weren't what Jeff had hoped they would be. In fact, if his sales didn't improve soon, he wouldn't be able to pay his booth rent and he'd have to close it down.

The notion was almost too much to bear. He couldn't process the thought of failing at something again so soon after losing Ella. Was he going to spend the rest of his life living as a failure?

"I ran into *mei freind* Miriam at the market today," *Mamm* began. "She said her *mamm* is feeling much better after that terrible bout of pneumonia."

As Jeff turned his thoughts toward everyone else's news, he felt his shoulders relax. He couldn't allow himself to worry about his booth right now. Somehow, God would see him through this season. He'd just keep praying for better sales so he could keep his business afloat.

"Gude mariye!" Phoebe greeted their cousins as she and Christiana stepped into the Coffee Corner booth the next morning.

"Hey there!" Bethany waved Christiana and Phoebe over to their table. "What a *wunderbaar* surprise." She hopped off her stool and pulled a fifth stool over to the table. "Would you both like *kaffi* and a donut?"

"*Ya*, please," Phoebe said. "What's your special flavor today?"

Bethany beamed. "Almond."

Phoebe clapped. "Yum! I'll help you, Bethany."

"Danki." Bethany smiled as they headed toward the counter.

Salina scooted her chair closer to Christiana. "Did you talk to your *dat*?"

"I did." Christiana couldn't stop her smile. "It took some convincing, but he approved my moving my business here."

"That's fantastic!"

"How did you convince him?" Leanna asked. "Oh, wait until Bethany gets back to tell us."

When Bethany and Phoebe returned, Christiana explained what happened.

"Did you ask that woman to come to the *haus* during supper?" Bethany asked, joking.

"No, but it would've been a great plan." Christiana handed Bethany money for the coffee and donuts. "I'm so excited. I need to go talk to the manager." She sipped her coffee and then took a bite of her chocolate donut.

"What are you going to call your booth?" Leanna asked.

"I'm thinking of calling it the Bake Shop." Christiana bit her lip while she waited to see if her cousins approved.

"I love it." Bethany held up her coffee cup. "Let's all toast the Bake Shop."

"Ya!" Phoebe said as they touched their coffee cups.

"It's going to be *wunderbaar* to be able to see each other every week at the market," Salina said.

"You need to let me come and work with you too," Phoebe said.

"Only if *Mamm* says it's okay. Remember, you promised to help with my chores," Christiana said, reminding her of their plan.

"But there will be a price for that." Phoebe grinned. "I get to come and help occasionally."

"I guess that's fair," Christiana said, and

everyone laughed. Then she felt as if someone might be watching her, and when she
turned toward the booth entrance, there
stood Jeff, looking at them. Her mouth
dried as heat crept up her neck.

He nodded at her, and she cleared her
throat and looked down at the table.

"Jeff!" Bethany waved at him. "How are
you?"

"I'm well." Jeff approached their table and
divided a look between them all. *"Gude
mariye."*

Christiana's cousins and sister greeted
him while she longed to crawl under the
table and hide. But when Jeff smiled, Christiana felt the tension in her neck release
slightly. He had a really nice smile, and he
seemed to be in higher spirits today. But
she still noticed a hint of sadness in his eyes.
Plus, he'd been rude to her yesterday.

"Would you like *kaffi* and a donut as
usual?" Bethany stood and walked to the
counter with him. "Today's special flavor is
almond."

"I'd love *kaffi* and a donut. Almond
sounds perfect," Jeff said. "That's the best
way to start my day."

"As long as Christiana doesn't spill your
kaffi on you," Leanna muttered, and Salina
snorted.

"Is he the guy?" Phoebe's question was a little too loud.

"Shh," Christiana hissed. "I'm already embarrassed enough." She glanced at Jeff, looking over her shoulder.

Is it too late to run out of here?

"*Ya,* that's the guy," Salina whispered. "And his booth is next to the one that's vacant."

"I know!" Phoebe chortled.

Christiana covered her face with her hands.

"Have a *gut* day," she heard Bethany say.

Christiana uncovered her face as Jeff moved past them, his eyes locking with hers before he exited the booth.

"Did you have to embarrass me like that?" Christiana glared at them all, but they chuckled.

"We were just teasing you, Christiana. It was all in fun," Salina said. "Besides, he smiled at you. I don't think he's holding the spill against you."

"He's handsome." Phoebe's smile was bright.

"Who's handsome?" Bethany climbed onto the stool beside her.

"Jeff." Phoebe nodded toward the entrance to the booth. "He's really handsome, and he smiled at Christiana."

"Can we please talk about something else?" Christiana moaned.

"So, when are you going to talk to Kent Dobson about the booth?" Leanna asked. "He's the manager of the marketplace."

Christiana felt the muscles in her neck relax as she smiled at her oldest cousin. "I was going to go talk to him after I finished *mei kaffi.*"

"*Gut.* You need to snatch up that booth before someone else does." Salina held up her cup. "Here's to our cousin joining us at the Bird-in-Hand market."

"Hear, hear," Bethany said.

Christiana touched her cup to her cousins' and sister's cups and smiled. She couldn't wait to get her booth set up. She just hoped no one else had already rented it.

3

"The previous renter sold knickknacks, and she left all her shelving and the counter." Kent Dobson gestured around the large booth with hands that made her guess he was in his mid to late forties — that and his graying brown hair. "I think you'd have plenty of room for your baked goods."

"I agree." Christiana poised her pen in her right hand and held a notepad in the other, ready to take more notes. "Would it be possible for me to set up a little propane oven to bake cookies during the day?"

Kent rubbed his chin as he gazed around the booth. Then he nodded. "I don't see why not."

"Great. I'd love to keep up with my inventory. If I can bake during the day, I might not run out as quickly as I do with my bake stand. Plus, I'd like to have the warm aroma of baking cookies in the booth all the time. Customers would probably enjoy that."

Christiana made another note on her pad. "This is perfect. I'll be able to spread out and have more room for all my baked goods than I do now."

"That's a good point." Phoebe fluttered around the booth, inspecting all the shelves. "We could create a cookie section here and then put all your pies over there." She pointed as she talked. "And your cakes could go over there. This is going to be so great." She turned to Christiana. "You have to ask *Dat* to make you a sign that says The Bake Shop." She looked down and clicked her tongue. "Well, hi there."

Christiana glanced over in time to see Phoebe rub a gray tabby's head.

"That's our market cat. Her name is Daisy." Kent held up his hands as he looked at Christiana. "I hope you're not allergic to cats."

"No, I'm not. And I've met her before. She likes to visit my cousins at their booths." Christiana bent and scratched behind the cat's ears.

Daisy purred and closed her eyes in response. Then the cat stood and stretched before sauntering out of the booth.

"Daisy acts like she owns the place. She makes her rounds and naps in certain booths. Many of the vendors keep snacks for her. I have a bed and a litter box for her in a little room outside my office." Kent clapped his hands. "So do you want to rent the booth?"

"Yes, I do. Thank you." Christiana tilted her head as she looked up at the man. "How much is the rent again?"

Christiana took more notes as they discussed the rental rate and other details about the market.

"How does all that sound?" Kent asked.

"Perfect." She signed the contract he handed her and then looked around the booth. "May I move in tomorrow?"

"Of course. I'd hoped to add an authentic Amish bakery to our market." Kent shook her hand. "We're happy to have you here. I think you'll be very successful."

"Thank you."

"Do you have any more questions for me?" he asked. She shook her head. "All right, then. I'm going to head back to my office. Please stop by anytime." With that, Kent left the booth.

Christiana made a list of supplies she'd need to set up her booth the next day. She was noting one last item when she heard Phoebe speak.

"Hi, I'm Phoebe Kurtz. *Mei schweschder,* Christiana, is moving her baked goods business here," Phoebe said. "She makes the best *kichlin* and *kuchen* in the county."

"It's nice to meet you," a man's voice said. "I'm Jeff Stoltzfus. I run the booth next door."

Christiana craned her neck to peer over her shoulder at Phoebe and Jeff as they shook hands.

"You have some really cool gifts over there," Phoebe said. "I remember noticing them the last time I was strolling around the market. You're so talented."

"Danki." He gave her a slight shrug and then turned to Christiana. "Hi. We haven't formally met. I'm Jeff." He held out his hand.

Christiana set her notepad and pen on a shelf and then shook his hand. "Hi. I'm Christiana, but I guess you know that. Again, I'm so sorry about your shirt. Were you able to get the stain out?"

"You don't need to apologize again." His expression was pleasant. *"Mei mamm* decided to work on the stain herself, so I'm sure it's already gone." He nodded toward Phoebe. "I heard you're going to open up a booth here and that your baked goods are well worth buying. Welcome to the neighborhood."

"Danki," Christiana said.

"Don't worry," Phoebe said. "She's not going to sell *kaffi.*"

Phoebe chortled, and Christiana bit back a groan. She loved her sister, but why did she have to humiliate her?

Jeff's lips twitched as he rubbed his chin. His expression eased the knots in her stomach. Perhaps he had a sense of humor. Perhaps they could even become friends.

"I didn't mean to overhear your conversation with Kent, but did you say you're moving in tomorrow?" Jeff asked.

"*Ya,* that's right." Christiana picked up her notepad and hugged it to her chest.

"How about I bring you *kaffi* tomorrow?" He turned up his palms. "I promise I won't spill it."

Christiana blew out a loud sigh. "I'm never going to live that down, am I?"

"I'm just kidding." His smile was warm. "Tell me about your baked goods."

"Well, I make the usual items you'd see at a bake stand — pies, cakes, cookies." Christiana retrieved her pen and fingered it. "They're pretty typical."

"No, they're not," Phoebe said. "Christiana collects cookbooks and tries different recipes. Our cousins suggested she move her business from her roadside stand to this booth because, among other reasons, her

63

bake stand is so busy. Last night we were eating supper when a customer knocked on our back door wanting to buy two pies even though the bake stand was closed."

"Wow. That's impressive." Jeff seemed to study her, and Christiana shifted her weight on her feet. "What are your biggest sellers?"

Christiana pursed her lips and envisioned her bake stand. "I'd say the most typical Amish recipes, like whoopie pies and shoofly pies."

"What about *kichlin*?" he asked.

"She sells out of those too," Phoebe said.

"Do you make macadamia nut *kichlin*?" he asked, rubbing his hands together.

"I do. Are they your favorite?"

"*Ya,* they are." He grinned, and she silently admired how that made his face light up. "You said your cousins convinced you to move your business here?"

"That's right," Christiana said.

"Who are your cousins? Would I know any of them?" he asked.

"You know them all." Christiana nodded in the direction of the Coffee Corner. "Bethany, Leanna, and Salina."

"Really?" His dark eyebrows rose. "I could tell you were close, but I didn't realize you were family."

"We are." Christiana glanced toward his

booth. "Why don't you show us what you sell?"

"Sure." He made a sweeping gesture toward his booth. "I have a variety of gifts made with wood and leather."

"What's your bestseller?" Christiana slipped her pen and notepad into her tote bag as she followed him out of her booth and into his. The sweet aroma of leather and wood filled her senses, and the old oak floor creaked under her feet.

"Probably the personalized leather bracelets the *Englishers* like. I have a manual stamping machine." He pointed to where it was sitting on a small table, and then he picked up a bracelet with the name Christy on it. As he held it out to her, a smile turned up the corners of his lips. "Here's one for you. Has anyone ever called you Christy?"

She laughed as she ran her fingers over the letters. "No." She met his gaze and shook her head. "That's not exactly true. *Mei daadi* once told my parents he thought Christiana was too long and they should call me Christy, but it didn't stick." She handed the bracelet back to him. "I can see why your customers would like these. They're really nice."

"*Danki.*" He turned toward one of the shelves. "They also like the leather belts and key chains."

Christiana followed him toward the back of the booth, where Phoebe was perusing personalized shelves and wooden trains. When a burning smell filled her lungs, she touched Jeff's hand. But then she quickly pulled her hand away as embarrassment filled her. How could she be so forward with a man?

He turned toward her, his eyes wide.

"I'm sorry," Christiana said as she folded her hands. "I didn't mean . . . I think I smell something burning."

"That's just my burnishing machine. I use it to cut leather." He pointed to the table in the back of the booth. A machine with two round ends sat on it. "It smells a bit. I apologize in advance, because you'll notice that a lot."

"That's *gut* to know." She glanced around the booth. "Phoebe was right. You are talented. How did you learn how to make all these amazing things?"

"*Mei daadi* taught me." He folded his arms over his wide chest. "I took an interest in the hobby when I was twelve, and he bought me my first set of tools. It's always been my favorite pastime. It's how I relax after working on *mei dat*'s dairy farm."

"That's neat. *Mei mammi, mei dat*'s *mamm,*

gave me my first cookbook. Baking is my favorite way to relax, even though it turned into a job too." Christiana scanned the booth again. "How long have you rented this space?"

"About a year."

"What inspired you to open it?"

"Ah. Well . . ." He pushed one hand through his curls. "I decided I needed to try something different and, I guess, make a change in my life. My parents suggested I sell my wooden and leather creations, so I opened Unique Leather and Wood Gifts here." He looked down at his shirt and wiped off what seemed to be invisible fuzz. When he looked at her, his expression was what she'd have to call sheepish. "I won't bore you with that story, though."

But she wanted to hear that story! Why did he need to make a change in his life? Was that why he seemed so sad? But she couldn't ask such personal questions when they'd just met.

"Christiana." Phoebe rushed over with a wooden sign. The words on it said The Smiths, Established 2005. "You should ask Jeff to make your sign for the booth."

"Oh no." Christiana shook her head. "It's lovely, but I don't want to trouble him."

"It's no trouble." He stood up straight.

"What would you like on it?"

"No, no." Christiana shook her head. "I'm going to ask *mei dat* to make it."

"She needs a sign that says The Bake Shop," Phoebe said. "Can you make one?"

"I'd be *froh* to do that for you." He pointed to the signs on the wall. "Which style do you like?"

"How much are they?" Christiana asked.

"Don't worry about the price." He walked over to the display. "Which one do you like best?"

"I like this one." Phoebe held up the sign in her hands.

Christiana nodded. "*Ya,* I agree."

"Consider it done." He took the sign from Phoebe. "I'll try to finish it by tomorrow."

"*Danki.* But, really, how much will I owe you?" Christiana looked behind him and found prices on the wall. "Is it that price over there?"

"*Ya,* but I'll give you a discount. How about fifty percent off since we'll be neighbors?"

"That's not right. I should pay full price."

A smile tugged at his lips as he pointed at Christiana. "You're stubborn, aren't you?"

Phoebe rolled her eyes. "You have no idea."

"Phoebe!" Christiana gasped.

Jeff tilted his head back and laughed, and the deep, rich sound caused Christiana to smile. He was even more attractive when he laughed.

A group of customers walked into the booth and began commenting on Jeff's items.

"We should go," Christiana told him. "I'll see you tomorrow."

"Have a *gut* day." Jeff gave them a little wave and then walked over to one of the customers. "Good morning. How may I help you?"

Christiana looked at him once more before walking away with Phoebe. Jeff seemed to have a secret or two, but maybe one day she'd be a friend he'd want to share them with.

"It sounds like the booth is perfect," *Mamm* said later that morning as she helped Christiana and Phoebe pack fresh baked goods into boxes.

"It is," Phoebe said. "And the man in the next booth is going to make her a sign that says The Bake Shop."

"Is he?" *Mamm* grinned. "Is he handsome?"

"Oh no. Please don't start." Christiana groaned. "I'm not looking for a boyfriend. I just want to sell my baked goods."

"He's the one she spilled *kaffi* on," Phoebe continued as she filled a box with macadamia nut cookies. "And, *ya,* he is handsome."

Christiana tried to ignore her mother's grin.

"That's very nice," *Mamm* said. "It sounds like you might have a new *freind* next door."

"*Ya,* I suppose so." Christiana added another box of cookies to the stack on the counter. "I need to get all my supplies together — my favorite *kichlin* recipes, my cash box, change, my two largest coolers, one for my ingredients — oh, and the two rolling baker's racks I bought today. I'm so glad to have them. Getting my fresh baked goods from my taxi into the market will be so much easier. Bringing home any baked goods I don't sell by the end of the day on Saturday will be easier too."

She pointed toward the large utility room off her mother's kitchen. "Since I'll be baking so much more at once — and *danki* so much for helping me — we'll have to set up a staging area in there so we can sort everything." She snapped her fingers. "Oh, I can't forget to buy a cash register. I'll have to go to the store later. All our cousins have one, and I noticed Jeff has one too."

"I think he likes you," Phoebe said.

"Phoebe, please stop," Christiana said, warning her. "I'm not interested, and I'm sure he isn't either. It would be nice to have a *freind,* but that's all I want. Besides, it would complicate things if I dated him and then it didn't work out. We're going to see each other three days every week."

Christiana turned toward the oven and checked the time. Another batch of cookies would be done in a few minutes. She continued packing cookies as her thoughts turned to Jeff. While she wasn't interested in finding a boyfriend, she did like the idea of being his friend. Maybe if they got to know each other, he'd tell her why he'd been so rude to her the day before. Maybe he'd share the reason for the underlying sadness she still saw in his eyes and why he'd needed a change in his life that led to opening a booth at the market.

But right now, she needed to concentrate on making her own booth successful.

Tomorrow she'd join her cousins at the Bird-in-Hand market and open her bakery. She could hardly wait to make her first sale.

4

The following morning Jeff held up the sign he'd made for Christiana's booth and ran his finger over it. He'd stayed late last night to make and then varnish it, and then he arrived at the market early this morning after finishing his chores on the farm earlier than usual.

He pursed his lips as he critiqued his work. It was good, but it wasn't his best effort. If he stared at it long enough, he could see the imperfections. But it was decent, and it would welcome Christiana's customers to her booth.

He laid the sign on his counter and peeked into Christiana's booth to see if she had arrived, but she wasn't there. The market was still quiet. He imagined her packing up her baked goods and traveling to the market. Would her family help her set up the booth today?

He rubbed at a knot on the back of his

neck as he recalled his conversation with Christiana and Phoebe the day before. He wasn't quite sure why he'd offered to make the sign. Perhaps it was Christiana's pretty smile, her enticing blue-green eyes, or the adorable smattering of freckles that marched across the bridge of her nose.

Something about her drew him in, something that almost encouraged him to share the true reason he opened the booth. But when he'd realized he was sharing too much, he stopped talking. He didn't want to open himself to more vulnerability.

He inwardly groaned. How could he even consider telling Christiana that his former fiancée dumped him and then married another man? It would be too embarrassing. But that's why he couldn't allow himself to trust another woman, to consider more than friendship with any woman. Anyone — even someone as nice as Christiana — could lead him on and then throw him away. He needed to concentrate on just becoming her friend, no matter how pretty she was. He was better off alone. Besides, a girl like her most likely had a boyfriend.

He stepped back into the booth and picked up the sign. Perhaps it was best if he put some distance between Christiana and him. He didn't want to risk becoming attached. He could leave the sign in her booth and then not worry about receiving any payment from her. It would be a onetime gift for his new neighbor, and nothing more.

Jeff set the sign on a shelf in her empty booth and then slipped back into his. He busied himself arranging his collection of wooden letters for his name trains, counting how many he had for each letter of the alphabet and recording it in his inventory logbook. He felt something soft on his leg, and he smiled when he found Daisy rubbing her head against his shin and purring.

"Hey there, Daisy." He patted the workbench next to him, and the gray tabby jumped up. "How are you today?" He rubbed her ear, and she tilted her head as her purr grew louder. "I bet you're looking for some treats, huh?"

He pulled a bag out of the bottom drawer of his workbench and set a few treats in front of her.

He laughed to himself as the cat happily ate. Then he glanced around, and his heart felt heavy. Why were his sales down for the whole past month? He didn't want to have to close his booth.

"Give me your honest opinion, Daisy." He placed a few more cat treats on the workbench. "Do you think I can bring my sales up to where they should be?"

The cat ate the last treat and then began licking her gray-and-white paws.

"What do you think I should start selling? What would attract more customers and guarantee my booth rent?"

Daisy moved from licking her paws to licking her legs.

Jeff snorted. "I'm talking to a cat about my business challenges. I've completely lost my mind."

As Daisy continued her bath, he rubbed her head. She glanced up at him before stretching to lick her back. Why was talking to this cat easier than talking to a human?

He knew the answer to that question. When he spoke to Daisy, he didn't have to worry about being judged as a dolt for not using the right words. If only he could find more courage and confidence. If only he could accomplish something great, like running a successful business. Despite his lifelong lack of confidence, he'd managed school, had some friends, and contributed to the family business on the farm. But he'd thought he'd sustained a relationship with Ella too — and look how that turned out.

Jeff pushed away his thoughts and finished inventorying his wooden letters. When he heard commotion in the booth next door, he stepped out into the aisle. A boy who looked about twelve was standing on a plastic crate and reaching high, attempting to hang the sign Jeff made from some hooks above the booth. Behind him, Christiana, her cousins, Phoebe, and an older woman seemed to be organizing.

When the boy teetered, Jeff rushed forward and grabbed him just as the crate flipped over.

"Whoa, there." Jeff gave a little laugh. "Why don't I help you hang that?"

"Danki." The boy gave him a sheepish smile and handed him the sign.

"What happened?" Leanna rushed over.

"I almost fell." The boy gestured at Jeff. "He caught me."

Leanna wagged her finger at him. "I told you not to stand on that crate." Then she looked at Jeff. "*Danki,* Jeff. This is *mei sohn,* Chester."

"Hi." Jeff could see the resemblance between mother and son. Chester had her light-brown hair and eyes. "I'll hang that for you." Jeff pulled a stool over from his booth and climbed up. When he'd hung the sign from the hooks, he jumped down and said, "There you go."

Chester looked up at the sign. "I wish I was tall like you."

Jeff laughed. "You should see *mei bruder.* He's six feet tall. He makes me look like the younger *bruder.*"

"Really?" Chester's eyes widened.

Jeff nodded. *"Ya."*

"Jeff." Christiana appeared beside him. *"Danki* so much for the *schee* sign."

She looked pretty today in her green dress and black apron. Her blue-green eyes seemed greener, and the red hair peeking out from underneath her prayer covering seemed even brighter.

He pushed the thoughts away as he smiled. *"Gern gschehne."*

She pulled a couple of bills from the pocket of her apron and held them out. "Here's your money."

He waved it off. "Consider it a house-warming gift."

"A housewarming gift?" She laughed, and he enjoyed the sweet sound. "That's generous, but it's not right. Take the money." She set it in his palm. "I insist."

He opened his mouth to protest, but the older woman joined them. He folded the stack of bills and shoved it into his pocket.

"Christiana, is this your *freind* Jeff you were telling me about yesterday?" the woman asked.

Warmth filled Jeff's chest. Christiana

already considered him a friend?

Christiana's expression transformed into an embarrassed smile as she gestured between him and the woman. "Jeff, this is *mei mamm,* Lynn. *Mamm,* Jeff made the *schee* sign Chester was trying to hang for me."

"It's so nice to meet you, Jeff." Lynn shook his hand. She had light-blue eyes and light-brown hair like Phoebe's, but Jeff saw the family resemblance in her thin nose. Where on earth had Christiana gotten that gorgeous red hair? Was her father a redhead?

"It's nice to meet you too." Jeff turned to Christiana. "Do you need help with anything else?"

"Well . . ." Christiana scanned the booth. Phoebe, Bethany, and Salina were still organizing baked goods on the shelves. "I think we have it handled, but *danki.*"

The sweet scents of pies, cakes, and cookies filled his senses as he took in the impressive display. He even saw some cupcakes.

Toward the back of the booth, Leanna was setting up the counter with a cash register and a cup that held pens and pencils. He thought the cash register was probably battery operated like his. Chester sat behind the counter on a cooler, off in a corner.

"Christiana," Bethany called. "This shelf is really loose. I think it might collapse if I put anything on it."

"Oh." Christiana frowned. "I don't have any tools here."

"I definitely have tools." Jeff jammed his thumb toward his booth. "I'll be right back."

"Danki." Her expression seemed to fill with relief. "Some deliverymen are coming later to install a propane oven for me. *Mei dat* wanted to be here, but he's working on a big *haus* project and couldn't come today."

"Is he in construction?"

She nodded. "*Ya.* He owns a brick mason business. Didn't you say your *dat* is a dairy farmer?"

"*Ya,* that's right." Jeff took some steps backward. "I'll be right back with tools."

As Jeff disappeared from the booth, Bethany sidled up to Christiana and bumped her with her shoulder. "He's awfully eager to help you, isn't he?"

"I think he's just being nice." Christiana looked toward the shelves. "You're all doing great. I appreciate the help."

"I'm *froh* to help. You helped me set up the Coffee Corner." Bethany wiped her hands down her black apron. "You know, I have an idea that might help you build your customer base."

"Oh *ya?*"

79

"What if I sold some of your *kichlin* and pie in the afternoon along with *mei kaffi*? I can tell customers you're selling more here, and it will drive some of them over to check out your baked goods."

"Oh, Bethany!" Christiana hugged her. "I love that idea. *Danki.* Your Coffee Corner is so busy that your idea will definitely help me."

"I hope so!" Bethany smiled. "Speaking of the Coffee Corner, I better get going. I have to check on the coffeepots."

"*Danki* again." Christiana touched her arm. "I'll be over for *kaffi* after I get organized."

"You're going to do great." Bethany gave her a quick hug. "I'll see you later." Then she hurried out of the booth.

Jeff reappeared with a small toolbox. "Which shelf is it?"

"It's over here. This one." Salina waved him over. "But I noticed one over there needs to be tightened too. I'll show you."

Jeff set to work securing the shelves, and Christiana walked to where Leanna had finished organizing supplies around the counter. Christiana circled behind it.

"*Danki* for helping with this." Christiana looked down at the shelves beneath the countertop. All her bags were neatly piled according to size.

"Gern gschehne." Leanna pointed to the cash register. "I turned it on and organized your money inside. The register tape is loaded too." She showed Christiana how the register worked. "This is better than using a cash box. People appreciate having a receipt too."

"Danki for suggesting I buy a register like yours. This is perfect." Christiana breathed a sigh of relief. She was almost ready to open.

Leanna tapped Christiana's shoulder and pointed. "Look at that."

Christiana followed her gaze to where Chester stood next to Jeff. As Jeff pointed, Chester turned a screwdriver and tightened the shelf in front of them.

"Isn't that sweet?" Leanna asked.

"Ya, it is." Christiana leaned forward on the counter and smiled at the friendship that seemed to be blossoming between Chester and Jeff.

Jeff's expression was warm as he watched Chester stick out his tongue in deep concentration. Jeff was a nice man, and he would most likely be a nice father someday. She rested her chin on the palm of her hand and studied his smile as she watched him instruct Chester at the second shelf. He

81

pushed that curl she'd noticed off his forehead, but it bounced back as if in protest.

"Christiana."

"What?" Christiana stood up and found her mother and sister staring at her.

"I'm trying to tell you we need to head home," *Mamm* said as she and Phoebe walked over to the counter.

"Can't I stay and help Christiana today?" Phoebe folded her hands as if saying a prayer. "I promise I'll work hard."

Mamm shook her head. "I'm sorry, but no. We have to start on chores."

Guilt weighed heavily on Christiana's shoulders as her younger sister's frown deepened. "Maybe you can help another day."

Phoebe nodded. "*Ya.* Maybe."

Christiana hugged her mother and sister. "*Danki* for helping today. I'll call a taxi when I'm ready to come home."

"Have a *gut* day." *Mamm* squeezed her hand. "I'm proud of you."

"*Danki.*" Christiana's voice quavered as she smiled.

"I need to get to my booth too," Leanna said. "I'll check in with you later."

Christiana hugged her cousin and thanked her again for her help. When she glanced toward the far shelves, she found Chester standing by them alone. Jeff had disappeared without saying good-bye. Once again, guilt washed over her. She had to thank him for hanging the sign and fixing the shelves. But why hadn't he told her he was leaving? Why was he so standoffish and quiet when he'd been friendly before? Did he not like her? But then why had he offered to make the sign?

Yet he hadn't brought the coffee he'd promised. Maybe he was just overall socially awkward. It was too soon to tell.

"Let's go, Chester," Leanna said. "I need your help stocking shelves."

"Okay." Chester waved at Christiana. "See you later."

"Bye, Chester. *Danki* for your help." Christiana waved as they left.

"I think I got everything organized." Salina walked over to the counter. "I need to head out, too, but I'll stop by later."

Christiana thanked her, and then she turned to the rolling baker's rack behind her and began unloading the rest of its contents. She set some baked goods on the counter and others on shelves. She had just put up the last box of chocolate chip cookies when the warm, delicious aroma of coffee filled her nostrils.

She spun to find Jeff standing behind her, holding two cups of coffee.

"Jeff. Hi." She pressed her hand to her chest. "You startled me."

"I'm sorry." He held up a cup. "This is for you. I promised you a cup of *kaffi* yesterday. Remember? This is your official welcome to the market."

She studied his dark eyes, the color of dark chocolate. He seemed eager to be her friend, but she couldn't help but feel now that whatever secrets he had were none of her business. Besides, some of his manners were a little questionable too. "This is kind of you, but I feel like I should pay you for *mei kaffi.*" She reached into her pocket for more money.

"No." He shook his head. "I insist."

"Fine, but I pay for your next cup." She nodded toward the far shelves. "*Danki* for the repairs and for being so nice to Chester."

His dark eyebrows lifted. "*Gern gschehne.* But why wouldn't I be nice to Chester? He's a great kid."

"I didn't mean it that way. He's just eager for a man to teach him things since he lost his *dat* three years ago. He looked *froh* while you were showing him how to use the screwdriver."

"Oh. I didn't know about his *dat.*" Jeff's smile flattened. "I'm sorry to hear that."

"I didn't mean to make you feel bad. I just wanted to thank you. You were a big help today, and I think Chester liked being your assistant." She sipped her coffee and then turned toward the entrance of the booth as voices sounded from the aisle.

"I think the market's open," Jeff said.

"Oh." She chewed her lower lip.

"It will be fine," he said as if reading her anxiety. "Your booth looks fantastic. I'll check on you later." He lifted his cup again and then left.

A group of women stepped into her booth, and one of them gasped as she glanced around.

"Look, Tootie," she said. "It's the Amish bakery that girl at the Coffee Corner told us was opening today."

"How wonderful!" Tootie exclaimed, and then she set her eyes on Christiana. "Hi! What flavors of whoopie pies do you have?"

Christiana set her coffee cup on the counter and then walked toward the front of the booth. "Good morning. What flavors are you looking for?" She squared her shoulders and smiled as excitement rushed through her. She was ready to help the first customers at her new bake shop.

5

Jeff stood outside the Bake Shop that afternoon and watched the crowd of customers grabbing baked goods. Just like all morning, a steady stream of them never stopped filing in and out of the Bake Shop. It seemed that Christiana's had become the most popular booth in the market — instantly.

He rubbed his chin and marveled. Christiana kept a pleasant smile on her pretty face as she checked out customers at the counter near the back of the booth. She seemed unfazed as the line of people ready to pay never seemed to shorten. He admired her patience and talent. Obviously, her baked goods were fantastic or customers wouldn't bother to buy them. The delicious, tempting smells of freshly baked cookies had wafted over from her newly installed propane oven to taunt him all day. His stomach had even growled several times as the aroma beckoned him to go buy some of those heavenly smelling treats.

He folded his arms over his chest and watched Christiana for a few more minutes, waiting to see if she would notice him. But she didn't seem aware that he was lurking outside her booth. He studied her attractive face. Surely she had a boyfriend.

But what did it matter? He would keep his distance and just be Christiana's friend if she needed him. Like he'd decided, he'd be friendly enough but not allow the opportunity to become attached. Maybe he'd talk to her later.

"Excuse me," a voice said behind him. "Do you run the Unique Leather and Wood Gifts booth next door?"

"*Ya,* I do." Jeff turned to face the woman. "How may I help you?"

"I'd like some personalized leather bracelets for my nieces and nephews."

Finally! A customer!

"Wonderful. Come tell me which designs you like best."

"It looks like you had a busy day," Salina said as she walked back to the counter in Christiana's booth later that afternoon. "You had a line every time I glanced over here."

87

"Busy? You could say that." Christiana stopped counting the money in her cash register and glanced around the booth. "I ran out of shoofly pies, chocolate chip *kichlin,* crumb *kuchen,* lemon bars, and chocolate *kuchen.*"

"It's a *gut* thing you have until next Thursday to restock. You have a lot of baking to do." Salina leaned on the counter. "You should probably plan for more customers next week. Not only will word get around about your booth, but it's Memorial Day weekend. We'll be inundated with tourists who'll be spending their time off in Amish Country."

"Oh." Christiana tapped her chin. "I'll have to get *Mamm* and Phoebe to help me bake even more, then. They offered to bake for me when I'm here, but I'm going to have to ask them to help more than I thought I'd need. How was your booth today?"

"It was busy for me too. I'm just about out of green peppers and celery." She cupped her hand to her mouth to stifle a yawn. "I'm worn out. We can walk outside together if you're ready to go home."

"*Ya.* I already packed up my leftovers. I just need to put my cash in my money bag." Christiana slipped the bills and change into the bag and then looked toward the exit.

"Have you seen Jeff this afternoon? I haven't seen him since this morning."

"*Ya,* I saw him talking to a few customers earlier."

Christiana removed a box of macadamia nut cookies from one of her racks. "I'm going to see if he's still in his booth. If he is, I'm going to give these to him before I call for my ride."

Salina grinned. "I think he'll like that. He seems to really like *you.*"

"Please don't start." Christiana narrowed her eyes. "He's just a *freind,* and nothing more. After he helped set up the booth this morning, he brought me *kaffi.* That's why I want to do something nice for him." She studied Salina. "What about you and Josiah Yoder?"

"What?" Salina's brow furrowed. "We're just *freinden.* You know our parents are close."

"Right." Christiana tilted her head. "I've seen how you two always talk after church."

"Trust me. He's not interested in me." Salina nodded toward her booth. "I'll get my coolers together and then wait for you here so you have some privacy with Jeff." She grinned again.

"Stop, Salina." Christiana frowned. "I'm not interested in him."

89

"Right," Salina deadpanned. "I'll see you in a few minutes."

Christiana carried the box of cookies to Jeff's booth and found him cutting pieces of leather at his workbench. The burning smell of the burnishing machine filled her lungs as she approached him.

"Aren't you getting ready to go home?" she asked.

He looked up at her and smiled. "Hi. I was just cutting some leather pieces for bracelets so I don't have to do it at my shop at home."

"You shouldn't stay late." She sat down on a stool next to him. "I haven't seen you all day. Have you been busy?"

"It's been okay." He shrugged. "Certainly not as busy as your booth. I saw your line earlier. It looked like it was never going to end."

"*Ya.*" She blew out a deep breath. "It's much busier than my stand ever was. I was glad I brought a sandwich so I could wolf it down when I had a chance. And the couple of times I visited the ladies' room, Salina asked customers to wait, and they did!" She held out the box. "I have something for you." She handed it to him. "Didn't you say macadamia nut cookies are your favorite?"

"*Ya,* they are." He pulled a wallet from

90

his pocket. "How much do I owe you?"

"Nothing. It's a thank-you for helping me this morning and then bringing me *kaffi.*"

"Are you sure?"

"Don't be *gegisch.*" She waved him off. "I hope you enjoy them."

"I will, and I might share them with my family too." He smiled, and her heart seemed to turn over in her chest.

"I'll see you next week." She stood. "Take care."

"You too."

As she headed back to her booth, she thought about how nice Jeff had just been. Maybe they could become good friends. But that was all. Her heart would just have to get over how handsome he was when he smiled.

"Jeff!" *Mamm* announced as he walked into his parents' kitchen later that evening. "How was the market today?"

"It was fine." Jeff couldn't worry his mother by admitting that the business was failing. Instead, he handed her the box of cookies, turning her attention to the surprise. "I brought dessert from my new neighbor." He turned toward the table where his brother and father sat awaiting their supper. Kathy, Nick's girlfriend, was setting a platter of Swedish meatballs on the table, and they greeted each other.

"Oh, *kichlin*," *Mamm* said. "Macadamia nut?"

"*Ya.*"

"The market has a bakery now?" Kathy asked as she set a bowl of egg noodles next to the meatballs.

"*Ya,* it just opened today. The booth beside mine was empty for a couple of weeks, but now a *maedel* is selling baked goods there." Jeff washed his hands at the sink. "She's already staying busy, so I believe her baked goods are fantastic. The smell of her cookies had my stomach growling all day long."

"That's nice that you brought us some of her *kichlin* to enjoy." *Mamm* set the box on the counter and grabbed a large bowl of salad. "You're just in time. We were just going to sit down." She put the bowl in the center of the table.

Jeff sat down across from Nick.

Kathy set bottles of homemade salad dressing on the table and then sat down beside Nick. They exchanged loving glances, and Jeff felt a familiar pang. How he missed having someone to love and confide in, but he dismissed the loneliness that teased him.

After *Mamm* sat down, they bowed their

heads in silent prayer before filling their plates.

"Who is the baker in the booth next to yours?" Kathy asked.

"Her name is Christiana. She had a bake stand that was too busy, so she decided to move her business to the market." Jeff sliced a meatball and then forked a piece into his mouth.

"By any chance, have you seen the *maedel* who dumped *kaffi* on you?" Nick smirked.

"Dumped?" Kathy said, her hazel eyes sparkling in the warm late afternoon sunlight pouring through the kitchen windows. "When did this happen?"

"Thursday," *Mamm* said, and then chimed in with the whole story. "I managed to get the stain out of his shirt, though."

"Oh no." Kathy placed a hand over her chest. "Did you get burned, Jeff?"

"A little." He shrugged as if it weren't a big deal, because it wasn't. "It was just an accident."

"Have you seen her again?" Nick asked as he lifted his glass of water.

Jeff nodded and forked a pile of noodles into his mouth.

"When?" Nick asked.

Jeff hesitated. For some inexplicable reason, he wanted to keep his friendship with Christiana a secret.

An awkward silence fell over the kitchen as Jeff debated how much to tell about Christiana. If he revealed that she had the booth beside him, Nick would tease him relentlessly. But Jeff was the older brother. Why should his younger brother's heckling bother him?

"She's the one who opened the bake shop next to my booth." Jeff shrugged again. "Now we're neighbors."

"Really?" Nick laughed. "The *maedel* who dumped *kaffi* on you now has the booth beside you? That's just hilarious."

"That *is* ironic," *Dat* said, agreeing.

"Were the *kichlin* her apology for the spill?" Kathy asked.

"No. They were more of a thank-you after I helped her set up this morning. I also made the sign for her booth last night."

"That's nice," *Mamm* said. "It sounds like she's become your *freind.*"

Jeff nodded. "She's nice."

"And *schee,* right?" Nick lifted his eyebrows.

"Excuse me." Kathy gave him a fake pout as she crossed her arms over her blue dress and black apron. "You're going to talk about another *maedel* in front of me?"

"You're the most *schee maedel* in the

94

world, *mei liewe*," Nick assured her. "I was just asking for *mei bruder*'s benefit."

"You'd better be." Kathy swatted his arm as *Mamm, Dat,* and Jeff laughed. Then she turned to Jeff. "Is she *schee*?"

His parents laughed again as Nick rolled his eyes.

Jeff snickered. "She is, but she's *not* the potential girlfriend you're all thinking she is."

"Why not?" Kathy's eyes seemed to fill with curiosity. "Does she have a boyfriend? Or is she married?"

"I don't know." Jeff scooped more noodles into his mouth.

"You should find out," Nick said.

"I'm not interested," Jeff said after he swallowed his mouthful. He shook his head and scooped salad onto his plate.

"*Sohn,* it's time to move on." *Mamm*'s tone was gentle as she handed him the salad dressing. "Ella did, and so should you."

Jeff gritted his teeth so hard that the muscles in his jaw ached. Why did she have to bring up Ella? And Ella didn't just move on. She left him!

Another awkward silence fell over the kitchen, and Jeff stared down at his plate as painful moments ticked by on the clock above the sink.

"These meatballs are just *appeditlich,* Joyce." Kathy's bright tone seemed forced. "I'd love to get the recipe from you."

"Of course, Kathy," *Mamm* responded. "I'll be sure to write it down before you leave. How are your parents doing?"

"They're just fine. *Danki* for asking. *Mei dat*'s shed business has been busy, and *mei bruders* have worked long hours with him at the shop."

While he finished his supper, Jeff lost himself in thoughts of Ella. She'd nearly destroyed him — and after he'd built her the exact house she'd wanted. He'd been so blinded by love for her that he'd never realized she'd somehow started pulling away from him. How could he have allowed her to have that much power over his emotions?

He'd never do it again. He'd never allow another woman to cut him to the bone like that again.

"Let's try these *kichlin,*" *Mamm* announced when everyone had finished eating.

"I'll put on the *kaffi,*" Kathy said.

"I can't wait to try these." *Mamm* set the box of cookies on the table in front of Jeff. "You try one first since the *kichlin* were a gift for you."

"*Danki.*" Jeff opened the box, and then he

96

chose which cookie he wanted before taking a bite. The sweet, delicious flavor tickled his taste buds and caused him to smile. "Wow."

"That *gut,* huh?" Nick chuckled as he grabbed a cookie. "I think I need one."

"Me too." *Dat* reached for the box.

"Save some for us," Kathy said, joking as she set coffee mugs on the table.

"Your girlfriend is talented," Nick said.

"She's not my girlfriend," Jeff muttered.

"I think she will be." Nick pointed a cookie at Jeff. "Just give it time."

Jeff sighed. If only life were as easy as his brother made it out to be.

Later that evening, Jeff stepped out onto the porch and looked toward the rock driveway. Nick walked hand in hand with Kathy toward his waiting buggy.

With a sigh, Jeff leaned forward on the porch railing and folded his hands. It seemed like only yesterday that Ella would join Jeff's family for supper. Then he'd take her home, and he'd cherished their long talks in his buggy and stolen kisses as they sat in her driveway.

But those days were gone now. Ella was married, and Jeff was alone. He tried to chase away the hollow feeling that still invaded his chest.

97

Nick opened the buggy door and helped Kathy climb inside. Then he turned toward the porch. "I'll be back soon."

"Be safe on the road," Jeff called. As the horse and buggy disappeared down the driveway, the screen door clicked shut behind Jeff. He craned his neck to see his father. "Are you ready to take care of the animals?"

"Ya." Dat nodded toward the dairy barn. "You know, your *mamm* means well," he said as they walked.

"What are you talking about?"

"When she said it's time for you to move on," *Dat* began, and Jeff sighed. "As parents, we find it hard to see our *sohn* unhappy."

"I'm not *bedauerlich.*" Jeff stopped walking and gestured around the farm. "I have a great life here. I have a *haus,* and I have my business at the marketplace." *Even though it's not going the way I'd hoped.*

"But you're lonely." *Dat* poked Jeff in his chest. "I know you go out to your shop every night after we care for the animals. It's your way of avoiding being alone in the *haus* you built for Ella, isn't it?"

Jeff swallowed. When had *Dat* become so observant?

"This *maedel* at the market may not be your future *fraa,* but it's okay for you to give her a chance. It's okay for you to move on with your life. You're entitled to happiness."

Jeff's throat suddenly felt as rough and dry as the sandpaper he used to create the wooden gifts he sold in his booth. "Okay."

"Gut." Dat looped his arm around Jeff's shoulders. "And while you're getting to know her, would you bring home more *kichlin?"*

Jeff laughed as he looked at his father. "Sure, *Dat.* I'll try."

6

The following Thursday morning Christiana
grunted as she gave the heavy rolling baker's
rack a yank, but the pesky wheels refused to
move from the back of the van. She huffed
and then pulled on the rack once again. It
broke free, teetering over the edge of the
van's floor.

"Whoa! Whoa! Whoa!" Jeff appeared
beside her and caught the rack as it began
to fall. He set it on the ground and then
lifted the second rack beside it, moving
them as if they were as light as a feather.
Then he slammed the van's door.

"Danki." She fingered the first rack and
cleared her throat. "I should have asked my
driver for help, but I forgot the racks are
especially heavy today. *Mei dat* helped me
load them. He's still a strong man."

"When I saw that rack break free, I
thought for sure you were going to drop it
and break your toes." He pointed to her

black shoes.

"I appreciate your help, and my toes do too." She waved to her driver, and the black van took off through the parking lot.

He reached for the first rack. "Let me push one of these for you."

"Oh, you don't need to do that." She shook her head. "I can come back for the second one."

"You have those tote bags too." He pointed to the bags sitting on the curb. "I insist."

"Okay."

He pushed the rack toward the market's back door as she pushed the other one, and they started across the parking lot side by side.

She looked over at him. "How was your week?"

"It was *gut.*" He smiled at her. "*Danki* for the *kichlin* you gave me. They were *appeditlich.* My family enjoyed them too." He leaned closer. "I didn't want to share them, but *mei mamm* made me."

She laughed. "I'm glad you all liked them."

"Next time I might not take your *kichlin* to my parents' *haus* at all. I might just hide them at *mei haus.*"

She tilted her head as she looked at him

101

again. He had his own house, but he wasn't married. She found herself stuck on that detail for a moment. "Did you say you work on your *dat*'s dairy farm when you're not here?"

He nodded. "*Ya,* I do."

"Who helps your *dat* when you are here?"

"*Mei bruder,* Nick. He's four years younger than I am."

"How old are you?"

"Twenty-eight."

"Oh." She took in his bright, intelligent eyes and that single curl that seemed to flirt with his forehead. She couldn't deny that he was handsome, and today he seemed so kind and thoughtful. He was also closing in on thirty. Why wasn't he married? Was she missing something? Or was it those sometimes-puzzling manners?

She ignored the questions and hefted her tote bags onto her shoulder. The answers weren't any of her business, and she hardly knew this man!

"Would you please push the button for the automatic door?" His question broke through her mental tirade.

"Right." Leaving her rack, she rushed up the ramp and pushed the button, which opened the door wide and allowed them to easily enter the marketplace.

"Danki." He pushed his rack inside, and she followed. Once again they pushed the racks, the main aisle wide enough to accommodate them side by side. "I suppose you do chores around your *haus* when you're not here." He nodded toward the baked goods. "And you bake."

"*Ya,* that's right. *Mei mamm* and *schweschder* sew and quilt, and sometimes I help them. But I'd rather bake than sew."

"It's going to be super busy this weekend. Prepare for an influx of tourists who came to spend the holiday weekend in Amish Country."

"That's what Salina told me, so I baked more than I would have. That's why these racks are so full."

"Do Phoebe and your *mamm* help you bake?"

She looked up at him, surprised by his interest. "*Ya,* they do. Does your family help you with your wood and leather creations?"

"No." One side of his mouth tipped up in a half smile. "They're supportive, but they don't make any of the items I sell." He pulled his rack into the booth and then pulled out a box of chocolate chip cookies. "Where would you like these *kichlin*?"

"You don't need to help me unpack." She pointed to the back of the booth. "Would you please just put the two racks back there?"

"I have a few minutes." He pointed to nearby shelves. "So *kichlin* over here?"

"How about you hand them to me?" she said, deciding she might as well concede.

For the next several minutes, Jeff handed her the contents of the racks, and soon her booth was restocked and ready for the day.

"Danki." She held out a box of macadamia nut cookies. "Would you like to take these as payment for your help? I promise I won't tell your family I gave them to you."

He laughed. "I appreciate the secrecy, but you don't need to pay me with baked goods you want to sell."

"Okay. How about *kaffi,* then? I'm planning to go visit with my cousins at the Coffee Corner before the market opens."

"You don't need to pay me at all. I'm just *froh* I was there to help before you broke a toe." He pointed toward his booth. "I need to get set up too."

"So you won't join me for *kaffi*?" Inwardly she groaned. Why had she sounded so needy — and interested? She couldn't be developing feelings for Jeff. *You just want to be his friend, remember?*

"I'll come by after I get set up, but you don't need to buy *mei kaffi.*"

"Okay." She smiled. "*Danki* again."

He nodded and then disappeared from her booth.

At the Coffee Corner she found her cousins sitting at their usual high-top table. When she entered the booth, Bethany hopped up and walked to the counter with her, and Christiana purchased a cup of coffee and a cinnamon donut.

"*Gude mariye.*" Christiana greeted her other cousins as she joined them at the table. "How are you all today?"

"Great." Leanna leaned forward and grinned. "And I see you are too."

"What do you mean?" Christiana asked before taking a bite of her donut.

"I saw Jeff helping you bring in your rolling racks this morning." Leanna winked at her.

"Is that so?" Bethany grinned. "You and Jeff, huh? *Gut* for you. He's a *gut* man."

"What?" Christiana shook her head. "No, no. It wasn't like that at all. I was struggling, and he helped me get them both out of the van. Well, he also helped me unload them."

"That's really sweet," Salina said. "I sure could use some help unloading my supplies."

"I don't think he likes me like that. We're

just *freinden*." Christiana sipped her coffee.

"I don't think that will last long," Salina said.

"I agree. I saw the way he looked at you last week when we were setting up your booth," Leanna said, chiming in.

"I saw it too," Bethany said.

"And he was so kind to Chester. Who wouldn't want a nice man like that?" Leanna added.

"Stop! I'm not interested, and neither is he."

"Why aren't you interested?" Bethany's brow furrowed. "What's wrong with him?"

"Nothing is wrong with him, although at first I wasn't sure. He seemed so rude." Christiana ran her finger over the top of the table to avoid their gazes. "I just don't have time for a boyfriend."

Salina snorted, and Leanna started to choke on her coffee.

"You're so *gegisch*." Bethany rubbed Leanna's back as she wiped her watery eyes. "You have time for a boyfriend if you make time for one." She turned to Leanna. "Are you okay?"

Leanna wiped her eyes and chuckled. "I am. I just wasn't expecting that response. Of course you have time for a boyfriend, Christiana. Why wouldn't you?"

"I'm just so busy." Christiana heaved a deep sigh. "If I'm not working here, I'm baking at home to get ready to come back here. Before I opened the booth, I was just as busy at home baking and running my stand. If I had a break from baking, then I had chores to do. Dating hasn't fit into my life."

"You have to make time," Bethany said. "That's the only way you're going to find someone to marry."

"What if I'm just not interested right now?" Christiana studied the liquid in her cup.

"Gude mariye," a sweet voice sang out.

Christiana looked up as a pretty brunette stepped into the booth. Christiana turned to Salina as her cousin pressed her lips together in a tight frown.

"Hi, Sara Ann." Bethany's greeting wasn't quite as chipper as usual. "Do you want *kaffi*? Today's special is caramel."

"Oh, that sounds delightful! Of course I want some!" Sara Ann's laugh was a little too loud as Bethany jumped up and headed to the counter. "I always need your *kaffi*, Bethany." She looked around the table and then stuck her hand out to Christiana. "Hi. I'm Sara Ann King, but you can call me simply Sara Ann." She laughed as she shook

Christiana's hand, and Christiana noticed she had lovely gray eyes.

"I'm Christiana." She managed a smile.

"I heard you took over that empty booth. How nice." Sara Ann's smile seemed a little forced too. "Do you live close by?"

"I live in Bird-in-Hand."

"Oh." Sara Ann looked around the table. "How do you know these ladies?"

"They're my cousins."

"Oh." Sara Ann's expression brightened. "How nice to have so many cousins. Are you married?"

"No." Christiana felt her eyes narrow. Why did Sara Ann ask so many questions?

"Neither am I." Sara Ann sighed. "But hopefully I'll find the right man someday." She gestured toward the booth exit. "I have a quilt booth next to Salina's booth. Welcome to the market."

Danki," Christiana said. "It's nice to meet you."

"Here you go." Bethany handed Sara Ann her coffee, and Sara Ann paid her.

"I'll see you all later. Don't be strangers." Sara Ann gave a dramatic wave and left.

Christiana examined her cousins' relieved expressions. "Why do you all seem *froh* she's gone?"

"Simply Sara Ann is our resident gossip,"

Salina began. "Don't tell her anything you don't want broadcast all over the market."

"That's exactly right," Leanna said. "She wants to know everything about everyone, so don't tell her anything personal. She's been hounding me to find out what happened to my husband, but I refuse to give her any information. That's too personal and too painful for her to use as fodder at one of her quilting bees."

Christiana nodded as her heart squeezed. She felt like Leanna's husband had died in that accident just yesterday, but it had been three long years ago. Her heart still broke for her cousin and Chester.

"Hi there!" Bethany's bright tone returned as Jeff stepped into the booth. "How are you?"

"I'm fine, *danki.*" Jeff's eyes found Christiana, and his handsome face lit up with a smile. "I told you I'd come by."

"I'll get your *kaffi* and donut." Bethany headed to the counter. "Now that you've switched to my specialties, I assume you want my caramel *kaffi* today."

"*Ya. Danki.*" Jeff approached their table and stood between Leanna and Salina as he leaned his forearm on it.

"You did say you'd come by." Christiana sat up a little taller as in her peripheral vision she spotted Salina smiling at her. "I was just telling my cousins how you saved me from the teetering rack."

"I was afraid she was about to lose a toe," Jeff said.

Leanna and Salina laughed.

"Here you go." Bethany placed a cup of coffee and a donut on the table in front of him, and he paid her.

"Are you ready for the rush this weekend?" he asked before sipping his coffee.

"No." Salina shook her head, and the ties from her prayer covering bounced off her shoulders. "I think I'm going to run out of produce too fast."

"I hope I run out of jams and jellies." Leanna held up her coffee cup. "Here's to a successful weekend."

"Hear, hear." Jeff touched his cup to Christiana's and then her cousins'.

Christiana studied his face, taking in his bright smile and the curl that flopped over his forehead. Her attraction to him was growing despite her determination to be only friends.

But not only did she not want to tell her cousins about the attraction, but she didn't want to admit his strange manner was holding her back. She went through her concerns again. The way he'd rejected her offer of an apology when she first spilled the coffee on him. How he sometimes seemed so awkward when they spoke. And why did he have his own home but was still single at nearly thirty? Something seemed a bit off about Jeff. Something she couldn't put her finger on.

Besides, she didn't need a relationship right now. She had to concentrate on her booth and make sure it was successful to convince her father to allow her to keep it open.

"*Ach* no." Salina glanced toward the clock on the far wall. "We need to get back to our booths. The doors will open soon."

"It's time to sell out of all our goods." Leanna gathered up her coffee cup and purse. "I'll see you later."

"Have a *gut* day," Bethany sang out.

Christiana walked with Jeff and Salina toward their booths.

As they rounded a corner to enter their aisle, Salina quickened her pace. "I'll see you both later. Have a *gut* day." She winked at Christiana before disappearing into her booth.

Christiana sucked in a breath, hoping Jeff hadn't seen the wink.

As they approached his booth, she turned to face him. "*Danki* again for your help this morning."

"I'm *froh* to assist anytime." He grimaced as voices sounded from across the market. "I think it's about to get crazy. Are you ready?"

"I'm definitely ready."

"See you later." He gave her a nod and then stepped into his booth.

As Christiana walked into hers, a knot of people came right behind her.

"Good morning," she said as she set her coffee on the counter and turned to face her first customers of the day. A smile overtook her lips. How she loved her booth and the chance to see her cousins so often. But, she had to admit, she also loved the freedom that having her business at the market gave her. She could concentrate on it without her father's strict oversight.

"How was your day?" *Mamm* asked as Christiana entered the kitchen that evening.

"Salina said it would be crazy, but that's not quite the correct adjective." She dropped into a kitchen chair as her feet throbbed. The aroma of a roast filled her senses. "It was beyond crazy. It was insanity."

"That busy?" Phoebe handed Christiana a glass of water.

"I ran out of everything and brought home empty racks. I'm going to have to get everything we made yesterday out of the freezer and make more *kichlin* tonight." She looked up at her sister. "And I really need your help. I thought I could handle this weekend alone, but I can't."

Phoebe turned toward *Mamm*. "May I please go with her tomorrow? Please. Please. Please!"

"*Ya.* You don't have to beg, Phoebe Kate." *Mamm* opened a cabinet. "Let's get a batch of *kichlin* in the oven before your *dat* gets home. The roast will be ready soon, and we can put the *kichlin* in. What should we make first?"

"Peanut butter *kichlin* seem to go fast." Christiana took a sip of water and then stood up. Oh, how her feet ached.

"Did you see Jeff today?" Phoebe asked.

"*Ya.*" While she gathered the ingredients for the cookies, Christiana shared how he helped her with her racks.

"That was so kind of him," *Mamm* said. "He seems like a very nice young man."

Phoebe grinned. "I think he likes you. He seemed so *froh* to help you when you moved in last week."

Christiana kept her eyes focused on making the cookie batter. How could she tell

113

her mother and sister that she didn't think Jeff was the man for her? Would that sound prideful?

Mamm sidled up to her. "What are you afraid of?"

"What?" Christiana met her gaze. "You think I'm afraid of Jeff?"

"I don't think you're afraid of Jeff, but I have a feeling you're afraid of falling in love."

"Love?" Christiana nearly choked on the word. "What makes you think I'm falling in love with someone I just met?"

"I didn't say that." *Mamm* pulled another mixing bowl from a cabinet. "You just seem to shy away from the idea of getting to know him and leaving open the possibility of falling in love."

"Where is this coming from?" Christiana stared at her mother. "You've never pressured me to fall in love before. Are you suddenly in a hurry to marry me off? Do you want to make my room into a second sewing room or something?"

Mamm chuckled. "Don't be *gegisch*. I'm not in a hurry to see you married, but I'd like to see you *froh*."

"I am *froh*." Christiana gestured around the kitchen. "I have my family and my baking. That's all I need right now. I'm only

114

twenty-five. I don't need to complicate my life with a relationship that probably won't last."

"Probably won't last?" Phoebe scrunched her nose as if she smelled stinky cheese. "Why would you say that?"

"None of my other relationships lasted more than a few months, so why would I even bother worrying about it?" Christiana stirred the batter. "I don't even know what it means to fall in love. Leanna talks about when she fell in love with Marlin and how she was certain he was the one God wanted her to marry. She said that's why they were married when they were only twenty. I've never felt that complete and overwhelming love for a man. My boyfriends were more like *freinden.* I couldn't see myself spending the rest of my life with any of the men I dated."

"It will happen when the time is right." *Mamm* patted her hand. "God will put the right man in your life when you least expect it. When I met your *dat,* I had given up on ever getting married."

"Really?" Phoebe asked.

Mamm nodded. "I had dated a few young men, and they were kind and *gut* Christians. I liked them, and I even considered marrying one of them. But it never seemed

115

quite right. I guess they didn't warm my heart the way a husband should." A smile turned up her lips. "But when I met your *dat,* I knew he was the one God intended for me." She touched Christiana's cheek. "You'll know when you find that man. God will tap you on the shoulder. He'll make sure you feel it in your heart."

Christiana swallowed against her dry throat. "We'd better get these *kichlin* ready for the oven."

Mamm's words echoed through her mind as she dropped the batter onto a cookie sheet. Would she really feel God's nudge when she met the man she was supposed to marry?

7

Jeff folded his arms over his chest and gritted his teeth as he stood at the front of his booth the following afternoon. Not only did the line into the Bake Shop snake down the aisle past his space, but other customers were weaving past the line, ignoring his booth entirely.

He craned his neck and looked back at the items lining his shelves, all seeming to wait patiently for customers to buy them — customers who would have to fight their way through Christiana's line to access his booth — *if they even noticed it.*

Blowing out a deep sigh, he turned back toward the chaos. Was Christiana giving away free samples today? What on earth had caused this madness? He pushed his hand through his thick hair. If only Kent Dobson had another empty booth, he would gladly move his business away from Christiana's.

But then I might not see her around the

market as much.

He swiped the thought from his mind. He had opened the booth to earn an income, not make friends.

But that wasn't true. He'd opened the booth to find an outlet for his heartbreak. Still, he wanted to sell his work, not just leave it on the shelves. But Jeff could never save his business if the entrance to his booth was constantly blocked.

His discouragement deepened as he made his way to the workbench at the back of the booth. He dropped onto a stool and pulled out a piece of leather. Soon he was cutting out a key chain in the shape of a cat.

"Excuse me."

Jeff looked up, startled. A woman about his mother's age was staring down at him. "I'm sorry. I didn't hear you come in."

"You looked like you were deep in concentration." She gestured toward the key chain. "You do amazing work."

"Thank you." He stood. "How may I help you?"

"I was looking at your personalized bracelets, and I think my granddaughters would love them." She pointed to the display. "I found their names there, so I'd like to purchase them along with a few key chains and wooden name trains."

"Great. Thank you." He waited at the counter with the cash register while she gathered the items she wanted to buy. After he rang up her purchases, she paid him, and then he deposited the gifts into a bag. "I'm glad you came in today." And he was. At least he'd had one customer today, and she'd bought several items.

"This market is wonderful." She slipped her change into her wallet. "I need to bring my sister here."

"That would be nice." He handed her the bag with her gifts, and she smiled.

"Have you eaten anything from that bakery next door?" Her smile widened. "That young lady is talented too. I had one of her peanut butter cookies. Oh my goodness!" She grinned as she held up another bag dangling from her arm. "I bought some for my grandchildren. They'll love them."

Jeff grunted. "Her baked goods are fantastic, but it would be nice if her line was a little shorter."

Her smile faded. "What do you mean?"

"Her line is blocking my booth." He pointed toward the mob of customers in the aisle. "You're the first person who's come in here all day."

"Oh." She looked over her shoulder, and then she smiled again. "I'm sure more people will come in. You have a marvelous selection too. Thank you. Enjoy the rest of your day."

"You too." Jeff leaned forward on the counter as the woman left. He glowered as she excused herself while weaving through the line of customers waiting for their chance to visit Christiana's booth.

He stood up straight. Maybe he could ask her customers to move away from his booth. But would that inspire them to peruse his store and purchase some of his gifts? No, probably not. His sales had been stagnant for nearly a month now. The line wasn't his only predicament.

Jeff groaned and made his way back to the worktable, trying to channel his frustration into creating more key chains. He needed to find a hot new item to sell, but what? He racked his brain and stared at his inventory, but the undercurrent of annoyance continued to nip at him.

Jeff's foul mood hovered around him like his own personal dark cloud.

Most of the day had been a waste of his time. He'd spent the remainder of the afternoon creating leather and wooden key chains, glancing at Christiana's crowd moving past his booth in their nonstop line.

He'd also continued to search his mind for an item to make that could boost his sales, but he'd come up blank. That one woman had been his only customer, and that reality caused his bad mood to fester. He was going to lose his business, the one thing that helped console his broken heart.

When he arrived home, he was greeted by his mother's and Kathy's perky dispositions as they cooked supper together, and their smiles only served to irritate him further. He answered their questions with brief retorts and then retreated to his workshop until Nick retrieved him.

While Jeff ate supper, he tried his best to keep his focus on his hamburger casserole instead of his brother's and Kathy's overt happiness. He longed to go back to his workshop and avoid his family until it was time for evening chores. He was in no mood to witness anyone's love. No, not today.

"Are you all right, Jeff?" *Mamm*'s question pulled him back to the present.

"Ya." Jeff nodded before sipping his drink.

"You seem rather grouchy." *Mamm*'s tone was hesitant, as if she feared Jeff's temper might snap.

"It was a long day." Jeff worked to keep his tone even.

"Was the market busy because of the

121

holiday weekend?" Kathy had gathered up their empty dinner plates and was putting the percolator on the stove.

Jeff rubbed his chin as he considered his response. "*Ya,* the market was busy."

"I'm sure you sold quite a few gifts," *Dat* added.

"No, actually, I didn't sell much at all. It was one of the slowest days I've had since I opened." Jeff gripped his glass of water and took a long drink.

"Oh. Well, uh, did you get any *kichlin* from Christiana?" *Dat*'s eyes seemed hopeful.

Jeff shook his head. "I couldn't get close to her booth once the market opened."

"What do you mean?" *Mamm* asked as she brought a chocolate chip cheesecake to the table.

"Her booth was busy all day. A line of people stretched in front of my booth all day long."

"No kidding." Kathy set mugs on the table for their coffee.

"No, I'm not kidding."

"I'm certain *she* had a profitable day," Nick said.

"*Ya.* At least one of us did," Jeff muttered.

Nick raised his eyebrows, but Jeff ignored the implied question.

"I'm sure you'll have more customers

tomorrow," *Mamm* said with a bright smile. "Let's sample this chocolate chip cheesecake. It's my first time trying this recipe."

"It looks fabulous." Kathy rubbed her hands together.

"I agree," *Dat* said.

But Jeff wasn't as interested in baked goods as usual. Not tonight.

Jeff approached his back porch just as a horse and buggy came to a stop at the top of his rock driveway. Lewis Blank, his best friend since school, climbed out of the buggy.

"Lewis." Jeff walked over and shook his hand. "It's great to see you. What brings you out here tonight?"

"I was out this way and thought I'd stop by. How are things?"

"Fine." Jeff pointed toward the porch. "Do you have a minute to sit?"

"*Ya,* of course."

"Let me get us some cold drinks." Jeff rushed into the house, where he grabbed two glasses of his homemade root beer before joining Lewis on the porch again. They sat down side by side in rocking chairs. "What were you doing out this way?"

Lewis took a drink of the soda and then set his glass on the small table between them. "I sort of had a date."

"What?" Jeff grinned. "When did you meet someone?"

"I ran into an old *freind* a couple of weeks ago, and we started talking." Lewis studied his glass as if to avoid Jeff's gaze. "And I went to visit her tonight."

"Who is it?"

Lewis looked up at Jeff. "Do you remember Renae Detweiler?"

"From youth group?" Jeff chuckled. "Of course I do. I've noticed her at church a few times. How's she doing?"

"She's great." Lewis pushed his rocking chair in motion. "She's twenty-eight and not married." He gestured between them. "Just like us. And she's still *schee* and sweet. I had a crush on her when we were eighteen, but I never had the confidence to ask her out."

"This is news to me." Jeff studied him. "Why didn't you ever tell me you liked her?"

"I don't know." Lewis shrugged. "I guess I was afraid you'd laugh at me." He cleared his throat. "Anyway, she's still great, and she's interested even after all these years. So I went to visit her tonight, and I'm going to go see her again tomorrow night."

"Wow." Jeff shook his head. "If your relationship progresses . . . I thought we'd be the last bachelors from our youth group."

"I never wanted that title."

"Neither did I." Jeff stared out toward his parents' house and then felt a new jolt of loneliness as he spotted Nick and Kathy walking to Nick's buggy. Soon Nick would ask Kathy to marry him, and then, he suspected, Lewis would eventually ask Renae. Jeff would be among the last few bachelors in his circle of friends and family.

"What's on your mind?" Lewis asked.

"Nothing." Jeff made sure to keep his tone light. "How's the lawn ornament business?"

"*Gut.*" Lewis picked up his glass again. "It was busy today, and we expect it to be even busier tomorrow. How's the market?"

"Fine." Jeff kept his eyes focused on his father's house.

"Fine?" Lewis angled his body toward Jeff. "That wasn't a very convincing response. What's going on?"

Jeff rested his left ankle on his opposite knee as he kept his gaze trained across the field. "Today wasn't a *gut* day."

"What happened?"

Jeff explained about Christiana's booth and how her long line of customers had blocked his booth all day long.

"I had one customer today." Jeff held up an index finger. "One. On a holiday weekend when the market was packed with tourists."

"Well, we can be *froh* for her that her booth is already so successful. You told me when you opened yours that you were taking a chance. She must be *froh* that she moved her business there."

Jeff pressed his lips together as he stared at Lewis. "That's all you have to say?"

"What do you want me to say?" Lewis shrugged. "You had a bad day. So what? We all have bad days. I think they're God's way of reminding us how blessed we truly are. Tomorrow will be better."

"It's more complicated than that." Jeff blew out a deep sigh. "The truth is sales were okay in the beginning, maybe because I was offering something new. But they haven't kept up. I'm afraid I'll have to close my booth." Saying the words aloud sent an ache radiating through his chest.

"Really? I had no idea."

"I was hoping sales would improve. I keep trying to come up with an idea for a new item that might help, but I can't think of anything that will bring people in. I've already filled my shelves with everything *mei daadi* taught me to make."

"Have you thought about visiting another market to get ideas?"

Jeff shook his head as he fingered his glass. "No. Maybe I should try that." He sighed again. "Still, it won't help to have new ideas if her line blocks my booth all day."

Lewis paused, and Jeff could almost hear the wheels turning in his friend's head. He could always count on Lewis to give him good, sound advice.

"How close are you to the *maedel* who runs the booth?" Lewis asked.

"I would say we're *freinden.* We talk."

"That's *gut.* What if you had an honest conversation with her? Ask her to help you come up with a solution so customers can access both your booths?"

Jeff considered this. "I suppose that might work." *If I were as confident and articulate as you are.*

"How much do you like her?"

"Why?"

Lewis's expression grew serious. "I know Ella hurt you, but you've been alone too long."

"Oh no." Jeff groaned and cupped his hand to his forehead. "Not you too. I don't need another lecture about how I need to move on and be *froh* because everyone else is."

"Whether you want to hear it or not, it's true," Lewis said, his tone insistent. "I'm already so much happier since I started seeing Renae, and if you found someone, you'd be happier too. We're not getting any younger."

"I know that." Jeff stared down at his root beer. "I'm just not ready."

"You need to push yourself."

"It's not that easy."

"Why not?"

"Because I'm surrounded by memories. They're everywhere." Jeff pointed to the floor. "Do you know why I built this wraparound porch?"

Lewis shook his head.

"Because Ella wanted it. Do you know why *mei haus* has one bedroom on the first floor and three on the second floor?"

"Because Ella wanted it."

"Exactly." Jeff pointed at him. "I start and end every day with my memories of her. I can't escape them."

"Things happen, but we move on. It's not your fault that she changed her mind."

"Maybe it was my fault. Maybe I hurt her somehow. I'll never know because she didn't tell me. All she said was that she couldn't marry me, and then she married someone else six months later." Jeff was aware of the despondency in his voice. "I don't know how to move on from that devastating blow to both my heart and my self-esteem."

"Have you prayed about it?"

"*Ya,* I pray about it all the time." His throat felt thick, and he cleared it. He had to get hold of his emotions before he said too much to Lewis. He couldn't bear the thought of getting emotional in front of his friend. "So what's your biggest seller this time of year?"

Lewis studied him for a beat, and then his expression relaxed. "The tourists love lighthouses the best. A few years ago, *mei bruder* convinced *Dat* to make lighthouses the size of our wishing wells, and they're a great success. We can't seem to keep up with the demand."

As Lewis told him more, Jeff tried to imagine what he would say when he talked with Christiana tomorrow. Tonight he would ask God to give him the right words. He needed a solution to the dilemma outside his booth.

8

"I'm so grateful you were here to help me this week," Christiana told her sister as she sat on a stool behind the booth's counter the following late afternoon. "There's no way I could have kept up with the flow of customers without you."

"Gern gschehne." Phoebe sat on the stool beside her, kicked off her shoes, and rubbed one foot. "I can't believe how crazy it was. Your shelves are empty again — except for one box of chocolate chip *kichlin*. I'm glad it's Saturday so we don't have to stay up late baking tonight." She gestured toward the empty shelves. "We didn't even get a chance to eat lunch." She rubbed the other foot.

"I'm sorry you were on your feet all day. We'll get all our chores done as soon as possible tonight so we can get to bed early. We have church tomorrow."

"It's not your fault." Phoebe cupped her

hand over her mouth to stifle a yawn. She perked up as she looked down. "Hi, Daisy. How are you?"

The cat meowed, and Phoebe jumped up. "May I give Daisy something to eat?"

"Of course. You know where I keep her bowls and food." Christiana smiled at the gray tabby. "How are you, Miss Daisy?"

The cat walked in circles around Phoebe's feet until she gave her a snack and some water from a cooler. Christiana turned her attention to the cash register and began to count the money. She looked up when her sister spoke, breaking her concentration.

"Hi, Jeff." Phoebe greeted him as he walked into the booth. "How was your day?"

"Long," he said.

"Hi." Christiana felt her smile wobble as she took in Jeff's frown. "We have one box of chocolate chip *kichlin* left. Would you like it?"

He seemed to hesitate, but then he nodded. "*Ya. Danki.* How much?" He reached for his back pocket.

"Just take it." Christiana pointed to the box as Phoebe handed it to him. "You can hide it from your family if you'd like to keep the *kichlin* all for yourself." She forced a smile in hopes he'd smile, too, but his frown didn't waver. "*Was iss letz?*"

131

"I need to talk to you." He approached the counter and set the box of cookies on it.

"Oh. Okay." Christiana studied his dark eyes, but she wasn't certain what she found there. Sadness? Frustration? Now what? Her stomach tightened.

"I've tried all day to get over here to talk to you, but I couldn't get your attention." Jeff gestured around the booth. "I don't think the stream of customers ever stopped coming."

"They didn't." Christiana shook her head. "You can see my inventory is wiped out. Phoebe and I are both exhausted."

"That's for sure," Phoebe muttered as she grabbed a broom from the corner and began to sweep the floor.

"I'm sure you are." He cleared his throat and seemed to ponder his words. "Have you noticed that your line of customers goes down the aisle?" He pointed outside the booth.

"*Ya,* I have. I'm surprised by how busy the Bake Shop has become already." Christiana placed her hands on the counter. "I thought I'd have to build up interest, but I think the sign *mei dat* put out where my bake stand was, inviting customers to come here, has already worked. I recognized a few of my regulars both yesterday and today."

132

"Right." Jeff rubbed his chin. "The interest has been overwhelming."

Christiana pursed her lips as irritation buzzed through her. He was stalling, and she was ready to pack up her empty racks and go home. The sooner she ate supper and did her chores at home, the sooner she could rest. "What are you trying to get at, Jeff?"

"Look, Christiana." He pushed the curl off his forehead, and it bounced back as if it were trained to sit there. "I don't know your situation, but I need my sales from this booth to at least cover my booth rent." A muscle ticked at his jaw. "I can't make money when your line blocks my business. Even if customers notice my items, they don't seem to want to lose their place in your line. But then they don't come back to my booth either. I had only one customer yesterday and only one again today. If this keeps up, I'll have to close my booth."

"I'm sorry." Christiana's stomach seemed to tie itself into a knot as she took in the crease in his forehead. "I didn't realize it was a problem."

"How could it not be a problem?" Frustration dripped from his words as he pointed outside the booth, and now she knew what she'd seen in his eyes — anger.

133

"Look," he said, "only a narrow aisle separates our booths from Salina's and Sara Ann's. With your customer line that long, I'm sure it's bad not just for me. It's bad for them too." He placed one hand on her counter. "Your booth isn't the only one in this market."

Christiana sat up straighter as her own anger engulfed her from the inside out. "I'm aware of that —"

"So we need to come up with a solution so your booth isn't the only one making a profit."

"I won't apologize for my baked goods being so popular, and I doubt Salina and Sara Ann's sales are being affected or they would *politely* talk with me about it. There's no need for you to speak to me with that tone just because *you* aren't making a profit."

He paused and took a deep breath. "I apologize for my outburst, and you have a point about your cousin and Sara Ann. But I don't come here for fun. I'm here to sell my goods and make a profit, just like everyone else. If we can't come up with a solution, this won't work."

"This won't work? *This?*" She leaned forward and did her best to pin him with a glare. "What does that mean? This isn't *your* market. You're just a vendor like I am." She pointed to her chest. "You can't make decisions about who's permitted to rent this booth."

He blinked as if he were caught off guard.

"I have just as much right to sell my items as you do." Her voice rose as her fury broke free. "At least my booth doesn't smell like I'm burning down the entire market. A few customers have asked me if something was on fire."

Jeff's mouth worked, but no words escaped his lips.

"I'm exhausted," she continued, her voice quavering. "My feet are throbbing, and my back aches, so if you don't have anything else to say, I'm going to pack up and go home. We've already called for our ride, and Phoebe and I have to be up early for church tomorrow."

He swallowed, and his Adam's apple bobbed. "Do you need help with your racks?"

Christiana stifled a sarcastic snort. "No. *Danki.*" She lifted her chin. "We can handle them just fine by ourselves. Have a *gut* night." Then she spun on her heel and began to gather what she needed to take home. Frustration pulsed through her veins as she kept her back to him until she finally heard his footsteps fade away.

She turned and found the box of cookies she'd given him still sitting on the counter. Then she put a finger to her lips, signaling Phoebe to be quiet. She didn't want her sister to make comments that might be overhead by any other vendors. They'd probably heard enough just now when she'd raised her voice. At least Sara Ann and Salina weren't in their booths, but no walls separated one vendor from another — just shelves and counters filled with product and goods.

When she and Phoebe were ready, they pushed her two rolling baker's racks outside to wait for their ride.

"I can't believe he said that to you," Phoebe hissed as they stood near the back of the parking lot. "How can he blame you for your booth's popularity?" She gestured widely. "In fact, he should be thanking you."

"Thanking me?"

"*Ya.* Customers have a *gut* chance to peruse his wares while they wait to go into your bakery. Maybe they don't come back to his booth because he doesn't have anything they want to buy."

"I don't think that's it." Christiana shook her head as her irritation morphed into disappointment. Jeff had ruined their friendship today. Perhaps her first impression of him was right — he was bad mannered and temperamental, and that was why he was still single at twenty-eight. Most likely he couldn't find a woman willing to put up with his foul moods. She stared at the ground and kicked a stone with the toe of her black shoe.

"He was just so rude," Phoebe continued, her voice too loud even for the parking lot. "The nerve of him! I really wanted to tell him off, but I knew you'd get upset with me."

"Who did you want to tell off?"

Christiana's head popped up as Simply Sara Ann appeared behind Phoebe.

Oh no. She was the last person Christiana needed to hear about her disagreement with Jeff today.

"Hi." Sara Ann set her two overflowing tote bags down on the ground and then held her hand out to Phoebe. "I'm Sara Ann King, but you can call me simply Sara Ann. And you are . . ."

"I'm Phoebe, Christiana's *schweschder.*" She nodded Christiana's way.

"How nice." Sara Ann's gray eyes sparkled. "Did I hear you say you wanted to tell someone off? What happened? I've been visiting with another *freind* who has a booth here. What did I miss?"

"Well, it was nothing —" Christiana started.

"It was Jeff," Phoebe said. "He barged into *mei schweschder*'s booth and gave her a hard time because her customer line blocks his booth. He said she's ruining his business because he had only one customer yesterday and one again today. I told Christiana that maybe the problem is what he's selling."

"Uh-huh." Sara Ann rubbed her chin and nodded her head.

"He said, 'This isn't going to work.'" Phoebe made air quotes with her fingers. "But it's not his job to decide who rents the booths. Some nerve!"

Christiana cringed and rubbed her forehead. Her sister was telling Simply Sara Ann everything! What would happen when Sara Ann made sure all the vendors knew about her argument with Jeff? They would be the subjects of the hottest gossip in the market!

"That certainly is something." Sara Ann looked as if she was trying to hold back a grin as she turned to Christiana. "Jeff was out of line. What are you going to do about it?"

Christiana shrugged. "Nothing. He's entitled to his opinion. He pays booth rent just like I do."

"Aren't you going to tell Kent that Jeff was out of line?" Sara Ann took a step toward her. "I think the manager ought to know about it."

"I don't." Christiana shook her head. "It's not a big deal. I'm not upset anymore." Where was her driver when she needed him? She glanced at Phoebe, who was staring at her with her brow furrowed.

"I would be furious if Jeff said that to me," Sara Ann said, continuing to offer her opinion.

Christiana looked out toward the road, and relief flooded her when the familiar black van steered into the parking lot. Just in time!

"Well, there's our ride." Christiana grabbed the first rack. "I'll see you next week, Sara Ann. Take care."

Sara Ann nodded. "It was nice meeting you, Phoebe."

"You too."

The van came to a stop beside them. Apparently sensing their exhaustion despite Christiana's insistence that they could manage, their driver helped them load the racks before they climbed inside. Rick Becker was a good man.

"Why did you act as if it was no big deal

when I told Sara Ann what Jeff said to you?" Phoebe whispered as the van bounced toward the parking lot exit.

Before answering, Christiana took in the rows of beautiful potted flowers that welcomed market patrons with their bright colors.

"Because Salina warned me that Sara Ann is the resident gossip at the market." Christiana was careful to keep her voice low as well. "I'm worried she's going to tell everyone in the market what happened today."

Phoebe seemed to study her. "Why does that bother you if you didn't do anything wrong?"

"I don't know." Christiana smoothed her hands over her apron. "I guess I don't like the idea of people talking about me. And I'm hurt that Jeff spoke to me that way."

"Why?" Phoebe said, prodding. "Because you like him?"

"No, I don't *like* him, not the way you mean." Christiana shook her head. "But I was starting to like him as a *freind,* and then he ruined that today." She stared past Phoebe, out the window. "It doesn't matter now since he's blaming me for his terrible sales."

They rode for several minutes with only the hum of the van's engine and country

140

music from the radio breaking the silence. Christiana looked out the window as the quaint Bird-in-Hand business area zoomed by. She took in the quilt stores, the gift shops, the hardware store, her favorite little bookstore, and the fire station. The Bird-in-Hand Family Restaurant was there too. This town was her home.

Christiana let her shoulders droop as her hurtful conversation with Jeff echoed through her mind. She could still see the disappointed expression that overtook his handsome face after she'd lost her temper. But what had he expected?

"I'm sorry." Phoebe's voice broke through Christiana's thoughts.

Christiana turned to her sister. "Why are you sorry?"

"Because I told Sara Ann everything." Phoebe sighed. "I should have respected your privacy."

"It's okay." Christiana touched her arm. "You're not the problem. You were only defending me. *Danki* for being on my side."

"I'm always on your side."

Christiana smiled. She was grateful for her sister despite her sometimes-impetuous nature.

"It sounds like Jeff had a really bad weekend," *Mamm* said as she sat at the table drinking tea with Christiana and Phoebe after supper. She pointed to the box of chocolate chip cookies. "This is all you have left today, but he had a total of two customers in two days? I can see why he's so frustrated."

"*Ya,* but he had no right to blame Christiana." Phoebe held up her mug of tea as if for emphasis.

"I suppose so, but we all get frustrated sometimes, right, Christiana?" *Mamm* asked.

Christiana nodded as her insides seemed to twist and tighten.

"And we all say things we don't mean, right?" *Mamm* added.

"He meant it. I could tell." Phoebe's expression indicated she was convinced.

"What's on your mind, Christiana?" *Mamm* asked.

"I forgive him, but I'm just so hurt." Christiana heard the tremble in her voice. "I thought we might become *freinden.*" She rested one elbow on the table and then her chin in her hand. "I feel so blindsided. But he was rude to me when I first met him, so I guess I shouldn't be surprised."

Mamm's expression grew warm. "It's not your fault that he had a bad day and took it out on you. But do you think you can find a

142

solution to customers blocking his booth?"

Christiana considered her mother's question. "I can at least ask them to not block other booths. Maybe put up a sign."

"Maybe that would work." *Mamm* smiled. "Why don't you try that next week and see if it works?"

"*Ya,* I will." Christiana tried to smile, but it felt more like a grimace. Even if her idea did work, she still believed their friendship was ruined. Forgiving Jeff didn't mean she could just forget what he did. How could she ever forget how he'd accused her of ruining his business?

They could never be friends if he wasn't even sorry. And for some reason, that hurt her to her core.

9

"I was surprised you didn't come for supper tonight," *Dat* said as he climbed Jeff's porch steps later that evening. "How was your day at the market?"

"It was the same as yesterday," Jeff said. *Only yesterday I didn't argue with Christiana.* He held back a groan as guilt and irritation warred within him.

"The same as yesterday?" *Dat* sat down on the rocker beside him. "Do you mean that business was slow due to that bakery next door?"

"Exactly." Jeff stared out toward the pasture, where the sunset streaked the sky with bright shades of red and orange that seemed to mock his grim mood.

"I'm sorry to hear that." *Dat* turned toward him. "What are you going to do about it?"

"Lewis came to see me last night, and when I told him about my dilemma, he sug-

144

gested I talk to Christiana about it. So today I did."

"And . . ."

"It didn't go the way I'd hoped." He sighed and pushed his hand through his curls.

"What happened?"

"I offended her."

"How would you do that?" *Dat* asked.

"I sort of lost my temper." He shook his head as his chest ached with embarrassment. "You wouldn't have been proud of me."

"Tell me what you said."

Jeff recounted the conversation as his father listened. When he finished, he sucked in a breath, awaiting his father's response.

"Well, you could always apologize and then ask her if you could come up with a solution together — this time more nicely." *Dat*'s expression was sympathetic.

"I don't think that will work." Jeff slumped back in the rocker as he recalled how angry she'd been. He thought he was just explaining his frustration to her, but then she bristled, and he lost his temper before she shut him down like a slamming door. In the end, he'd hurt her. "I blew it with her. Our friendship is over now, so I doubt she'll even talk to me."

"Jeffrey, we all have days when we're irritated and say things we don't mean. We're human, and we all fall short of the glory of God. Just apologize and then ask her if together you can figure out how customers can access both of your booths." *Dat* made it sound so easy. "Didn't you say she's a nice *maedel*?"

"*Ya*, I did. But you didn't feel the frustration and anger coming off her. She just about threw me out of her booth."

Dat smiled. "Your *mamm* has been just as irritated with me at times, and she's forgiven me."

"But you and *Mamm* are married. She *has* to forgive you. This is different." Jeff ran his hand down his face. "It's all my fault. I have a short temper, and it got the best of me today. To make matters worse, I always worry I'll say the wrong thing, which makes conversations even tougher. Now I've ruined any chance I had of becoming *freinden* with her."

"I doubt that. I'm sure she'll give you another chance if you ask for forgiveness."

Jeff let his head fall back and smack the back of his rocking chair. He longed to erase the memory of the hurt in Christiana's pretty blue-green eyes. A wave of guilt threatened to pull him under and drown him.

"She'll have forgotten about it by the time Thursday rolls around," *Dat* continued. "Why don't you take her a cup of *kaffi* from that Coffee Corner and ask her if you can talk it over. Tell her you're sorry for losing your temper and ask her if you can talk about the situation like civil adults. She'll be *froh* that you came back to apologize."

"Okay," Jeff said, agreeing just to appease his father. "I'll try that."

"*Gut.*" *Dat* smiled.

But Jeff had a hunch that winning back Christiana's friendship wouldn't be that easy.

"Gude mariye," Christiana said, greeting her cousins as she approached them in the Zook family's kitchen the following morning before the church service.

"How are you?" Bethany gave her a hug.

"I'm all right." Christiana stretched her aching neck and tried to smile.

If she were completely honest, she'd tell them she'd tossed and turned all night as she mentally replayed her argument with Jeff and her irritation and hurt smoldered. But she didn't want to recount the story. She wanted to forget the entire situation.

And she might even want to move her business back to the bake stand at her house to avoid seeing Jeff Stoltzfus ever again.

"Why did you leave the market in such a hurry yesterday?" Salina asked. "When I came back to my booth, you and Phoebe had already left without saying good-bye."

Christiana blew out a puff of air. So much for forgetting what happened and moving on.

"Was iss letz?" Leanna asked.

"I had words with Jeff just as we were closing up the booth, and then Phoebe and I got out of there as fast as we could."

Her three cousins gasped in unison and took a step toward her.

"You had words?" Bethany asked.

"What did you argue about?" Leanna asked.

"What did he say?" Salina added.

Christiana took a deep breath and then recounted her conversation with Jeff as they all listened with their eyes wide. "And to make matters worse, Phoebe shared it all with Sara Ann in the parking lot."

"Oh no." Leanna groaned. "The entire market will know about it before we open on Thursday."

"*Danki* for the encouragement," Christiana deadpanned.

"If your business is doing so well, maybe you should raise your prices." Bethany rubbed her hands together.

"*Danki,* but I think you're missing the point, Bethany," Christiana said. "Jeff really hurt my feelings. He said if my customers don't stop blocking his booth, it isn't going to work — as if he has the power to get the Bake Shop kicked out of the market."

"He was probably just upset because he expected to have *gut* sales over the holiday weekend," Salina said.

"You're taking his side?" Christiana exclaimed.

"No, I'm not." Salina shook her head. "I just think maybe you should give him the benefit of the doubt. You said he kind of hedged before he got to the point of his visit. He might not have meant to be so harsh with you."

"Salina has a point," Leanna said.

Christiana huffed. Maybe she should have kept the conversation to herself.

"He could have been nicer about it," Christiana insisted as her irritation rose to the surface. "He was downright rude. I was hoping we could be *freinden,* but I'm not interested if he's going to behave like that. I can't be *freinden* with someone who's that ill-tempered and judgmental. I'll never go

149

out of my way to talk to him again."

"Gude mariye," Sadie Yoder said as she came up behind Bethany and Leanna. She was a member of the congregation. "How are you all this morning?"

"I'm well." Bethany gave Sadie a hug. "How about you?"

As Bethany and Leanna began a conversation with Sadie, Salina took Christiana's arm and gently pulled her away from them.

"You have feelings for Jeff, don't you?"

"Why would you ask me that?"

Salina frowned. "Because you looked so *bedauerlich* when you said you can't be his *freind.*"

"It's not that." Christiana shrugged. "I've seen sadness in his eyes, and I've wondered if I could help him. But I can't help him if he's going to be rude to me. He told me he's twenty-eight and single, and I can see why. Why would any *maedel* put up with being treated that way?"

"I think you're being too hard on him."

"I don't think you'd feel that way if he'd accused you of ruining his sales."

Salina waved off her comment. "Stop being so prideful, Christiana. Maybe he didn't mean to be so tough on you. Maybe he was just having another bad day. Give him a chance to make it up to you."

Christiana had just opened her mouth to protest when Bethany cut in.

"Sadie just told me she overheard a customer at her hardware store say I sell the best *kaffi* in Lancaster County." Bethany grinned. "What a *wunderbaar* compliment for her to share. She didn't even have to tell me, but I needed a lift today. I had some grumpy customers this week."

"It *was* nice for Sadie to share that, Bethany." Salina kept her eyes on Christiana as she spoke. "Sometimes a *freind* is there for you when you need them most."

Christiana pursed her lips. It was easy for Salina to say that when she wasn't the one accused of ruining someone else's business.

But what if Jeff needed a friend? Was she being prideful by not giving him a chance?

The following Thursday Jeff took a steadying breath and then stepped into the Coffee Corner with a smile plastered on his face.

"Gude mariye," Bethany sang out. "How are you today, Jeff?"

"Fine. *Danki.*" He nodded at Leanna and Salina, who both nodded back. When he turned his gaze to Christiana, he found her studying her coffee cup. Any hope he'd had sagged. She was giving him the cold shoulder, and he felt so guilty. He'd managed to ruin another relationship, but at least this time he knew how he'd done it.

"Today's special is French vanilla. Would you like a cup?" Bethany walked with him to the counter.

"*Ya.* Please." He leaned on the counter and then peeked over his shoulder to where Christiana and her two other cousins whispered. Most likely he was the subject of their conversation. Bethany seemed friendly enough, but were the others conspiring to put him in his place? Had Christiana told them what happened?

His cheeks burned with embarrassment. If only he had the courage to finally apologize, but he couldn't find the nerve to attempt it when she was surrounded by her cousins. He couldn't stand the idea of her rejecting him in front of anyone. And what could he even say to Christiana to smooth things between them? He didn't have the right words.

"How is your week going so far?" Bethany said as she poured his coffee. Her expression was bright as usual. He tried to smile, but he couldn't.

"*Gut.* Yours?"

"Just peachy." She put his cup and a donut on the counter, and he gave her his money. "You have a great day, now."

"Danki." Jeff took his purchases, wishing he didn't have to walk past the table where Christiana and her other cousins sat.

As he approached, their conversation ceased, and once again Christiana turned her attention to her coffee. He nodded at her cousins, who at least didn't pretend as if he weren't there, and left for his booth.

After drinking his coffee and downing the donut, he was rearranging a belt display when Sara Ann entered his booth.

"Gude mariye," she said as she smiled at him. "How are things at your *dat*'s farm?"

Salina and Bethany had warned him long ago that Sara Ann was a gossip, but he'd already known that. They lived in the same district, and everyone in their congregation knew what she was like. He would never say anything he wouldn't want shared. At least she'd never told anyone at the market about Ella leaving him — he didn't think. Even Sara Ann had to have a heart.

"Things at the farm are *gut.*" He forced a smile, and then he started reorganizing his key chain display so he'd look busy. Maybe then she'd leave.

"How has business been here?"

He stilled and studied her. Did she already know the answer to that? If so, was she hoping to get more details to spread around?

No, he wouldn't allow her to use him.

"It's been fine. How about yours?" He tried to keep his tone even.

"Business is *gut.*" She brightened. "I sold six quilts over the weekend."

"Huh." He tried to ignore the river of envy that flowed through him. So Sara Ann's booth really did do just fine despite all the attention given Christiana's, and he had a feeling Salina's did too.

"I heard you and Christiana had a disagreement."

Jeff gritted his teeth as he took in her expression, suddenly smug. She'd been leading up to this.

So Christiana was talking about him — and to a gossip. Why did that hurt him so deeply?

"Who told you that?" He had to know.

"Christiana's *schweschder* told me when they were leaving the market that day. She was really upset about it too." Her pretty face became animated as she recalled the conversation. "She said you were frustrated that the Bake Shop line blocked your booth, and that you had only two customers that Friday and Saturday. Is that true?"

Jeff folded his arms over his chest as he looked at her. A wave of shame rolled over him, and he didn't respond.

"I guess it is true," Sara Ann said. She twirled a ribbon from her prayer covering around her finger. "What are you going to do to improve your sales? I assume you can't pay the booth rent if you don't." She pointed to his shelves. "And you have quite a bit of inventory."

"That was a holiday weekend, and I'm sure her business won't always be as busy as it is now. It's probably just getting extra attention because it's new."

"I suppose so, but I'm certain word about how *wunderbaar* her baked goods are is traveling fast. I heard a few customers say her pies are the best they've ever tasted. They also said she makes superb lemon bars. I'll have to try them. Have you had them?"

"No." He felt his eyes narrow. Was she trying to provoke him?

"I need to take some home to my family. *Mei dat* loves lemon bars. I've tried to make them, but I don't get them quite right." She looked over her shoulder and then back at him. "How are your parents doing?"

First the farm and now his parents? "Fine." He thought he might get whiplash from her quick change of subject.

"And your *bruder* and his girlfriend?"

"They're just fine too."

"That's nice." She looked over her shoulder again, and she waved at Christiana and Salina as they walked by.

His guilt raised its ugly head again as Christiana walked with Salina to her booth. They stopped there and kept talking.

How he longed to interrupt their conversation and apologize, but his fear of rejection kept him cemented in place like the coward he was. Besides, Sara Ann was still there.

"Oh, I wanted to tell you something," she said. "*Mei mamm, schweschder,* and I went to a quilting bee yesterday."

"Uh-huh." Jeff looked past her at Christiana.

"Well, you'll never guess who was there." When he didn't respond, she said, "Jeff. Did you hear me?"

"What?" He turned toward her.

"Guess who was at the quilting bee." She stuck her lower lip out in a pout.

"I don't know. Who?"

"Ella." Her smile widened. "She looked *gut.* She looked *froh* too." Her expression suddenly took on a look of concern, but he didn't think it was genuine. "What happened between you two to make her leave you like she did? I never heard."

Something inside him froze. So that's why

156

she'd come. Sara Ann's mundane questions were just leading up to that one. Did she really think he'd tell her anything about Ella, allowing her to gossip about what happened even more than she probably already had among her friends?

He turned away and started rearranging his display of leather bracelets, his hands vibrating with fury. He shouldn't think the worst of Sara Ann, but at the moment, he couldn't help it.

"The market is going to open soon," he muttered as the donut he'd eaten turned sour in his stomach. "I need to finish getting ready."

"I never understood why she picked John Lantz over you," she said. "I would have chosen you any day. John has no personality. He reminds me of a wet mop."

Was that supposed to make him feel better? Or more open to discussing this with her? Because it didn't. John might have the personality of a wet mop, but he won Ella over and convinced her to marry him. Apparently, a wet mop was better than the house Jeff had built for her.

Jeff banished the thought. He had to calm down.

"Well, I suppose I should get ready as

well," Sara Ann said. "Have a profitable day."

As Sara Ann flittered across the aisle to her quilt booth, Jeff spotted Christiana walking from Salina's booth toward hers. Their gazes entangled, and his heartbeat ticked up. She nodded, but when he returned the gesture, she looked at the floor.

He took a step toward her booth, but then he halted when a half-dozen customers came around the corner. Without hesitation, they filed into the Bake Shop, their excited voices bouncing off the marketplace's walls.

This chance to apologize to Christiana was gone, too, and now he had to wait until the next opportunity presented itself.

He just hoped his courage would appear as well.

10

"You look hungry." Salina walked up to Christiana's counter later that afternoon and handed her something in plastic wrap.

"What's this?" Christiana asked.

"Lunch." Salina nodded at it. "It's half a turkey and cheese sandwich."

"Danki." Christiana hopped up on a stool as Salina pulled over a second one.

"You've been busy again today," Salina said between bites. "I saw a line every time I looked over here."

"I know." Christiana pulled two bottles of water out of a cooler at her feet and handed one to Salina.

"You sound disappointed." Salina opened her bottle and took a drink.

"I'm not disappointed about the business." Christiana gestured toward her shelves. "My baked goods are selling, and I've noticed repeat customers coming in. I'm just disappointed the line is still block-

159

ing Jeff's next door. I put out a sign asking people not to block any other booths, but the line looks the same to me. I don't know how else to help him." She took a bite of the sandwich.

"Why don't you talk to Jeff about it?"

Christiana shook her head as she chewed and then swallowed. "I've forgiven him, but I have nothing to say to him until he tells me he's sorry."

Salina lifted an eyebrow. "Have you always been this stubborn?"

"I don't know. You tell me." Christiana grinned, and they both laughed. "I'll take that as a *ya.*"

"You still care about him," Salina said.

"I care about his business, but he was rude to me. I think he should approach me first. I saw him looking over at me this morning when I was talking to you at your booth." Christiana gestured toward her cousin's farm stand. "But he didn't come over. He needs to make the first move."

Salina nodded. "I guess that's fair."

"*Ya,* it is. And when I looked out into the aisle earlier, I saw those two *maed* who work at the candy booth staring at me as they walked past. I think news about my argument with Jeff has spread, and I suspect Sara Ann started it. Maybe it will all blow over soon, but it might not if Jeff refuses to apologize." Christiana just hoped he would make the effort to fix things between them before thoughts of him drove her to the brink of insanity.

"How has your week been?" Jeff asked Christiana as he stepped into her booth the following Thursday morning. The delicious aroma of her baked goods filled his senses. He'd missed her cookies.

Christiana stopped rearranging a display of pies and turned around to look at him. She looked stunning in a black apron and a bright-green dress that accentuated the green in her eyes. She studied him for a moment, and then her expression relaxed — slightly. "Okay. How has yours been?"

He squelched the urge to cheer. Those were the most words she'd uttered to him since he'd been so rude to her two weeks ago. Of course, this was the first time he'd mustered the nerve to do more than greet her in the morning.

"It's been okay," he said.

When she turned her attention back to her pies, he wondered if she was inventing work to avoid looking at him.

"I need to thank you," he blurted.

She stilled and then faced him. "Thank

me for what?"

"Your customers still form a long line, but they're leaving a gap in it, and I've had more customers come in. I think your sign asking them not to block other booths helped."

"Oh. *Gut.* I didn't realize they were doing that. I'm glad they followed my instructions."

He nodded as they stared at each other, and then he rubbed the back of his neck as he searched for something else to say. Why was talking to someone so difficult for him but so easy for people like Lewis and Nick? He'd had that problem even before he and Ella started dating. But now he needed to restore whatever friendship he and Christiana had before he'd lost his temper with her. Unfortunately, he still couldn't find the words.

"It sure feels like June out there," he finally said. "The weather has warmed up quite a bit."

Ugh. He gave himself a mental head slap. The weather was such a banal subject, but it was better than silence between them.

"There you are!" Bethany announced as she, Leanna, and Salina stepped into the booth, ruining his chance. "When you didn't join us for *kaffi,* we decided to come find you." Bethany looked at Jeff and gave him a little wave. "Hi, Jeff."

"Hello." He held up his hand in greeting as disappointment whipped through him.

"I have a fresh pot of *kaffi* waiting in the Coffee Corner," she told him. "I made white chocolate–flavored *kaffi* today" — her smile brightened — "*and* fresh chocolate donuts. Aren't they your favorite?"

"They are. *Danki.*" Jeff studied Bethany. Did she ever get sad? Or was she bright and sunny all the time? He had a feeling she could find a silver lining in any cloud. "I'll come by in a few minutes."

"Fantastic," Bethany said.

Jeff looked over his shoulder and found Christiana engrossed in a conversation with Salina and Leanna. He gave Bethany a nod and started for his booth.

He looked back at Christiana one last time. His shoulders sagged. Would she ever trust him again? Not if he couldn't find a way to apologize.

"What was he doing here?" Leanna asked as Jeff disappeared into his booth.

Christiana shrugged. "He asked me how my week was going. Then he thanked me for asking the customers to not block other booths."

"I saw that your sign's working," Salina

said. "Your customers aren't blocking Jeff's booth anymore, at least not like they were."

"He said they've been leaving a gap so other customers can get in and out of his booth. He also said his sales have improved." Christiana acted as if it wasn't a big deal, but she was grateful that her customers had respected her request.

"That's fantastic," Bethany exclaimed, just a little too loudly. Like Simply Sara Ann, she needed a volume setting on her voice, but Christiana adored her anyway.

"He sounds like he's trying to say he's sorry about hurting your feelings," Salina said.

"Maybe, but he still hasn't said the words." Christiana tried not to sound as disappointed as she felt.

"Some people struggle with that, so they try to *show* you they're sorry," Leanna offered. "Marlin always had a tough time telling me when he was sorry," she said. "Chester is the same way. He'll offer to help me in the kitchen or weed my garden instead of apologizing."

"That's sweet," Bethany cooed.

"I wish someone would offer to weed my garden," Salina quipped.

"You should be nice to Jeff," Leanna continued. "I think he's really trying."

"I wasn't rude to him," Christiana said, insisting. "I didn't ignore him. I answered him."

"*Gut,*" Leanna said.

"So are you all coming for *kaffi*?" Bethany pointed in the direction of her booth. "I need to get back."

"I have work to do here." Christiana pointed toward her pie display. "I think I'll just drink some water."

Bethany crossed her arms over her black apron and raised her blond eyebrows.

"Are you avoiding Jeff?" Bethany said, as if to challenge her. "Or do you not like *mei kaffi*?"

"I love your *kaffi,* Bethany. Everyone does."

"So what's the problem?" Bethany lifted her chin.

Out of the corner of her eye, Christiana spotted Salina's grin. Was Salina enjoying this interrogation?

"I just need to make sure I have all my baked goods out. I don't get much of a break once the market opens."

But that wasn't the whole truth. She *was* avoiding Jeff. She was confused by her conflicting feelings for him. On one hand, she felt sorry for him because she still found a sadness in his eyes. But on the other hand, she was still hurt by how he'd spoken to her. As she'd been taught, she'd finally forgiven him. But she longed for him to say he was sorry. She was also afraid of where her feelings would lead if he did apologize. Yes, she was confused, and avoiding him seemed to be the best solution to her dilemma.

"You should give Jeff a break," Bethany said. "I think he deserves it."

Christiana blinked at her cousin. What did she mean?

"Let's go get our *kaffi,*" Leanna said as she and Bethany started to leave. "I'll drink a cup for you, Christiana."

"I'll talk to you later." Salina gave Christiana a hug and then disappeared with their other cousins.

Jeff stepped into the Coffee Corner and was surprised when he didn't see Christiana sitting at the high-top table. He'd assumed he'd have another chance to talk to her here, and he hadn't noticed her in her booth when he'd walked past it.

Still, he was relieved she hadn't given him only a cold, curt response to his questions earlier. Although progress was slow, he was at least taking baby steps, as his *mamm* would say.

"I know you want a chocolate donut," Bethany said as she walked to the counter with him.

He smiled. "And you know that's the truth."

She handed him the donut and then poured his cup of coffee.

"Danki." He handed her money. "I'll enjoy this."

"Do me a favor, Jeff," Bethany began as she made his change. "Don't give up on Christiana. She's stubborn, but she'll come around."

Jeff paused as he studied Bethany's sunny expression. "What do you mean?"

She waved him off with a laugh. "You don't have to play dumb with me." She leaned forward and lowered her voice. "I know you hurt Christiana's feelings, but I also know you've been trying to apologize to her."

"How did you know that?"

"Christiana has told me a few things, and I can read between the lines. Christiana is stubborn, but she has a *gut* heart. Just promise me you won't give up on her."

A bit taken aback by Bethany's urging, Jeff took a sip of coffee.

"Promise me," Bethany said, insisting.

"Okay. I promise."

"Gut." Her sunny smile was back. "Now, you have a great day."

As Jeff walked back to his booth, drinking his coffee and relishing its chocolaty taste, he contemplated Bethany's words. Maybe Phoebe had told all the cousins about his rift with Christiana, too, but how did Bethany know so much about what had happened since? Oh, who was he kidding! He was aware that women shared everything, and most likely, Christiana had told her cousins about his lame attempts to talk to her.

Did that mean she cared about him — maybe even beyond friendship? His stomach fluttered at the thought, but he finally had to admit it appealed to him. Did he have a chance with her?

His elation faltered. Maybe so, but she could still change her mind like Ella had.

"How are things with Christiana?" Lewis asked as he sat across from Jeff that Sunday at the meal following their district's church service.

"Not that great." Jeff shook his head as he picked up a pretzel and popped it into his mouth.

"What do you mean? When we last talked, you said you were going to discuss how her

168

line of customers was blocking your booth. Did you talk to her?"

Jeff rubbed at one temple. "*Ya.* Well, that didn't go the way I planned." He explained everything that had happened. "Then on Friday a mutual *freind* at the market, her cousin Bethany, encouraged me to not give up on her, but Christiana isn't the problem. I am. I still can't seem to come up with the courage to apologize to her — and our argument was two weeks ago! She hardly acknowledges me, but I guess I can't blame her."

Lewis shook his head. "And you wonder why you're still single."

Jeff guffawed. "Wow. *Danki* for being so supportive."

Lewis tossed a pretzel at him, and it bounced off Jeff's shoulder before hitting the barn floor. "Why are you such a moron?"

"What's that supposed to mean?"

"Why haven't you tried a different angle?"

"Like what?"

"How about you invite her to have lunch with you?" Lewis snapped his fingers. "Or you could make her a gift. You're the one who makes that amazing stuff tourists love so much."

Ideas popped into Jeff's head. Why hadn't

he thought of that?

"Do you care about her?" Lewis asked.

Jeff hesitated. He not only didn't want to admit that he cared about Christiana but also that he was afraid to risk having his heart broken again.

"She's not Ella."

Jeff bristled at Lewis's casual remark. He ate another pretzel and decided to change the subject. "I saw Renae before the service started, and she said hello to me. How are things going with her?"

Lewis's expression brightened. "Great. She invited me to have supper with her family last night."

"Really?" Jeff asked.

"I had a great time. Her *dat* is funny. I enjoyed talking with him." Lewis's expression warmed. "I really care about her, and I'm going to ask her to be my girlfriend." He lifted another pretzel. "In fact, I believe I'm falling in love." He gave a laugh that sounded nervous. "Who would have thought, huh?"

"Ya." Jeff hated the thread of jealousy that churned in his gut. Would he ever feel that way again? Or would he forever be a bachelor, living alone in the house that felt too big?

"Listen," Lewis said, "back to Christiana

— I can tell you're interested in her as more than a *freind*. You just don't want to admit it because you've been hurt. But you should finally apologize, and then, like this Bethany suggested, give her the chance to forgive you and be *freinden* again. Maybe try that gift or lunch idea — or both. If you don't, you'll always wonder if she could've been more than just a *maedel* you annoyed at the market. Sometimes friendship leads to more."

"Fine. I'll find a way. It's only right," Jeff said. "And I think you're right about the gift or lunch. I can't just apologize. I have to try to make it up to her somehow. But if she rejects me, I'm giving up."

Lewis nodded. "That's fair."

11

"Thank you for coming in today," Christiana told the older woman as she handed her a bag of assorted cookies Thursday morning. "I hope you'll come back soon."

"I sure will, sweetie. This is my favorite shop here at the market. I'll see you again next week."

"Great." As Christiana gave her a little wave, she saw Jeff standing at the entrance to her booth. His intense expression sent an unexpected shiver dancing up her spine. "Jeff."

She glanced around the booth, and when she found it empty for once, she walked over to him.

"What are you doing here?" she asked him.

"I was wondering if you ever take a break for lunch. Your booth has been so busy . . ."

"Why do you want to know?" She searched his eyes.

"There's a nice area beyond the parking lot in the back." He pointed in that direction. "It has picnic tables and a *gut* view of the trees."

She stared up at him, confusion raining down on her. He politely greeted her when she saw him, but now what was he doing? She couldn't keep up with his moods!

When she didn't respond, his expression hardened and he shook his head.

"Never mind," he muttered as he turned toward his booth.

"Wait!" She grabbed his arm and spun him toward her. Had that been rejection in his eyes on top of the sadness she still saw there? It nearly split her in two. "Why were you asking me about lunch?"

He harrumphed. "Because I've been trying to figure out a way to apologize to you after acting like such a jerk —"

She lifted her chin and smiled. "Apology accepted."

"What?" He searched her eyes as his mouth went slack.

"All I ever wanted was to know you were sorry."

He ran his hand down his face. "That's all? I thought maybe I'd have to make it up to you somehow."

"I forgave you soon after our disagreement, but I was still hurt. Your apology frees us both to be *freinden* again." She grinned. "If you're asking me to have lunch with you, I'd love to. I'm tired of working straight through the day anyway. What time? I did bring a lunch."

"So did I. How about one thirty since we always have a rush of customers at noon?"

"Okay. I'll put a sign up saying I'm closed from one thirty to two. My customers can adjust." She glanced over her shoulder to see more customers arriving. "I'll meet you at one thirty."

"Great." He smiled, and her pulse sped up.

"What inspired you to open your bake stand?" Jeff asked Christiana as she sat across from him at a picnic table. She looked so pretty sitting across from him with a warm smile brightening her face.

"Well, I always loved to bake. *Mei mammi, mei dat*'s *mamm,* taught me how when I was little." She shook a handful of chips onto her paper plate next to her ham sandwich and then handed him the bag. "When she passed away a few years ago, she left me her favorite cookbooks. I started baking to work through my grief of losing her. Then I started selling baked goods to neighbors. I also began collecting cookbooks as a hobby, buying them at yard sales and used bookstores. Trying new recipes is fun for me."

She popped a chip into her mouth, chewed, and swallowed. "My baking business sort of got out of hand when my neighbors started placing orders. *Mei mamm* suggested I open a roadside stand so I could be a little more organized. *Mei dat* built the stand, and I started selling baked goods just about every day but Sunday. Then my cousins suggested I move the business here."

"That's a neat story." He put the last bite of his roast beef sandwich into his mouth.

"What about you? Did you say your *daadi* taught you how to make leather and wood items?"

He nodded as he swallowed. "*Ya,* it's the same story, really. *Mei daadi* taught me, and then he bought me my tools. I was visiting the market with *mei mamm* about a year ago, and she suggested I open the booth." He picked up an apple. "Are your cousins your closest *freinden*?"

"*Ya.*" She dabbed at her mouth with a napkin. "Salina, Bethany, and I are close in age. Leanna is a little bit older, but we're all close."

"And Phoebe is your only sibling?"

"Right. She's seven years younger than I

am, but we get along really well. I think the world of her." She pointed her sandwich at him. "You told me you have a younger *bruder,* Nick. Does he look like you?"

"*Ya* and no." He sighed. "He has dark hair and eyes like mine, but he was blessed with straight hair instead of this." He pushed back the curl on his forehead, but it landed in the same place. "He doesn't have to try to beat his hair into submission every morning."

"Aww." She shook her head. "How could you possibly complain about your hair? It's gorgeous."

"Gorgeous?"

"*Ya.* It is." She pointed to his head. "I love that one curl. It's adorable."

Compliments? He hadn't expected any of those today. "He's also taller. He's nearly six feet."

"Wow." Her eyes widened. "Is he married?"

"No, but he has a serious girlfriend. I wouldn't be surprised if he asked her to marry him soon."

"That's nice. What about you? Do you have a girlfriend?"

"No." He pushed past the image of Ella that popped into his mind. "I sure don't. Do you have a boyfriend?"

"No." She shook her head, and he did his best to hide his surprise.

A *maedel* as pretty and wonderful as she was should have been snatched up by a young man in her church district by now.

But she wasn't just pretty. She was kind and thoughtful. She was easy to talk to, and she already seemed like a dear friend. He felt a closer connection with her than he ever had with Ella, and they'd planned to marry. Christiana was different, and she was special. She wasn't afraid of speaking her mind or following her dreams. She was courageous and strong willed.

She smiled, and he admired her striking eyes and the riot of freckles on her nose. How he longed to see more of that bright-red hair peeking out from under her prayer covering. She was beautiful, and she was smiling at him.

He forced a swallow as his throat thickened. He couldn't allow himself to fall for another beautiful woman who would change her mind after he'd given her a piece of his heart. If he had failed with Ella, why wouldn't he fail with Christiana?

Her smile faded, and she tilted her head. "Are you okay?"

"*Ya.*" He reached into his pocket and fingered the gift he'd made for her last night. A gift for a *friend.* "I have something for you."

"You do?" Her eyes sparkled. "What is it?"

"You might think it's *gegisch.*"

"I'm sure I won't." She rubbed her hands together. "I love surprises. What is it?"

"Hold out your hand and close your eyes."

"Okay." She followed his instructions.

He pulled out the wooden key chain that said Christy, and then he set it in her hand, closing her fingers around it. He allowed his fingers to linger against hers for a moment, enjoying the warm feel of her soft skin. Then he pulled his hand away.

With her eyes closed, she moved her fingers over the wood. "May I look now?"

"Ya." He chewed his lower lip, hoping she'd approve of the gift.

Her eyelids flipped open, and her pretty pink lips turned up in a wide smile. "You made me a key chain." She looked over at him and laughed. "It's *wunderbaar.*"

"You like it?"

"*Ya,* I do!" She laughed again and turned it over in her hand. "Christy."

"I thought if I made one that said Christiana it might not fit into your pocket."

She laughed again. "*Danki* so much." She reached across the table and squeezed his hand, but then her smile flattened into a thin line. "I'm sorry for being so terrible to you."

He felt his brow pinch. "What do you mean?"

Christiana sighed. "I realize now that I haven't been fair to you. You've tried to be nice to me, and I was so determined for you to apologize that I rejected you. You deserved better."

Jeff stared at her, speechless.

"Leanna told me she was sure you were trying to apologize and that some people have trouble saying the words *I'm sorry.* She said her late husband was like that and Chester is too. Bethany said I was being too hard on you, and Salina said I overreacted the day you were upset about the line blocking your booth."

She stared down at the key chain. "*Mei mamm* also said you were just frustrated and didn't mean to lose your temper. They all were right. I was being stubborn, determined that you had to apologize before I would be *freinden* with you again. And I definitely misjudged you. I have a bad habit of making snap judgments about people, and it's not right. I'm sorry."

Jeff was overwhelmed as he listened to her. She'd talked about him to her cousins and her mother. Maybe that meant she *did* care

179

about him.

"You're not answering me, so I guess you agree." She looked up at him, a sheepish expression on her face.

"I'm just surprised. I was certain you didn't even like me after the way I lost my temper."

"Like I said, I was hurt, and I wanted to hear you say you were sorry, but I never gave up on you completely."

"I'm glad." *I'm relieved.*

They ate for a few moments as an amicable silence fell over them. Jeff breathed in the warm June air and the sweet smell of the grass. The sun heated the back of his neck as a butterfly fluttered past their table. Birds sang happily in the nearby tall oak trees.

When they had finished eating, Christiana pulled out a ziplock bag filled with macadamia nut cookies and handed them to him.

"Your dessert." She smiled. "And you don't have to share them with your family."

"Danki." His heart warmed. "My favorite." He opened the bag and handed her one.

"Danki." She took a bite and then seemed to study him. "Remember the first day we met and I dumped the *kaffi* on you?"

"How could I forget?" he said, joking.

"Right." She shook her head and her

cheeks flushed bright pink. She was adorable! "You mentioned you were already having a bad day. Why was it so bad?"

He shifted in his seat as panic gripped
him. He wasn't ready to tell Christiana
about Ella, and he might never be ready.

"It was just a bad day." He tried to shrug
it off, but her bright, intelligent eyes seemed
to assess him.

"Sometimes you seem so *bedauerlich.*"
Christiana leaned forward, and now kindness and concern seemed to shine from her
eyes. "Why is that?"

Jeff wanted to run and hide from her
direct questions. They made his skin itch.
She was too intuitive, too sweet.

"I think it's time for us to get back." He
shoved his lunch bag into a nearby trash
can. "We don't want to lose customers
because we're away too long."

"Right." She nodded but seemed uncon-
vinced. He was certain she could see right
through his facade.

They cleaned up the table and then
walked back into the market.

"*Danki* for having lunch with me," he said
when they'd reached their booths.

"I had a great time." She held up her key
chain. "And *danki* again for *mei wunderbaar*
gift."

181

"*Gern gschehne,* Christy." He liked the sound of her nickname. Would she allow him to keep calling her that? Would it be his special name for her?

What was he thinking? He didn't want to get too attached to Christiana, even if he did feel his attraction to her deepening as she grinned at him.

"I'll talk to you later, okay?" she asked.

"I look forward to it." As he stepped into his booth, happiness surged through him despite his fears. No, he wouldn't risk his heart again, but he was still grateful she'd given their friendship another chance.

The afternoon flew by for Christiana as she helped a constant stream of customers and contemplated her lunch with Jeff. She kept the key chain he'd made for her in the pocket of her apron and stroked it periodically. She smiled when she recalled how he'd called her Christy. He felt like a friend, a true friend, and she wanted to get to know him better. She'd tried to get him to share more about himself, but he seemed to shy away from telling her. She couldn't ignore the sadness in his eyes, and she yearned to know why he was so unhappy. How could she get him to trust her with those secrets that seemed to be buried so deep?

Salina stepped into the booth at closing time. "How was your day?"

"Busy again." Christiana moved her piles of bills from the counter to her money bag as Daisy sat beside the cash register. "I think it's going to stay like this. As you can see, I need to bring a lot more baked goods tomorrow."

"But you do have a helper." Salina gestured at the cat, who blinked up at her.

"*Ya*, I do." Christiana laughed.

"It looked like you had an interesting lunch today," Leanna said as she walked up to the counter with Bethany close behind her.

Bethany divided a look between Leanna and Christiana. "What did I miss?"

Christiana shrugged and zipped the money bag shut. "I just had lunch with Jeff."

"Oh *ya*?" Bethany walked up to the counter. "Tell us more."

"We took our lunches out to one of the picnic tables and talked. It was nice." Christiana reached into her apron pocket and touched the gift he gave her.

"What made you get past your hurt?" Leanna asked.

"He finally made an apology, and I told him that I accepted it." Christiana turned her attention to a list she'd made on the

183

counter, trying to avoid their curious stares.

"What did you talk about?" Salina sidled up to her.

"We talked about our families and things like that. We were just getting to know each other." Christiana jotted one more note about what fresh baked goods to bring tomorrow. "He's a really *gut* guy."

"So you finally admit that you like Jeff?" Bethany said, prodding.

Christiana held up both hands and looked each of her cousins in the eye. "Let's all slow down. Right now, Jeff and I are *freinden.* I'd like to just take my time and get to know him." *And find out why he's so sad.* "I need you all to respect that and not tease me or make comments, okay?"

"*Ya,* of course," Bethany said.

"I understand," Leanna added.

"Great." Christiana hefted her tote bags onto one of the racks. "I need to get going. My ride is probably already waiting for me. I'll see you all tomorrow." She pointed toward the aisle.

Bethany and Leanna said good night before heading out of the booth.

Christiana gave Daisy a good-night head rub and then started to push the two racks. Salina grabbed her arm and yanked her back, causing her to stumble. "Hey."

184

"Your ride can wait a minute. Tell me what you're not telling Leanna and Bethany." Salina wagged an accusatory finger at her. "I can tell when you're holding back."

Christiana hesitated, and then she fished the key chain from her apron pocket. "He gave me this."

"Christy?" Salina grinned as she took the key chain. "How adorable."

"I know. I love it." Christiana was sure she was beaming. "He said if he'd made one that said Christiana, it wouldn't have fit in my pocket."

Salina laughed as she handed the key chain back to her. "You really like him."

"*Ya,* I think I do." Christiana studied the key chain. "But I want to get to know him better. I don't want to rush into anything."

"Right." Salina nodded. "I'm glad you two finally talked. I can tell how much better you feel now that he's apologized."

She touched Salina's arm. "But I mean it when I say I want to take it slow. I don't want to get ahead of myself and get too attached before I truly know him."

"That makes sense." Salina squeezed her hand. "Have a *gut* night."

"You too."

"So he invited you to lunch and also gave

185

you a gift." *Mamm* beamed as she scrubbed another pan. "How generous."

"I thought so too." Christiana picked up a dish from the drain-board and dried it with her towel. "I think I'm going to invite him to lunch tomorrow. I'll pack a picnic basket." She began a mental list of what she'd take — lunch meat, rolls, macadamia nut cookies . . .

"I'm just glad he finally apologized," Phoebe announced as she swept the floor. "I didn't like how he spoke to you when he complained about the customer line. He was rude, and you didn't deserve it."

Christiana smiled at her younger sister. "I appreciate how you defend me, but I lost my temper too. And I misjudged him. I wasn't innocent."

Phoebe stopped sweeping. "*Ya,* but he started it. He provoked you. Remember that."

"Maybe so, but it's time to move on." Christiana turned to her mother as Phoebe resumed her task.

"What does his *dat* do?" *Mamm* asked.

"He's a dairy farmer. His younger *bruder* works on the farm when Jeff is at the market just like Phoebe works here when I'm there. Jeff has his own *haus* on the farm."

"Who's Jeff?"

186

Christiana spun to find her father standing in the doorway that separated the kitchen from the family room. "He's *mei freind* from the market."

Dat studied her for a moment while fingering his light-brown beard. "You can't date him until I meet him."

"I didn't say I wanted to date him," Christiana said. "I'm just getting to know him."

"Just remember that he has to ask for my permission." *Dat* wagged a finger at her. "You have to follow the rules, or you'll be back here selling your baked goods at the roadside again."

She nodded. "I understand."

"Gut." Then he disappeared through the mudroom, and the screen door clicked shut.

"Never mind your *dat.*" *Mamm* patted her arm. "I know you won't do anything behind our backs."

"Right, *Mamm.*" Christiana sighed. What she didn't tell her family was how much Jeff intrigued her. Still, she needed to know more about him before she'd even consider dating him. She just had to figure out how to inspire Jeff to open up.

12

"Gude mariye." Christiana stepped into Jeff's booth the following morning and found him working in the back, his burnishing machine humming.

As she crossed the worn, creaky oak floor, the burning smell of the machine filled her lungs and caused her to take a deep breath. She cleared her throat.

He looked up at her and then turned off his machine. "Hi. *Wie geht's?*"

"I'm well." She smiled and looked at the pieces of leather on his workbench. "What are you making?"

He picked up a wallet and handed it to her. "What do you think of this?"

"It's beautiful." She turned it over in her hand and then ran her fingers over the three letters in the corner. *"A-B-C?"* She looked at him. "What does that mean?"

"They represent initials. I've been trying to think of something I can create to boost my sales, and last night it hit me. My customers seem to like personalized items the best, *and* I also sell a fair number of wallets. So wouldn't they buy wallets with initials? I could take special orders."

She grinned. "Wow. That's brilliant!"

"You think so?" She found his hesitant expression endearing.

"*Ya,* I do. I'm sure they'll boost your sales."

"*Danki.*" He set the completed wallet on the workbench. "What brings you over this morning?"

"I was wondering if you want to have lunch again today. I packed a picnic basket with enough food for two."

"Really?" His expression was warm and genuine. "That would be *wunderbaar.* What time would you like to meet?"

"How about one thirty like yesterday?"

"Perfect."

She pulled her key chain from her pocket and jingled the keys she'd added to it last night.

He smiled. "So you like it?"

"I do. It's perfect."

"I'm glad to hear it, Christy." He winked at her, and her insides did a little dance. "I'm glad it's useful."

189

She gave him a wave. "I'll see you at one thirty."

"I'll look forward to it."

"I couldn't decide what kind of lunch meat to bring, so I brought a little of everything." She pulled out small ziplock sandwich bags as they sat at the same picnic table they'd chosen the day before. "I have turkey, ham, and roast beef." Then she pulled out more ziplock bags. "I baked bread, but I wasn't sure which kind you'd like, so I made a variety. I have wheat, white, and rolls."

He grinned. "You're amazing."

"I have cheeses too. Cheddar, American, and provolone."

"Wow. This is too much. The bread looks *appeditlich*. Actually, everything does." He shook his head. "I'll take roast beef and provolone on a roll."

"Coming up." She started building his sandwich, and he watched in awe.

"Has your booth been busy?" she asked.

"It has." He smiled because the words felt so good to say. "Two customers were interested in my personalized wallets. Plus, I took two custom orders for signs. The wallets and signs need to be ready by noon tomorrow, so I might have to stay late tonight."

"Oh, that's a shame."

"Not really." He shrugged. "I don't mind staying late for a sale."

"What will the signs say?"

"They're wedding anniversary gifts for the woman's *kinner*. Each one will have their last name and then the date her sons were married. So it will say Reynolds 2015 or something like that. The wallets are also wedding anniversary gifts that two women ordered for their husbands. They'll have the husbands' initials on them."

"Those are thoughtful gifts." Christiana held out the sandwich. "Here you go."

"*Danki.*" He took a bite, chewed, and swallowed. "This is *appeditlich,* Christy."

"I have chips too." She pulled a bag of chips from her basket and handed it to him.

He opened it and took a handful. "*Danki.*"

"*Gern gschehne.*" She began making a sandwich for herself — turkey and cheddar. "Tell me more about your *grossdaadi* — the one who taught you how to work with wood and leather."

"Oh." He was surprised by the. request. "Well, he was a dairy farmer like *mei dat,* and he had a little shop in the back of his barn where he tinkered with leather and wood. But he didn't sell what he made. That was just his hobby. He enjoyed unwinding in his workshop after a long day on the farm, like I do now."

"What did he do with the items he made?"

"He'd give them to the grandchildren or the neighborhood kids who stopped in to see the cows." Jeff smiled as visions of his grandfather filled his mind. He recalled his booming laugh, his wide smile, and his warm demeanor.

She leaned forward. "What's that smile for?"

"I hadn't thought about that in a long time. It's a nice trip down memory lane." His gaze tangled with hers, and then something passed between them — something warm and familiar and comforting.

Friendship? Or something more?

The last thought caught him off guard, and he bit back a trembling gasp.

"How long ago did he pass away?" Christiana asked, seeming oblivious to his inner confusion.

"Six years ago," Jeff said.

"I'm so sorry. It's difficult to say good-bye to a loved one, especially one who's had such an impact on your life." She shook her head and took another bite of her sandwich.

"What about you?" he said after she'd swallowed. "Tell me more about your *mammi,* the one you told me taught you

192

how to bake."

"She passed away five years ago. She was *mei dat*'s *mamm.* I used to bake with her at least once a week, and we had the most amazing talks. She told me about what life was like when she grew up, and she shared her favorite recipes with me."

"What was your favorite thing to make with her?"

"Oh, her carrot *kuche* with cream cheese icing. It's fabulous." She put her hand to her chest. "I'll have to make one for you."

Jeff grinned. "I'd love that. Tell me more about her."

They spent the rest of their lunchtime sharing stories about their grandparents. Jeff was glad it was another gorgeous June day so they could eat outside. The sun was warm and cheery, and the birds serenaded them from the trees lining the parking lot.

When they arrived back at their booths, Christiana gave him another stunning smile. "*Danki* for joining me today."

"I'm glad you invited me. Let's do it again tomorrow, but I'll bring lunch this time."

"I'd like that."

As she walked away, Jeff felt a stirring in his chest. But he steeled himself against it. He could be only a friend to Christiana. Not that she wanted anything more, but

193

with his history of failure, he was too afraid that even a hint of romantic entanglement would turn out badly.

Christiana hummed to herself as she packed up her supplies the next day. She'd sold most of her baked goods, and she'd enjoyed another lunchtime with Jeff.

Today he'd brought two big helpings of his mother's tuna casserole, which had been both delicious and filling. She'd brought snickerdoodle cookies to share, and they spent most of their time talking about their favorite childhood memories.

When they shifted to more recent events, Jeff still seemed to be holding back. He was hiding something, something important, but she couldn't seem to find the key to unlock his trust.

She wasn't going to give up, though. After all, she was stubborn to her core. She was determined to find out what caused the underlying sadness she saw in Jeff's dark eyes.

After her packing was finished, she pushed the two baker's racks over to Jeff's next door. She noticed a young Amish couple who looked to be in their late twenties standing just inside Sara Ann's booth. They were facing her. The man was average-looking with dark-brown hair and a matching beard, but the woman, petite with blond hair and light-colored eyes, was quite beautiful. She held a quilt while Sara Ann fawned over it, running her fingers over the stitching and praising her own work.

Christiana smiled to herself as she turned away. Sara Ann seemed to enjoy garnering attention, and she'd go to great lengths for it.

Dismissing her thoughts of Simply Sara Ann, Christiana parked her racks at the entrance to Jeff's booth and then stepped inside.

"Hi, Jeff." She waved at him as he made his way toward her from the back of the booth. "I just wanted to tell you to have a nice Sunday tomorrow and a *gut* week. I look forward to eating lunch with you again . . ."

Jeff's attention wasn't focused on her. His dark eyes were cool, and his face clouded with a deep frown as he glared at something behind her, his hands fisted at his sides.

"Jeff?" she asked, but he kept staring. "Jeff? Are you okay?"

She craned her neck to see what had captured Jeff's attention, but all she saw was Sara Ann still talking with the couple.

Her mind whirled. Jeff had been bright

and sunny at lunch, so his change in demeanor caught Christiana by surprise. Had Sara Ann done something to upset him?

"Jeff?" she asked again, her tone measured and soft. "Are you all right?"

His eyes cut to hers, but his expression remained stony.

"Was iss letz?" she asked. "You're scaring me."

"You should go." His voice was raspy.

She opened her mouth, but then she closed it as she felt her heart begin to crack.

"Go," he repeated. "I can't talk to you now."

Before she could respond, he pivoted and walked toward the back of his booth.

Christiana's eyes burned as he walked away from her, leaving without an explanation. Maybe *she'd* done something to upset him, but when? Had she said something at lunch that made him angry once he thought it over?

She fought back tears. Why did his strange behavior, popping up again, cut her to the bone?

Because I care about him. He's become important to me.

But she didn't want to care about him. Why had she allowed her heart to cross the line? Now she had to suffer the consequences. Perhaps she'd been right about him before. He was too prone to being moody and rude. Why had she let herself become attached?

Peering at him as he stood at his worktable with his back to her, she waited a few beats, hoping he'd turn around, apologize, and explain his odd behavior. But when he didn't, Christiana returned to her baker's racks. No, she didn't want to care about him, but she couldn't seem to help it.

As she made her way to the parking lot, she sent up a silent prayer.

Lord, please heal Jeff's heart toward me and help us find a way for our friendship to work. If it's not your will, then please help me mend my heart. Jeff has found a way to break it.

"I thought I might find you out here."

Jeff looked up from the worktable as *Dat* stepped into the shop in Jeff's barn that evening. "Hi, *Dat.*"

"Have you eaten?" *Dat* sat down on an empty stool beside him.

"No, but I'm not very hungry."

"Your *mamm* thought you'd join us for supper tonight. She made country fried steak especially for you since you enjoy it so much. There's plenty left if you change your mind."

197

Jeff nodded as guilt, his constant companion since he'd left the market, swelled, twisting his insides. "*Danki,* but I don't think I'll eat tonight."

Dat studied him, and Jeff fidgeted under his stare. "Tell me what's wrong, *sohn.*"

Jeff cleared his throat and stared down at the piece of leather he'd been cutting. "I saw her today."

"Who?" *Dat* leaned close to him.

"Ella." Jeff's voice quavered as renewed heaviness filled his chest. "Ella and her husband were in the market. When I saw her, I lost it, just like I did one day when I saw them at the hardware store. All the anger and hurt came back like a raging river. I couldn't handle it, *Dat.* They were at the booth right across from mine." He paused. "Worse, I took it out on Christiana."

He met his father's warm gaze as his always-present ache turned to grief. "I'm sure I hurt her. She came to my booth to talk to me, and then I saw Ella behind her. I just froze. I couldn't function." The memory of the pain in Christiana's eyes sliced through him like a knife to his soul. How could he have hurt such a sweet, wonderful friend? She'd never forgive him this time.

"Did you tell her why you were upset?"

"No." Jeff worked to clear his thickened throat. "She asked me what was wrong and if I was all right, but I couldn't speak. When I found my voice again, I was too upset to talk, so I asked her to leave." He closed his eyes as the truth poured out of him. "No, I *told* her to leave. I was too embarrassed to tell her about Ella. How could Christiana have any respect for me if she knew my fiancée dumped me?" The words were painful to admit aloud, even to his father.

Dat clicked his tongue. "Don't be *gegisch, sohn.* If Christiana is truly your *freind,* she won't blame you for Ella's decision. You built Ella a beautiful *haus* and prepared yourself to marry her. She's the one who left. You did nothing wrong."

Jeff squeezed the bridge of his nose. If only the past was as easy to accept as his father thought it was. His parents, Nick, Lewis — they all seemed to be on the same page.

"Why don't you go apologize to her?" *Dat* said. "Do you know where she lives?"

"No, I don't." Jeff rubbed his eyes with the heels of his hands. "Why would she forgive me? This is the second time I've hurt her. The first time I rudely complained about her line of customers, and this time I was rude to her without any explanation.

Why would she even trust me again? I'm obviously not stable."

"You're too hard on yourself, Jeffrey." *Dat*'s expression warmed. "You just had a bad day."

"But I have a bad day every time I see Ella."

"Give yourself time."

"I've had more than a year, but I'm still a mess, *Dat*. I don't know how to deal with it. You'd think I'd be over it by now, but I'm not. And now I probably ruined any chance to have a meaningful friendship with Christiana."

"You're not a mess, Jeffrey." *Dat* gripped Jeff's shoulder and gave it a little tug. "You're just still hurt."

"I know. How do I get over it? I don't know how to move on."

"Have you tried praying about it?"

Jeff nodded. "Many times."

"Keep trying. Ask God to heal your heart."

"And what should I do about Christiana?"

"Tell her why you behaved that way and explain that you never meant to take it out on her. Tell her how much her friendship means to you and that you'd like to try again." *Dat* grabbed his shoulder again and gave him a gentle shake. "Tell her she's important to you and that you want to work on your friendship."

"Right." Jeff nodded as if his father's advice would be simple to take. "I'll do that."

"Gut." Dat stood. "How about you come and have some of your *mamm*'s country fried steak? I know it would make her *froh* to see you enjoying it."

"I'll be there soon. Let me just finish cutting out this leather piece for a wallet I'm making."

Dat paused and then nodded. "Fine. Don't take too long, though."

"I won't. I promise." Jeff waited for *Dat* to disappear from his shop, and then he covered his face with his hands. He was broken, and he needed the Great Healer to help him. Closing his eyes, he opened his heart in prayer.

"God," he whispered, "I need help. No matter what *Dat* says, I am a mess. I can't see Ella without completely breaking apart, especially when she's with her husband. I've been building a special friendship with Christiana, but I'm certain I ruined it today. If it's your will, please help me repair my friendship with her and figure out how to be strong around Ella. Guide me to where I'm supposed to be."

Jeff opened his eyes, swiped his hand

down his face, and then stood.

As he strolled toward his parents' house, he wondered if Christiana would give him another chance.

Did he even deserve another chance after the way he'd behaved?

13

"How are things with Jeff?" Leanna asked Christiana on Tuesday as the four cousins began to assemble sandwiches at Bethany's parents' house. "You've been eating together at the market, right?"

"Ya." Christiana lifted two slices of bread from the plate in the center of the table. How she loved these cousin lunches when the four of them got together away from their businesses and even away from the rest of their families. Bethany had suggested this one, perhaps sensing that Christiana could use some extra time in their company.

"Tell us more," Bethany said, prodding from across the table. "I don't suppose he's talked to your *dat* about dating you yet?"

"No, he hasn't. He wouldn't. We've just been *freinden.*" Christiana sensed Salina watching her as she shook her head and selected a few pieces of roast beef from another plate.

"Did something happen?" Salina's tone was serious.

"*Ya*, you could say that." Christiana set the pile of lunch meat on one slice of bread.

"What happened?" Salina touched her arm.

"He changed on Saturday." Christiana shrugged as if Jeff's behavior hadn't moved her to tears during the short ride back to her house Saturday or caused her to cry herself to sleep.

"What do you mean by *changed*?" Bethany's sunny smile faltered.

Christiana shared her story, and then she took a bite of her sandwich and awaited her cousins' assessment of the situation.

"He was staring at Simply Sara Ann?" Leanna scrunched her nose as she looked at Bethany. "Why would he look at her like that?"

"Maybe she said something that made him angry?" Bethany shrugged and then scooped a pile of macaroni salad onto her plate.

"I don't know."

"He wouldn't answer you when you spoke to him?" Salina asked.

Christiana shook her head as she swallowed another bite of her sandwich. "Not until he told me to leave."

"I think it had to do with Sara Ann and not you." Salina held up a finger. "Maybe something is going on between them, and I think you should ask him what it is."

"You do need to talk to him," Leanna said, agreeing. "You two were getting close, so I doubt it had anything to do with you."

"That might be true, but he took it out on me." Christiana heard her voice wobble. "Even if it wasn't my fault, he still hurt me again."

"What are you saying?" Bethany's expression was full of concern.

Christiana picked up her cup of water. "I'm saying I don't think I want to deal with his mood swings and temper. No matter how much he means to me, I don't appreciate never knowing where I stand with him." A knot of disappointment and hurt expanded in her throat, and she tried swallowing water past it.

"You care about him." Salina rubbed her back. "I'm so sorry he hurt you again."

"I'm fine." Christiana tried to smile, but she failed. "I've been praying for him, and I hope he finds happiness, but I just can't help him anymore. I can't let him hurt me. My heart can't take it."

Salina looped her arm around Christiana's shoulders. "You have us."

205

"That's right." Bethany squeezed Christiana's one hand while Leanna took the other.

"Always," Leanna said.

Christiana's eyes filled with tears as she smiled at her cousins. What would she do without their love and support? She never wanted to find out.

As she walked to her father's buggy later that afternoon, Christiana heard a horse pull up behind her and someone calling her name. She turned.

"Christiana!" Reuben Esh hopped out and jogged to her. "I saw you from the road!"

"Hi, Reuben." She smiled at her old friend from school. "How are you?"

"I'm fine." He worked to catch his breath. "I'm really out of shape since I sit in a store all day. Even a short jog isn't a *gut* idea." He chuckled and flashed a warm smile.

Christiana recalled that before his family moved to another district, Reuben had been one of the nicest boys in her school. They were the same age, and he'd always gone out of his way to be kind to her, whether they were in the one-room schoolhouse or playing outside.

"I heard you opened a bakery booth at the Bird-in-Hand marketplace," he said.

"*Ya,* that's true."

"My three-month anniversary with my girlfriend is coming up next weekend, and I thought I might get her something sweet as a gift." He rubbed his hands together. "I also heard you make the best peanut butter pie in the county."

"*Danki.*" Christiana shrugged. "I'm not sure if it's the best in the county, but I can save you one. Why don't you come by on Thursday? I'll have one ready for you."

"Great!" Reuben grinned. "I'll see you then."

Christiana reached into her pocket and touched the key chain Jeff had given her. What would she say to Jeff when she saw him at the market?

"Lewis." Jeff stepped out of his barn to see his best friend Wednesday evening. "What brings you out this way?"

The mid-June sunset filled the sky with vivid hues of orange and yellow above him, and the air was heavy with summer humidity. The cicadas sang their happy song as fireflies began their nightly dance through the skies.

"*Mei mamm* asked me to drop off a quilt for your *mamm,* so I thought I'd see how you're doing. Your *dat* said you were in your workshop."

"Why don't we sit and catch up?" Jeff gestured toward his back porch. "How's Renae?"

"She's *gut.*" Lewis's smile was more like a grin. "She's really *gut,* actually. I'm thinking about asking her father if I can marry her."

"Really?" Jeff stopped and turned toward Lewis, who nodded. "Wow. That's great, but isn't it a little . . . soon?"

"I don't think so." Lewis shook his head. "I think when you know, you just know, no matter how long it's been. My parents dated for only a couple of months before *mei dat* proposed, and they're still happily married. Sure, they have their disagreements at times, but their relationship is still going strong."

Jeff shook his head as they continued toward the porch. Even though Lewis had previously indicated Renae might be the one, he still wrestled with his best friend getting married so soon — or at all. "Wow. I never expected you to decide to get married this quickly."

"Why not?" Lewis gestured widely. "We're not getting any younger. Besides, I'm ready to settle down and start a family. Aren't you?" He sank into a rocking chair.

"I don't know. I thought I was last year."

Jeff sat down beside him as he recalled the scene at the market with Ella. "But apparently it wasn't in God's time."

Lewis's smile flattened. "Stop thinking about Ella. I keep telling you, it's time to pick yourself up and move on." He pointed behind him. "You have a lot to offer a *maedel.* You have this *haus,* this farm, and your business at the market. Don't let Ella's decision color the rest of your life."

Jeff snorted. "It's so easy for you to say that."

"What do you mean?"

"I mean you have no idea what it feels like to be dumped," Jeff snapped, and Lewis's eyes widened. "I'm sorry. I didn't mean to raise my voice."

"What's going on with you?" Lewis's expression held concern.

Jeff blew out a sigh. "I saw Ella at the market on Saturday. It took me by surprise. She was with her husband."

"What happened?"

Jeff told him. "And when I froze, I couldn't speak. All the anger and hurt came back again, and I felt like I was drowning. And then I hurt Christiana's feelings. I know I did. She looked at me as if I'd punched her."

"What did you say to her?"

"I told her to leave." Jeff stared out toward his parents' house. "I've hurt her feelings more than once now, so she's probably given up on me. I've ruined any chance I had with her." Guilt whipped through him, hard and fast, stealing his breath for a moment.

"Whoa." Lewis held up his hand. "What do you mean you ruined any chance you had with her? Did you ask her to date you?"

"No." Jeff shook his head. "I think we should just be *freinden.* But we'd been getting to know each other. We had lunch together each day last week, and we talked a lot."

"You say you just want to be *freinden,* but I get the feeling you really like this *maedel.*"

Jeff nodded and took a big breath. "*Ya,* I do, but now I don't think —"

"Jeff, this is huge." Lewis angled his body toward him. "You've been moping around for more than a year, pining over Ella."

"I don't pine. *Ya,* I've been hurt, but I don't mope either."

"*Ya,* you do. Now let me finish. You've finally found someone you care for. Maybe Christiana is the one God sent to heal your heart. And maybe to build a future with."

Jeff shook his head. "I don't think so."

"Why not?"

"Because I keep hurting her. I keep messing up." Jeff forced himself to speak past the heavy feeling that felt like a sinking rock in his soul. "I lost my temper with her when her customers were blocking my booth, and then I lost it on Saturday when I saw Ella and took it out on her. I have such a tough time controlling my emotions, and I keep saying the wrong thing to her. How can I be in any position to date her? Why would she even want to date me?" He jammed a finger in his chest. "I can't see my ex without completely snapping."

"You'll get through this. God will carry you through. Pray for his help and guidance."

"I have. But I still feel as guilty and broken as I did on Saturday."

"You need to talk to Christiana," Lewis said. "Tell her the truth. Explain what Ella did to you and how you're still struggling to get over it. If she's the person you think she is, she'll forgive you. She'll understand."

"I don't know. *Dat* told me I should tell her about Ella, too, but I don't think I can bring myself to tell her the whole story." He looked straight into his best friend's eyes. "Lewis, Ella didn't just leave me. She left me *on our wedding day.* What will Christiana think? Even more, why would she

211

want to date a loser who can't control his temper?" Jeff fell back into his chair. "I've blown it."

That day flashed into his mind. How could Ella have done that to him? *How?* But he didn't want to think about her now. He wanted to repair his relationship with Christiana, and he shoved those wedding day memories away.

"Jeff, let her decide whether you've blown it. And have faith that she'll forgive you. We're taught to forgive, so give her a chance to show you that she still believes in your friendship."

Jeff rubbed at a tense muscle in his shoulder as he considered Lewis's words. He longed to believe Christiana would give him another chance, but how would he find the right words to apologize? He'd never really found them the first time he hurt her. She'd just known he was trying to say he was sorry. And how would he explain what Ella had done to him without falling apart?

He would pray about it. Only God could grant him the courage and the right things to say.

The muscles in Christiana's shoulders tightened when Jeff walked into the Coffee Corner the next morning. She gripped her

212

coffee cup as she sat with her cousins at their usual high-top table. Her eyes locked with his, and her stomach tied itself into a knot.

"Gude mariye," Bethany sang out as she hopped down from her stool and walked over to Jeff. "How's your morning so far?"

"Fine." Jeff broke his gaze with Christiana and followed Bethany to the counter. "What's your special flavor today?"

"Irish cream." Bethany's voice remained perky. "Would you like a cup?"

"*Ya,* please." Jeff pulled out his wallet.

"Are you going to talk to him?" Salina's voice was soft beside Christiana.

"I don't even know what to say." As Christiana studied Jeff's back, all kinds of emotions rushed through her — disappointment, anger, resentment, rejection. How could a man she barely knew affect her so deeply? "He owes me an explanation for the way he treated me, but I doubt I'll get one."

"Maybe you should give him some grace," Leanna said. "I still doubt he was upset about something you did. You've been nothing but a *freind* to him."

"Maybe he needs you more than you know," Salina said, chiming in.

"Why is everyone taking his side?" Christiana said.

Salina held up both hands. "Hold on. I'm not taking his side. I just remember what you said about him seeming so *bedauerlich.*" She hesitated for a moment. "I love you, Christiana, but sometimes you jump to conclusions without getting the whole story."

Leanna nodded. "That's true. I remember you being angry with Bethany for a week because you thought she'd taken your favorite doll. You were about nine. Then you found it in your *dat*'s workshop, right where you'd left it."

Christiana blinked and her shoulders slumped. "That is true."

"I remember that too," Salina said. "Maybe Jeff is dealing with something difficult and you can be a blessing to him instead of making assumptions about his behavior."

Christiana sipped her coffee. Had God brought her into Jeff's life to help him? Was that what Salina was trying to tell her might be the case?

But if that were true, why did Jeff keep rejecting her?

Jeff handed a customer her change and then her purchases later that morning. "Thank you for coming in today. I hope your grandchildren enjoy their personalized clothing hooks."

"Oh, they will." The woman ran her hands over her bag. "When I was younger, every item with my name on it was always sold out."

"Really?" Jeff asked. "What is your name?"

"Jennifer." The woman sighed. "I clearly remember trying to find a toothbrush with my name on it, but the store had sold out of them. I had to buy a kit with stickers and put the letters on a toothbrush myself. Of course, once the letters got wet, they never stuck right again." She chuckled and pointed to her bag. "That's one reason I enjoy buying personalized items for my grandchildren. I want them to have something special with their name on it."

He grinned. "That's nice."

The woman glanced down at the counter and picked up one of his sample wallets. "My goodness. Is this a personalized wallet?"

"Yes, it is."

"What a fantastic gift." She tapped her chin. "These would be wonderful birthday gifts for my sons in a couple of months. Could I order some for next week?"

"Of course." Jeff pulled out a notepad. "What would you like the initials to be?"

215

He wrote down her instructions, and then she paid a deposit for the wallets. "I'll have those ready for you."

"Perfect."

"I'm glad you came in, and I hope you enjoy the rest of your day."

"I sure will." The woman smiled and then left.

Jeff followed her to the booth entrance and turned toward the Bake Shop. His pulse kicked up as he remembered his brief encounter with Christiana in the Coffee Corner this morning. He'd wanted to apologize, or at least ask her if they could talk later, but he lost his nerve.

You're a coward.

Jeff gritted his teeth. Yes, he was a coward. He needed to talk to her and explain why he'd been so cold last week. He needed to be honest with her and ask for her forgiveness. But he was afraid she'd reject him.

He closed his eyes and gathered any courage he could find deep inside of himself. Then he took a trembling breath and walked over to her booth. He stopped dead in his tracks when he found her talking to an Amish man who looked to be around her age.

Jeff's eyes widened as he witnessed Christiana smiling and laughing with the man as he picked out a pie. The man said something to her, and she giggled and then handed him another pie.

Their interaction seemed familiar, as if they knew each other well. Christiana's smile and laugh were warm and comfortable.

She liked this man. She trusted him. She *liked* him.

Jeff meant nothing to her. She had forgotten about him. She'd moved on.

The contents of his stomach seemed to curdle as something like a sense of betrayal snaked around his insides. Christiana and the man walked to her counter together, their conversation continuing as he paid for his purchase. Then she gave him a sweet smile and a little wave as he backed away.

When the man turned and reached Jeff, he gave him a pleasant smile. *"Gude mariye."*

Jeff mumbled a response before the man walked away.

"Jeff." Christiana's smile faded as she walked toward him. "What are you doing here?"

He opened his mouth to speak, but then he turned without a word and walked toward his booth.

"Wait." She started after him. "Wait a minute!"

But Jeff kept going and headed to his workbench.

"You are unbelievable!" She'd followed him. He turned to see her eyes narrowed and her finger pointing. "You have the nerve to be rude to me last week and then walk away from me today? I can't be *freinden* with someone who treats me like this. I've tried, Jeff, but I can't do it anymore." Her voice was thick. "I'm done." Then she turned on her heel.

Had Christiana just walked right out of his life? Good. He didn't need to let another woman in only to have her choose someone else.

14

Jeff carried a lantern as he stepped out of his barn later that night and trudged to the pasture fence. Fireflies flittered around him like floating confetti, mocking his foul mood.

He set the lantern at his feet and then leaned forward on the fence. He looked up at the bright stars twinkling above him and heaved a deep sigh as anger and disappointment threatened to tear him into a million pieces.

"Did you talk to Christiana today?" *Dat* came up beside Jeff and set his own lantern on the ground beside Jeff's.

"Not the way you mean."

"I can tell by the look on your face that something happened," *Dat* said. "Talk to me, *sohn.*"

Jeff kept his eyes focused on the sky. "I found her flirting with another man. She might not have lied when she said she didn't have a boyfriend, but from what I saw today, she knows someone she'd like to be her boyfriend."

"Are you sure?" *Dat* asked.

"What does it matter? I've been used again, just like Ella did." He gritted his teeth as his body vibrated with anger and humiliation.

"Wait a minute." *Dat* turned toward him. "Did you ask her anything about that man?"

Jeff blinked. His anger seemed to slip away, but he was still frustrated. "No."

"So how do you know you're not misinterpreting what you saw?"

Jeff pointed to the ground as his frustration boiled over. "I know what flirting looks like. And why wouldn't she flirt with him? She could have any man she wanted. She's *schee,* funny, and *schmaert.* She's also a *gut* listener and a kind person. She's special, more special than any *maedel* I've met. That man would be a moron if he didn't like her. And because I was rude to her when I saw Ella, she's done with me. She told me so."

Dat tilted his head as his expression seemed to warm. "You're not truly worried that she might like someone else. You're worried that you're not *gut* enough for her. Ella made you feel like you're not worthy of finding someone to love you."

Jeff opened and closed his mouth as his thoughts spun.

"I never told you the story of what happened before I met your *mamm*." *Dat* leaned forward on the fence and looked out toward the dark pasture. "I'd been dating a *maedel* for four years. Her name was Rosemary. We grew up together and then went to youth group together. I thought she was the love of my life. I planned to marry her and then move her here since my parents said they would give me their *haus* and move into the *daadihaus* on *mei bruder*'s farm."

"What happened?" Jeff turned toward his father.

"I asked her *dat*'s permission to propose, and he said *ya*. So I took her out on a picnic and asked her to marry me." He paused. "And to my surprise, she said no."

"Why?"

Dat pressed his lips together and rested his chin on his palm. "She said she cared about me but didn't love me enough to marry me. She said she would always remember me fondly, but she didn't want to be *mei fraa*."

Jeff shook his head. "I'm so sorry she hurt you like that, *Dat*."

"I survived it. I was down for a long time, and I lost confidence in myself. I think

221

that's what you're feeling — not just hurt but a lack of confidence. And it's hard for you to trust another woman."

Jeff swallowed and then nodded.

Dat smiled. "But it all turned out the way God intended. I met your *mamm* about six months later. I was scared to trust her, but she helped me realize that Rosemary wasn't God's plan for me. She showed me what it was like to love someone who loved me in return." He touched Jeff's arm. "You need to allow yourself to trust someone new."

Jeff felt as if his head were spinning. "I had no idea you went through this. Why didn't you tell me when Ella left?"

"I didn't want to deflect from what you were going through. I thought bringing up my heartache would sound as if I wasn't supporting you. I didn't want to make it about me when you needed my sympathy. I'm sorry."

Jeff spun and leaned back against the fence. "You were wrong, *Dat.* What you just told me has done the opposite. I feel a little better knowing you understand how I feel."

"I do understand, but I can't stand to see you so *bedauerlich.* You need to let your heart heal and trust again. You need to tell Christiana how you feel and what happened with Ella."

Jeff looked down at the ground and kicked a stone with the toe of his boot. "Sometimes I feel like I can't express myself well. I tend to say the wrong thing and drive people away. That was true even before I was with Ella."

"Be honest with Christiana about that, too, and see where the conversation leads. That's what you need to do first. Give yourself a chance to really get to know her before you decide she's not who you thought she was." *Dat* patted his shoulder. "You're worthy of love, *sohn.* God loves you. He'll send you the perfect mate." He picked up his lantern and started toward the house. "*Gut nacht.* Get some rest."

Jeff looked out at the pasture as his father's words soaked through him. Could he trust again? Could he find the right words to tell Christiana not just about his past but about his feelings for her?

He didn't know the answer, but he yearned to find out.

"So I told him I can't be *freinden* with someone who treats me that way," Christiana told her cousins at the Coffee Corner the next morning. She took a long drink of Bethany's mint mocha as if the hot liquid would solve the mystery of Jeff Stoltzfus.

"He glared at you when you were selling Reuben a pie." Salina said the words slowly as if analyzing their meaning.

"Well, I wasn't looking then, but he certainly glared at me after Reuben left," Christiana said.

"Maybe he was jealous of Reuben?" Bethany offered her theory with a shrug of her slight shoulders.

"I was wondering the exact same thing," Salina said.

"Why would Jeff be jealous of Reuben?" Christiana asked. "Jeff has never indicated that he likes me that way. Also, I told him I don't have a boyfriend."

"Maybe he does like you, but he's been afraid to tell you," Leanna said. "When I started dating Marlin, he admitted he'd liked me for a while but was too afraid to ask me to date him. He thought I liked someone else."

"But sometimes Jeff acts as though he doesn't like me at all. Did Marlin do that?" Christiana asked.

"No, but he acted *naerfich*. Maybe you're mistaking Jeff's nerves for something else."

Salina pressed her lips together and shook her head. Christiana suspected Salina was holding something back.

"What are you thinking, Salina?" Christiana asked.

"I still think you should give him grace. You said you could tell he was sad when you first met him. Maybe he's going through a tough season. You don't know what he's dealing with. Maybe he needs everyone to cut him some slack."

Christiana swallowed more coffee, hoping to drown her threatening guilt. No, she would not allow Salina to make her feel guilty. Jeff was rude to her when she'd done nothing wrong — twice. If God *had* sent her to help Jeff, Jeff wasn't cooperating.

"Did you sell a lot of jams and jellies yesterday?" Bethany asked Leanna.

"*Ya,* I did." Leanna smiled. "I'll have to make more next week. I'm finally running out of my cranberry apple jars."

"Ooh." Bethany grinned. "That's my favorite."

Christiana was grateful that Bethany had changed the subject. She was tired of thinking about Jeff and her disappointment in him. She cared about him, but she longed to tamp down those feelings. They couldn't be friends, even if they had to see each other three days every week.

She studied her coffee while her cousins chatted about their own businesses. When she saw movement out of the corner of her

225

eye, she looked up and found Jeff staring at her. Her jaw tightened. She was tired of his playing games with her, and she wasn't going to allow his sad eyes to manipulate her any longer.

"I need to get set up," Christiana muttered as she hopped down from the stool. She brushed past Jeff, marching to her booth without looking back.

Humiliation hung on to Jeff like a second skin as Christiana glared at him before moving past him and out of the Coffee Corner booth.

"Gude mariye," Bethany sang out with her usual perky tone as she walked over to him. "Do you want the special *kaffi* today?"

"Ya."

"How are you?"

"Fine. You?" He walked with her to the counter.

"It's another *schee* day at the market." Bethany gave him his chocolate donut. "I hope you like mint mocha *kaffi*. My cousins seem to."

"I'm sure I will. All your flavors are *appeditlich*." He handed her some money once she'd given him his coffee. *"Danki."*

"Have a *gut* day." Bethany gave him a little wave.

If only he could have a fraction of her positivity to get him through this day.

He nodded at her and then started toward the booth exit, aware of her cousins' stares. He heard one of them whisper something to the other, and his ears felt as if they might spontaneously combust.

"Jeff." Salina trotted over and matched his steps as they walked toward their booths. "May I speak with you?"

"Sure." Jeff could hear the hesitation in his voice as dread pooled in his gut.

"Wait." She stopped and turned toward him, and he halted. "I don't want Christiana to see us."

Uh-oh. He nodded.

"I know this is none of my business, but I want to say something."

"Okay." He swallowed.

She glanced toward their aisle and then lowered her voice. "You should talk to Christiana."

"You think she wants to talk to me?" He gestured toward the Coffee Corner. "She obviously didn't want to have anything to do with me a few minutes ago."

"I know, but just listen." Her expression almost seemed to be pleading with him not to walk away. "She's really upset about what happened yesterday."

"That's kind of obvious," Jeff deadpanned.

"If she didn't care about you, would she be upset?"

"You think she cares about me?" He studied her expression, looking for any signs of a lie.

"Would you be upset about losing a friendship if you didn't care about that person?" Her blue eyes challenged him.

He glanced past her toward Christiana's booth.

"Just do me a favor and try to talk to her. That's all I ask."

"Okay," he finally said.

"Danki."

As Salina walked away, Jeff silently asked God for help again. It was time he worked through his fear and just did what he needed to do — whether or not Christiana would care.

"Gude mariye," Simply Sara Ann said as she swept into the Bake Shop booth and smiled. "You were busy yesterday, weren't you?"

"*Ya,* I was. Weren't you?" Christiana set a chocolate cake with peanut butter icing on a shelf and then turned toward Sara Ann.

After leaving the Coffee Corner to avoid Jeff, Christiana had hoped to have a few minutes of peace and quiet before the customers arrived. But Sara Ann's arrival had ruined that notion.

"I was." Sara Ann joined her at the shelf. "Ooh. Chocolate *kuche* with peanut butter icing. My favorite." Her smile was a little too friendly. "If you have any left at the end of the day, I'd like to purchase one to take home to my family."

"Okay." Christiana put another cake on the shelf. "Do you need something else?"

"Actually, I want to ask you something." Sara Ann looked over her shoulder and then leaned in closer. "Did I see you and Jeff having another disagreement yesterday?"

Christiana pivoted to face her. "Why would you ask that?"

"I don't know." Sara Ann shrugged. "I just noticed some body language when Jeff left your booth at one point, and you looked upset after you followed him. You still looked upset when you left last night."

Christiana studied Sara Ann as questions about her motives whirred through her mind. Did Sara Ann have feelings for Jeff? Did she want to gather more gossip to share with other vendors? Or did she really care about them?

"You know," Sara Ann began as she moved closer to Christiana, "Jeff went through a tough time about a year ago."

"What do you mean?" Christiana's words were measured.

"Let's just say someone he cared about broke his heart."

"How?"

"It's really not my secret to share." Sara Ann took a step back. "I think Jeff should tell you."

A group of customers stepped into Christiana's booth.

"I should get going. Have a *gut* day." Sara Ann smiled and then walked away.

As Christiana turned her attention to the customers, new questions plagued her. If Simply Sara Ann was telling the truth, maybe Salina was right. Maybe Christiana should give Jeff a chance to explain his confusing behavior. She still didn't understand how he could be so rude, but deep down she'd always known he had a reason for the sadness she saw in his dark eyes.

"What did you mean when you said Marlin was too afraid to ask you out because he thought you liked someone else?" Christiana asked Leanna as they ate lunch at the high-top table in the Coffee Corner that afternoon.

Leanna chewed and swallowed a bite of her tuna fish sandwich and then took a drink from her bottle of water before answering. Around them, customers sipped coffee and ate donuts while Bethany worked the counter. The sweet aroma of mint mocha filled the air.

Christiana had invited her three cousins to eat with her today, but Salina's Farm Stand was too busy for her to take a break, and Bethany's line of customers didn't seem to end either. Christiana was grateful Leanna had agreed to close her Jam and Jelly Nook to visit with her.

"Well, I think that's all there was to it. For some reason, he thought I liked someone else." Leanna grinned and shook her head. "He was so *gegisch,* but we were also very young. I had liked him from the time I was thirteen years old, but I was always too *naerfich* to tell him."

"Oh."

"Do you think that might be why Jeff got upset yesterday?" Leanna asked. "Maybe he got the wrong impression about you and Reuben?"

"I don't know, but it's occurred to me." Christiana looked down at her liverwurst sandwich. "I had a strange visit from Simply Sara Ann this morning."

Leanna groaned. "What did she have to say?"

"She said she noticed that Jeff and I seemed to be arguing again yesterday. And then she told me someone broke Jeff's heart about a year ago. That's all she would tell me, but she pretty much confirmed I'm right that he seems *bedauerlich* all the time."

"Huh." Leanna rested her elbow on the table. "So maybe Salina was right when she suggested you give him another chance."

"*Ya,* I guess so." Christiana touched her bottle of water, moving her fingertips through the condensation.

"What else is bothering you?"

Christiana sighed. "You know I've only dated a couple of men, and those relationships didn't work out."

Leanna gave her a little smile. "Maybe that's because they weren't meant to work out. Maybe God hadn't led you to the right man yet."

"Maybe." Christiana took a bite of her sandwich.

"I'm not suggesting you marry Jeff, Christiana. I'm just suggesting that maybe you should talk to him or at least let him talk and listen."

Christiana nodded as her throat suddenly dried. She was barely able to swallow her food. *"Ya."*

"Gut." Leanna smiled. "How are things at

232

your booth today?"

"Busy as usual." Christiana closed her eyes for a moment. "But I really needed this break."

"I did too."

As their conversation turned toward the market, thoughts of Jeff lingered in the back of her mind. She resolved to listen to him the next time he approached her.

Now she just had to wait and hope.

15

Jeff rubbed the back of his neck as he stood at the entrance to the Bake Shop late that afternoon. A constant stream of customers had kept him busy all day long, and his hope for his booth had been renewed. The wallets were a success, and when a customer asked about personalized leather journal covers, a new product had been born in his mind. He planned to design a journal cover tonight.

But even with his new success, thoughts of Christiana had lingered at the back of his mind as he contemplated what Salina said.

He'd spent all day trying to work up the nerve to talk to Christiana, and now he stood watching her pack up her supplies.

Her back faced him as she loaded empty boxes and serving platters onto one of her baker's racks.

When she faced him, she gasped, cupping her hand to her mouth.

"Jeff." She pressed her hand to her chest. "I didn't know you were standing there. How — how are you?"

She was so pretty that he couldn't speak for a moment. He stared at her, his courage dissolving. Then he stood a little taller. He could do this. His father had faith in him. Lewis had faith in him. Salina even seemed to. Now he had to find faith in himself.

"I'm okay. You?"

"I'm okay."

An awkward silence passed between them.

"Do you want something?" she finally asked. Her expression seemed more curious than annoyed.

"I have a lot to tell you. Could I please give you a ride home today?"

She paused and then nodded. "Okay. Just give me a few minutes to call my driver and cancel my ride."

He was so shocked by her agreement that he felt off-balance for a moment.

"Why don't you finish getting ready to go, and we'll talk in your buggy," she suggested.

"*Ya,* that's perfect."

Thirty minutes later, they were riding side by side as he guided his horse out of the parking lot toward the road. Out of the corner of his eye, he could see Christiana sitting erect with her hands folded in her lap.

"What do you want to talk about?" she asked after giving him directions to her house.

"I want to apologize for my behavior yesterday," he began as he kept his gaze fixed on the road ahead. "But first, I need to tell you that I have a difficult time trusting people."

He interpreted her silence as an invitation to continue. "I was engaged a year ago," he said.

He heard a small gasp escape her lips. "You were?"

"Ya." He paused. "Her name is Ella, and we dated for a few years. We were going to be married, and I built her a *haus* on *mei dat*'s farm. She told me what she wanted, and I built it. It even has the wraparound porch she said she'd dreamt about since she was a little girl."

He gripped the reins tighter. "We were going to build a life there. She talked about having a big family, and she even had names picked out for our future *kinner.* Life was going to be perfect, she insisted. I was supposed to take over the farm when *mei dat* retired, and she said she was looking forward to being a farmer's *fraa.*"

"What happened?" Her voice was full of curiosity.

"She changed her mind on the day of our wedding."

"Are you kidding?" Christiana's voice rose. "She broke up with you on your wedding day?"

Oh, how he hated to recount this story! Yet Christiana deserved to hear the truth. He took another deep breath and nodded. "She came to *mei haus* two hours before the wedding was supposed to start and called off not only our wedding but our relationship." He halted the horse at a stoplight and then turned toward her, fearful of her reaction to his painful secret.

"Wait a minute. I'm trying to understand this. Ella backed out on you on your wedding day after you had built her a *haus*?" When he nodded, her expression grew fiercely angry. "How could she do that to you after all you'd done to prepare a life for her?"

His shoulders relaxed at her support of him.

"That's despicable," she snapped.

"I know. That's why I've been so hesitant to trust people. I'm still recovering from the way she treated me. And since then, my instinct is to expect the worst from others."

"So that's why you opened your booth," she said, seeming to put all the pieces together. "You said you needed a change in your life."

"Exactly."

"And that's also why you seem so *bedauerlich.*" Her expression warmed as she pointed to his face. "I see it in your eyes."

He was stunned silent for a moment. When he looked out the windshield and found the light had turned green, he guided the horse through the intersection.

"Why were you so upset when I came to see you at your booth last Saturday?" she asked.

"Ella and her husband were at the market. I saw them just as you walked over to me. They were over at Sara Ann's —"

"Hold on. She broke up with you on your wedding day and then married someone else?"

"That's right."

"When did she marry him?"

"About six months later."

"Jeff," she said, "I am so sorry."

"Danki." He stared straight ahead so he could avoid looking into her kind eyes again, but her concern felt like a balm to his battered soul.

"Had you told me why you were upset, I

would have understood."

"I'm sorry about that." He blew out a puff of air. "I never meant to hurt you."

"It's okay. I understand now. I noticed them with Sara Ann that day, looking at a quilt. I'm sorry she hurt you so badly."

He pressed his lips together. He didn't feel worthy of Christiana's precious friendship, a friendship he thought he'd lost. "After she broke up with me, *mei bruder* said it was probably better that we didn't get married because she wouldn't have been *froh.* Still, it hurt me back then, and it hurts me now." He felt vulnerable, almost naked, revealing so much of his broken heart to her. But at the same time, it was a relief to admit the truth.

"I can't even imagine how much it hurt." Her voice was soft, almost reverent.

"So that's why I've been such a terrible *freind.* I want to trust you, and I want to get to know you. But there's still this voice in the back of my head that tells me you could hurt me." He hated the tremble in his voice. "I like you, but I'm *naerfich.*"

"I like you too."

He smiled, but then he recalled the man in her booth yesterday. "May I ask you something?"

"Of course."

"You said you didn't have a boyfriend, but you were flirting with that man who came to your booth yesterday and bought a pie. Who was he?"

"You must be talking about Reuben. I wasn't flirting with him." She laughed.

He bristled. "It looked like you were."

She waved off the comment. "He came to buy a pie for his girlfriend. It's their three-month anniversary." She clicked her tongue. "Is that why you glared at me?"

"Ya." He felt heat crawl up his neck.

"Jeff, he's just *mei freind.* We've known each other since we were in school."

"Did you date him?"

"No, we never dated, but he was always nice to me."

"Do you like him that way?" The words tasted bitter on his tongue.

"Jeff, are you jealous of my friendship with Reuben?"

Jeff didn't know what to say. What a foolish mistake he'd made!

"I promise you I'm not interested in him," she said. "I've had only a couple of boyfriends, and the relationships never lasted very long. They ended it after a couple of months."

He briefly shut his eyes. Why would a man in his right mind break up with Christiana?

240

"I used to wonder if something was wrong with me," she said.

"There's nothing wrong with you." He tried his best not to smile at her silly comment. "They obviously were the ones with the problem."

"That's nice of you to say."

As he led the horse onto her street, past the rolling patchwork of lush, green pastures, disappointment filled him. He wanted to ride around for hours so their conversation could continue. Now that Christiana knew the deepest of his secrets, he wanted to know her in the same way.

"That's my driveway." She pointed ahead. "I'm so glad you gave me a ride home."

"I'm grateful you agreed to give me another chance." He led the horse up her driveway toward the large, two-story brick home.

"I'm sorry I misjudged you — again. I know that day at the picnic table I apologized to you for the same thing, but my cousins have been trying to tell me that I'm still too quick to judge and assume the worst."

"I'm glad we're both giving the other another chance." He halted the horse by the path leading to the back porch. "I'll help you get your supplies."

"Danki," she said.

He unloaded her rolling racks and then walked to the back porch beside her. He nodded toward the ramp her father had built for her. "Do you want me to take these up for you?"

"No, *danki.* I can handle them." Christiana turned toward him and smiled. "But would you like to stay for supper?"

He blinked, surprised by the invitation. How he'd love to share a meal with her and her family! If only he hadn't promised *Mamm . . .* "*Danki,* but *mei mamm* is expecting me at her *haus.* Maybe another time?"

"Okay." She nodded. "Be safe going home."

"I will." He turned to go but then stopped when she called his name.

"I promise I will be a *gut freind* to you," Christiana said. "Just give me a chance to prove it, okay?"

His chest swelled with warmth as he took in her stunning smile. "I want to be a *gut freind* to you too."

"Of course. *Gut nacht,* Jeff."

With a spring in his step, he headed to his buggy. Maybe he could learn to trust again with Christiana's help.

"Christiana!" *Mamm* called as she walked

into the kitchen. "You're late. I was starting to worry, but then I heard you bring your baker's racks into the mudroom." She set a platter of pork chops on the table as Phoebe carried over a bowl of rice.

"Jeff gave me a ride home." Christiana set her tote bag on the floor.

"How did that happen?" Phoebe asked.

"He wanted to talk to me." Christiana told them how he explained that he had trouble trusting people ever since his fiancée left him, but she withheld the most intimate details Jeff told her.

"I want to help him learn how to trust again," Christiana said. "We're going to give our friendship another try." Her heart seemed to perform a little flip at the thought.

"That's *gut,*" *Mamm* said, "but take it slow."

"*Ya.* We will." But she'd be lying if she said she didn't already wonder if their relationship could grow into something more.

"That's *wunderbaar!*" Phoebe clapped her hands.

Dat appeared in the doorway. "What's *wunderbaar?*"

Christiana's happiness dissolved as she took in her father's grim expression. He'd

243

already made it clear that he wanted to meet her future boyfriends, but Jeff wasn't her boyfriend. He was only a friend who had driven her home.

"Christiana said she had a nice talk with her *freind* Jeff." *Mamm* stressed the word *friend.*

Dat studied Christiana, and she felt herself wilt under his intense gaze. "Is this the same Jeff who has the booth next to yours?" he asked.

Christiana nodded.

"Did I see you get out of his buggy when you got home?" *Dat* asked.

Uh-oh. "He gave me a ride home only so we could talk. We had a misunderstanding, and he wanted to explain why he —"

"What have I told you about not dating before I meet and approve the man?" *Dat*'s voice boomed off the cabinets in the large kitchen.

"We're not dating." Christiana held up her hands to calm him. "I meant it when I said we were just *freinden.* I want to get to know him better before I consider something more serious with him."

"I decide if he's worthy of dating you." *Dat* pushed his finger into his chest. "I forbid you from accepting any more rides from him before I meet him."

Christiana nodded. "Okay. I won't."

"Gut." Dat looked at the table, where Phoebe had added a bowl of corn and a basket of rolls. "This meal smells *appeditlich.* Let's eat."

As they sat down to enjoy their supper, Christiana imagined Jeff asking her father's permission to date her. Would that day come soon?

A knock sounded on Jeff's back door. He crossed the kitchen and then headed through the mudroom. He pushed open the screen door and found his brother standing on the porch.

"Hi," Nick said. "Are you busy?"

"No." Jeff pushed the door open wide. "Come on in."

"Danki." Nick wrung his hands as he stepped into the mudroom.

"What's going on?" Jeff studied his brother as he pushed his shaking hands through his dark hair. "Why are you so jittery?"

"Because I've decided to ask Kathy to marry me."

Jeff grinned. "That's fantastic." He pointed to the table. "Let me get us a cold drink."

Nick sank down into a chair, waiting for Jeff. Soon he brought them two mugs of root beer and sat down.

"When are you going to ask her?"

"I'm going to go see her *dat* tomorrow. I just wanted to talk to you first."

"Really?" Jeff smiled. "Did you tell *Mamm* and *Dat*?"

Nick shook his head. "I want your opinion before I tell anyone else."

Surprised, Jeff rubbed his chin. "*Danki,* but why do you need my opinion? This is your life, not mine."

"*Ya,* but do you think it's too soon? We've been together only a year. How do I know if it's the right time?" Nick took a long drink.

"You're asking me?" Jeff gave him a half shrug. "What do I know about relationships? My wedding didn't even happen." He gestured around the large kitchen that had also been one of Ella's dreams. "I'm living in a *haus* I built for a *maedel* who married someone else."

"*Ya,* but you're my older *bruder.* I care about what you think."

Jeff looked down at his mug and then up at Nick again. "You and Kathy obviously love each other very much, and I think you'll have a *gut* marriage." He glanced around his house, and the familiar loneliness crept in. He'd been smiling ever since he dropped Christiana off at her house, but

246

if he assumed their friendship would grow into more, he was getting way ahead of himself.

"What?" Nick leaned forward. "You look like you want to say something."

"Why don't you and Kathy move in here?" Jeff gestured around the kitchen again. "This place is too big for me, and I'd love to see this *haus* have a family to enjoy it."

Nick's expression clouded with a deep frown. "Though that's a kind offer, you need to stop being so negative."

Jeff winced as if his brother had hit him. "Excuse me? What do you mean by that?"

"You act as if you're going to be alone the rest of your life because Ella left you. *She* left *you*. That was her decision, but that doesn't mean your life is over." Nick pointed at him. "I keep telling you. We all keep telling you. You need to pick yourself up, dust yourself off, and find someone new. You've grieved for a while now, and it's time to move on."

"I know." *Easier said than done, though.* "So where are you going to live?"

"I haven't figured out a long-term plan, but her parents already hinted they'd let us live in the *daadihaus* on their property. That will work for at least a few years."

"Or you could buy this *haus* from me,"

Jeff said, making his offer again.

Nick raised an eyebrow.

"Okay, okay." Jeff took a drink of root beer.

"What about Christiana?"

"What about her?" Jeff tried to sound casual.

"Have you talked to her?"

Jeff nodded before taking another drink.

"And . . ."

"I took her home tonight, and we had a nice long talk. Our friendship is back on track."

"See?" Nick held up his mug. "You think you'll be alone in this *haus* forever, but you won't. God will lead you to your *fraa*. Just pray about it."

Jeff nodded. "All right. I will, but that doesn't mean he's chosen Christiana for me." Then he smiled. "So tell me what you're planning for Kathy. And when are you going to talk to her *dat* tomorrow?"

After Nick left, Jeff tried to imagine his own marriage. Did God have a wife for him? And if so, would Jeff know her when he met her? If the woman was Christiana, wouldn't he already know?

Jeff longed to share his home with a special woman, and he hoped against hope that he would someday. But until then, he didn't look forward to being a bachelor while Nick and Lewis enjoyed married life.

didn't look forward to being a bachelor
while Mick and Rita were married life

16

On Tuesday afternoon Christiana and Phoebe stepped into the Bird-in-Hand Family Restaurant and waited at the podium.

"I'm starved." Phoebe peered toward the tables and booths, and then suddenly her eyes widened. She tapped her sister's arm. "Christiana! Isn't that Jeff in that booth by the window?"

"Where?" Christiana looked around the dining room, and her pulse ticked up when she spotted Jeff sitting with another man. He looked to be about Jeff's age, and he had dark hair and eyes too. "*Ya,* I think it is Jeff. I wonder if that could be his *bruder?*"

"Let's go say hello." Phoebe started toward the booth.

"Phoebe. Phoebe, no!" Christiana trailed after her. "They might not want to be interrupted."

"Hi, Jeff." Phoebe smiled as she reached

the booth. "How are you?"

"Phoebe." Jeff looked surprised. His gaze moved past Phoebe, and his smile broadened when he saw Christiana. "Christy. Hi!"

Christiana's stomach fluttered when he used her nickname. "Hi, Jeff. We didn't mean to interrupt your lunch." She smiled at the other man. "Phoebe and I were just out shopping" — she lifted two shopping bags — "and we thought we'd stop in for something to eat. Phoebe spotted you over here."

"I'm so glad you did." Jeff gestured to the man across from him. "Christiana and Phoebe, this is *mei freind* Lewis."

"Nice to meet you." Lewis gave Christiana and Phoebe a nod. "Jeff came to see me at my lawn ornament shop, and I reminded him that he still owes me lunch."

"I do not owe you lunch. You're making that up so you don't have to pay for your meal." Jeff chuckled and then smiled up at Christiana again. "Join us." He scooted over on the bench seat and then patted the empty space beside him.

"No, we don't want to intrude —"

"We'd love to." Phoebe smiled as Lewis slid over and she sat down beside him.

Christiana cringed with embarrassment as she slipped into the seat beside Jeff, but

251

then she told herself to just enjoy having lunch and getting to know Jeff's friend.

"We were about to order," Lewis said.

"We'd better pick something out." Phoebe perused the menu. "What's *gut* today?"

"Everything is always *gut* here. I'm going to have my usual." Christiana smiled at Jeff. "What a coincidence to run into you here."

"I was just thinking that." He pointed to the bags at her feet. "Where did you go shopping?"

"We went to the fabric store, and then I bought some new pans for *mei kichlin.*" Christiana pointed at his bag. "How about you?"

"I needed supplies for my booth since business has been picking up, and Lewis's shop is next to the hardware store."

"I hear you make the best baked goods in all of Bird-in-Hand, maybe in all of Lancaster County," Lewis said to Christiana. "Jeff was just telling me about your *wunderbaar* macadamia nut *kichlin.*"

"Were you?" Christiana felt giddy at the thought of Jeff talking about her.

Phoebe winked at Christiana from across the table.

"*Ya,*" Jeff said as he shot Lewis a look. Was he embarrassed?

The server arrived. After distributing

water in glasses, she took their orders and walked to the kitchen.

"So, Phoebe," Lewis began, "do you like to bake like your *schweschder* does?"

"I do, but she's the best baker in the *haus,*" Phoebe said. "I'm better at sewing and quilting."

"Really?" Lewis asked. "*Mei mamm* likes to quilt too."

While Lewis and Phoebe settled into a conversation, Christiana turned toward Jeff, and when her leg brushed his, a tremble raced to the place their bodies touched. She tried to ignore the excitement bubbling through her, but she longed to reach over and hold his hand. Now that he'd told her about his past, she felt so much closer to him.

"We were both so busy on Saturday that we didn't get to talk, not even on a break for lunch. It's going to be even crazier at the market next week with the Fourth of July being on Saturday," Jeff said. "Are you ready for another busy holiday weekend?"

"I suppose so." Christiana fingered her glass. "Phoebe and I are going to start baking when we get home and get as much as we can in our freezers ahead of time. I bought more baking sheets so we can have more *kichlin* ready to go into the oven at a time."

"That's a *gut* idea."

"Have you prepared for a rush?"

"*Ya.* I'm going to have more plain bracelets and wallets ready to go. I also started making leather journal covers. That way I just have to personalize them while the customers shop around the other booths." He picked up his glass of water and sipped from it.

"Those items sound great."

"*Danki.*" Jeff sat up a little straighter. "The wallets have boosted my sales, so I thought I'd give the journal covers a try too."

She glanced over at Phoebe, who was now talking with Lewis about someone named Renae. She turned back to face Jeff. "How's your family?"

"They're all *gut.*" He seemed to hesitate for a moment. "*Mei bruder* got engaged on Sunday."

"Really?" Christiana clasped her hands. "That's so exciting." Then she stilled as she recalled their conversation in his buggy. "Are you okay with that?"

He paused and then nodded. "*Ya.* Why?"

"It must be difficult for you to think about your *bruder* getting married after what happened to you."

His expression warmed. "That's really thoughtful, but I'm okay. I'm *froh* for him. Kathy is great, and I think they'll be *froh* together."

"*Gut.*" Christiana studied his eyes and didn't find any sadness there. Was their renewed friendship already helping to heal his heart?

When their food arrived, they all bowed their heads in silent prayer and then began eating.

"How long have you known Jeff, Lewis?" Christiana asked as she cut into her meat loaf.

"How long?" Lewis grinned at Jeff. "We met in first grade when we were seven years old."

"That was a long time ago." Jeff shook his head as he picked up a french fry and popped it into his mouth.

"Tell us some stories about Jeff as a kid," Phoebe said as she picked up a section of her club sandwich.

"Hmm." Lewis rubbed his clean-shaven chin. "One time he tripped while running on the playground and ripped the back of his pants."

"No!" Phoebe said with a cackle.

Jeff groaned and covered his face with his hands. "You had to tell that story?"

"Ya." Lewis laughed. "The teacher had to sew his pants for him."

Christiana tried not to laugh. "You must have been so embarrassed."

"You have no idea. The kids teased me about it for weeks."

"Tell another story," Phoebe said.

"Well, another time he brought a frog to class to show one of the *maed,*" Lewis began.

"Stop," Jeff warned, pointing a fry at him.

"The frog got loose in the classroom, and the teacher was furious," Lewis continued. "It took the class probably thirty minutes to find it and take it outside."

"I had to clean the classroom for a week as punishment," Jeff said.

Christiana and Phoebe chuckled.

"Your turn, Lewis. How about I share some embarrassing stories about you?" Jeff said. "How about the time you were trying to get a girl's attention, so you ran after her and then tripped and fell in a puddle? Or that time in youth group when we took a few girls fishing, and you fell out of the boat?"

Christiana couldn't stop grinning as Jeff and Lewis spent the rest of lunch sharing stories about their adventures in school and youth group.

When they had all finished, they shared a couple of pieces of oatmeal pie before the server brought the check.

Christiana pulled her wallet from her purse. "How much is Phoebe's and my portion?"

"I've got it." Jeff put a pile of bills on the check and handed it to the server.

"Please, let me pay for ours." Christiana held out some money.

"No, no." He gently nudged her hand away, and when their skin brushed, she felt a thrill rush up her arm. "It's my treat today."

"So I can pay another time?" she asked.

"Probably not, but I'll say *ya* if that makes you feel better." He smiled, and her heartbeat galloped.

"Danki," Christiana said.

"Gern gschehne."

Christiana climbed out of the booth, and she and Jeff started toward the restaurant exit together, walking behind Phoebe and Lewis.

"I'm so glad you joined us for lunch," Jeff said. "I'd like to spend more time with you."

"How about I bring us lunch on Thursday?" she offered.

"Perfect."

They walked outside together.

"Well, I need to get back to work. It was nice meeting you." Lewis shook Phoebe's hand and then turned to Christiana to shake hers. "It was very nice to meet you too. I've heard a lot about you."

"Really?" Christiana cut a glance to Jeff as he shot Lewis a warning look. "That's nice to know."

"I hope to see you both again soon." Lewis gave a little wave, and then he loped across the parking lot.

"Do you two need a ride home?" Jeff asked.

"No, *danki.*" Christiana shook her head, remembering her father's words. "Our driver will be here in a few minutes, but I appreciate your offer."

"Okay." Jeff smiled. "I'll see you Thursday."

Christiana and Phoebe thanked him again for lunch before he ambled back to his waiting horse and buggy.

"Lewis is an interesting man. He told me all about his girlfriend, Renae," Phoebe said once they were sitting in the back of their driver's van. "And Jeff is so nice," she gushed. "And so handsome."

"I know." Christiana peeked out the window to avoid grinning at her sister.

"He really likes you too."

I hope so. Christiana pretended to be fix-ated on the stores they passed.

"Was iss letz?" Phoebe bumped her shoul-der against Christiana's. "I thought you'd be in a better mood after seeing Jeff today. It was such a special treat."

"Ya, it was."

"So what's wrong?"

"I'm trying not to get too excited about the possibility of dating him."

"Why not?"

"Because Jeff's had his heart broken and he's hesitant." Christiana looked down at her lap and smoothed her hands over her apron. "Plus, you know how strict *Dat* is. I might get my hopes up only to have *Dat* tell him no if he asks to date me."

Phoebe's forehead puckered. "Why would *Dat* tell him no?"

"I don't know." Christiana shrugged. "I just don't want to get too excited until it happens."

But deep down, Christiana knew it was too late. Jeff had once broken her heart, but now that it was mended, he'd stolen a piece of it.

"Gude mariye." It was Thursday morning, and Christiana walked into Jeff's booth car-rying a fresh cup of *kaffi* and a donut. "I

259

brought you some breakfast."

"Wow." Jeff was certain he wore a goofy grin. "This is so nice, but I can get my own *kaffi* and donut."

"I know, but you paid for lunch on Tuesday. And you made it clear that you wouldn't let me pay the next time." She held out the cup and chocolate donut. "I thought I'd thank you with your usual morning meal. And you're going to love the flavor of *kaffi* Bethany made today." She grinned. "It was sort of my idea."

"Okay." He sipped the coffee, and his eyes widened. "Macadamia nut?"

"Uh-huh." She folded her hands as if saying a prayer. "Do you like it?"

"I love it. You suggested it?" He took another sip.

"I did." She bit her lower lip and shrugged, her adorable expression sheepish. "I thought you might enjoy it."

"Danki." He sipped more coffee and then took a bite of the chocolate donut. "This is the perfect breakfast. Where's your *kaffi*?"

"In my booth." She nodded toward the Bake Shop. "Are you ready for the crowds today?"

"I think so." He set the cup on his worktable. "How about you?"

"I brought Phoebe in to help me today.

She offered to run the booth while we eat lunch." She held up her hand. "That's if you want to eat together at the picnic tables. If it's too busy and you don't want to take a break, we can skip lunch today."

"I'd love to take a break — even if it's a short one." He couldn't allow an opportunity to spend time with her go by.

"Gut." She spoke as she backed away. "I'd better go. Phoebe and I are still stocking shelves."

"*Danki* again for the breakfast surprise."

"Gern gschehne." She tossed the words over her shoulder.

"Christy," he called, and she spun toward him, grinning. "May I give you and Phoebe a ride home?"

She pressed her lips together and hugged her arms to her chest. "I'm sorry, but not today."

"Why not?" He took a step toward her as an alarm pinged in his mind.

"Well . . . *mei dat* doesn't want me to accept rides from any men before he's met them. I'm so sorry."

"Oh no." Guilt overtook him as he walked toward her. "Did I get you into trouble last week when I gave you a ride home?"

She shook her head. "Not really, but he warned me not to do it again." She paused.

261

"I'm so embarrassed." She pressed her fingers to her forehead.

"Don't be."

"He's really strict, and I have to obey his rules."

"I understand. I won't pressure you."

"Danki." She looked up, and her eyes met his. "I'll see you at lunch."

"Make lots of sales," he called after her as she headed to her booth.

Jeff smiled as he realized how much his fear of rejection had diminished. He imagined the day he'd ask Christiana's father if he could date her, and he had a feeling that day would come soon.

17

Jeff walked into Christiana's booth at lunchtime a week later. "I have a surprise for you, Christy. I've closed my booth for lunch, and I'd love to take you out today. Do you have time?"

Christiana smiled as she thought of how their friendship had grown just in the past week. They'd had lunch together every day at the market the week before. They talked and laughed. She couldn't wait to see where this relationship might lead.

"*Ya*, I have time. Phoebe is with me again every day this week because of the Fourth of July crowds. She'll be back from her lunch break in a minute. Where are we going to eat?" Her heart fluttered as she retrieved her purse.

"I thought we could go to that diner next door. Their service is pretty quick, so we won't be gone long."

"Great."

When Phoebe returned, they walked across the parking lot to the diner, where they sat in a booth by the window.

"How is Nick?" she asked after they ordered their food.

"He's *gut.*" Jeff gave a little smile. "He and Kathy are excited about their wedding. They're planning it for around Thanksgiving."

"Oh, how exciting." Her smile faded as she studied his eyes. "Are you still okay with that?"

"Of course I am." He smiled. "Nick and Kathy are going to live in the *daadihaus* on Kathy's father's farm until they can build a *haus.*" He shrugged. "It will be strange to not have Nick around every day, but I'm sure I'll see him." He took a drink of water and then looked at his glass. "I offered him *mei haus,* but he said no."

"Why would you give away your *haus*?"

"Because I live in it alone, and he's getting married. He needs the room more than I do."

Christiana tilted her head as she studied his face. "But don't you think you'll get married someday?"

"I hope so, but his wedding is in only a few months. He needs a *haus* now. I could move back in with my parents and figure out where I'm going to live when the time is right." He took another drink of water.

Christiana's heart sank a little. Jeff obviously didn't see himself getting married anytime soon. Did that mean he wasn't interested in being more than her friend? She took a deep breath and tried to ignore a pang of disappointment.

"What did Nick say when you offered him your *haus*? I mean, besides no," she asked.

Jeff gave her a sheepish smile. "He told me to stop being so negative. He said I'll meet someone and that I'll need the *haus* eventually." He picked up his BLT and took a bite.

"Oh." She rubbed at an imaginary itch on her nose. "Do you believe that?" She picked at her club sandwich.

"I'm starting to." He smiled, and her shoulders relaxed slightly.

They spent the rest of lunch talking about the hot July weather and their customers at the market. When their sandwiches had disappeared, they shared a warm brownie smothered in vanilla ice cream. Soon it was time to walk back to the marketplace.

"*Danki* for lunch," Christiana said as they headed toward their booths. "But next time I'm going to pay."

"No, I don't think so." Jeff grinned. "It's

265

my job to pay."

"We'll see about that." She gave his shoulder a playful swat. "Go sell a lot of wallets and journal covers."

"And you go sell your baked goods. But do save me some macadamia nut *kichlin.*"

Christiana took in his handsome profile and adorable curly hair. She loved the idea of being more than his friend. She'd have to wait to see if he'd ask her father for permission, but he might always want to be only friends. She had to be prepared for that.

Jeff sat on a stool in Christiana's booth Saturday morning and glanced at the wind-up clock on one of her shelves. He'd arrived early to put his plan into action. He'd wanted to do something special to show her how much he cared for her, and he'd racked his brain for a creative idea.

Then it hit him late last night. He'd surprise her this morning with more than just coffee and a donut. He set his alarm an hour earlier than usual, and then today he quickly took care of his morning chores before heading for the market.

Daisy the market cat hopped up on the stool next to him and rubbed her head against his arm. *"Gude mariye,* Daisy. *Wie geht's?"*

The cat meowed and blinked up at him. He found the bowls and dry food Christiana kept for Daisy and gave her food and water before returning to the stool.

A few minutes later, he heard the wheels from Christiana's baker's racks scraping across the oak floors. He stood and walked to the entrance just as she stepped inside.

"Jeff." Her eyes widened, and a smile lit up her beautiful face. "What are you doing here so early?"

"I have a cup of *kaffi* for you." He handed it to her.

"Danki." She took a long drink. "It's *appeditlich.*"

"It's hazelnut flavored. I added a lot of creamer and sweetener, just the way you like it." He slipped his hands into his pockets.

She glanced down at Daisy. "I see you gave Daisy her breakfast." She bent down and rubbed the cat's head. Then she looked up at Jeff. "Are you okay?"

"Ya." He rubbed his chin. "I was just wondering if we could go for a walk before we get ready for customers. Today's the Fourth, so we won't have much time."

"Go for a walk?" She lifted an eyebrow.

"Ya." He shrugged. "We could walk around the park once or twice and just talk before

our day gets started."

"Oh." Her smile was back. "That sounds nice." She glanced at the clock. "I think we have about thirty minutes to spare. We'd better go now. Phoebe went to the Coffee Corner. I'll leave her a note."

His pulse took on wings as they walked to the nearby park and started down the path.

"Did you have a nice evening last night?" she asked as they walked side by side.

"I did." He nodded. "Lewis came by to say hello."

"Oh?" She looked over at him. "Did you have a *gut* visit?"

"We did. He's been dating one of our old *freinden* from youth group, and they've been getting serious. He's thinking about proposing to her."

"Wow. So your best *freind* is talking about getting engaged, just like your *bruder* did."

"Ya." Jeff chuckled. "I asked Lewis if there was something in the water making everyone want to get married."

She laughed. "Do you think he's going to talk to his girlfriend's *dat* soon?"

"I think so. The first time he told me what he was thinking, I suggested it might be too soon. He said he didn't think so, but he's been mulling it over ever since. Last night he *asked* for my opinion." Jeff snorted.

"Both *mei bruder* and my best *freind* ask for my advice about their futures as if I have some special insight. When I tried to get married, it fell apart. What do I know about planning a future?"

To his surprise, Christiana stopped walking.

He spun to face her. *"Was iss letz?"*

Christiana's expression clouded. "I see why your *bruder* thinks you're too negative."

Jeff felt his lips press into a flat line as worry coursed through him. "Are you angry with me?"

"No, but I'm frustrated with you." Christiana pointed her coffee cup at him. "You have no faith in yourself. You still blame yourself for what Ella did to you, but it wasn't your fault. Ella changed *her* mind. You're a kind and *wunderbaar* man who deserves happiness. Don't let her choice ruin the rest of your life."

He stilled as her encouraging and caring words sent a strange sensation twirling through him. Her kindness soothed his broken heart.

And she thinks I'm wunderbaar?

"Let's walk before we run out of time," she said. She started down the path again, and he trailed after her.

They were silent for a beat as they walked

along, and his thoughts spun with possibilities.

"What do you see in your future?" he asked.

"*My* future?" She seemed stunned by the question.

"*Ya.* What do you want?"

"Well, I'd like to fall in love and get married someday." She looked straight ahead as she spoke. "I'd like to have a *haus* and *kinner.* And I'd like to keep selling my baked goods somehow. I wouldn't be able to go to market until the *kinner* grew up, like Leanna can now because Chester is older. But maybe if I could get my husband to build me a stand, I could sell them certain days of the week." She suddenly stopped, and her cheeks turned red. "I guess I'm rambling. I'm sorry."

He smiled as he took in her adorable expression. "You're not rambling. It's interesting to hear what you want in your future." *Will I be a part of it? Do I want that?* More excitement overcame him. Was this a message from God?

"What about you?" Her question invaded his thoughts. "What do you want?"

He took a deep breath. "I'd love to fill *mei haus* with a family." Saying the words out loud broke down the wall he'd built around his heart. It was as if he'd suddenly been set free of the grief Ella had caused in his life.

"I'm certain you will someday." Her smile was nearly as bright as the morning sun.

"I hope so."

"Don't give up. God has the perfect plan for all of us." She nodded toward the market. "But first, we'd better hurry. We need to get back and finish setting up."

They swiftly returned to the market, the cheerful potted flowers greeting them as they approached the heavy front doors made of glass. They stepped into the building over the worn, creaky oak floors as the aromas of lunch meat, coffee, and candy filled Jeff's senses.

He smiled at Christiana as they walked to her booth together.

"This was the perfect way to start my morning," she said. "*Danki* for the *kaffi* and the walk."

"I'm so grateful you joined me." Without thinking, he reached up and touched her cheek, taking in her smattering of freckles. "You're so *schee.*"

She sucked in a breath as her eyes widened.

"If Phoebe is willing to manage the crowds by herself for a little while, would you please

271

have lunch with me today?"

"Ya." Her voice sounded hoarse. "I'd love to."

"Gut." He let his arm drop to his side. "Have a *gut* morning."

As he walked to his booth, he felt as if he were walking on air. He was falling for Christiana, and unless it was his imagination, she seemed to like him as more than a friend. He just hoped she wouldn't change her mind about him the way Ella had. How would he live through another heartbreak?

"Okay, Christiana." Bethany leaned over the arm of the rocking chair on Leanna's parents' porch and tapped her cousin's arm. "Tell us everything about Jeff. We know you had lunch with him again this week, and we saw you walking into the market with him yesterday morning. What's the deal?"

Christiana grinned as she gripped her glass of iced tea.

It was Sunday afternoon, and the sun was bright as the warm aroma of moist earth filled her senses. Since Leanna's parents had hosted church today, Christiana and her family were spending the rest of the day with her mother's side of the family. Leanna and Chester had moved in with her parents after Marlin died so they could help support her and their grandson.

Christiana always enjoyed her visits with her mother's family. She and her cousins would find a place to talk while their mothers visited in the kitchen, their fathers talked in the barn, and Phoebe visited with their younger cousins by the pasture fence. They laughed and chatted as the hours slipped by too quickly.

"Well, Christiana?" Leanna's light-brown eyebrows careened toward her hairline. "What's going on between you and Jeff?"

Christiana settled back in her rocking chair and pushed it into motion with her toe. "We had lunch together all three days at the market, and early yesterday morning he was waiting at my booth with a cup of *kaffi* for me. We went for a walk in the park and talked before the market opened."

"What did you talk about?" Salina asked.

"Everything." Christiana looked down at her lap and smiled.

"What's everything?" Bethany swatted her arm. "Come on. Stop teasing us."

Christiana mentally debated how much to share. By now her cousins all knew about Ella, but she'd never betray Jeff's trust by sharing his most intimate feelings.

"He shared that his best *freind* is talking about getting engaged, and then we talked

273

about our hopes and dreams. It was nice." Christiana sighed.

"Really?" Leanna's expression brightened. "Sounds like it's getting serious."

"I wouldn't say that." Christiana's smile faded. "I mean, he does seem attentive and *froh* to spend time with me, but I can't be sure he wants to date me."

"Why would he have lunch with you every day and take you on a walk if he didn't want to date you?" Salina asked.

"Exactly," Bethany said, jumping in.

"He's had his heart broken. Maybe he just needs a *freind.*" Christiana fingered the hem of her apron.

"I disagree," Leanna said. "He wouldn't be so eager to see you if he only wanted to be your *freind.* He seems to seek you out. I've noticed he's completely focused on you when you're together."

"Would you go out with him if he asked you?" Salina asked.

"*Ya,* I would, but he has to get *mei dat*'s permission first."

"Are you worried about that?" Salina asked.

"You know I am." Christiana sighed. "Your *dat* is our bishop, but he's not nearly as strict as *mei dat* is. *Mei dat* says he'll know who the right man is for Phoebe and for

274

me. Assuming Jeff asks, what if he says no to him?"

Salina shook her head. "I don't think your *dat* would say no."

"So let's just assume he gets your *dat*'s permission," Bethany began, "and then he asks you to be his girlfriend. Would you say *ya*?"

"Of course I would. I care about him. I think he's a *gut* man. I just don't know if he's ready for another relationship yet." Christiana sipped her iced tea as her thoughts moved to how her lungs had seized when he touched her cheek. She'd felt as if lightning had struck her. She'd never felt such a strong attraction to her former boyfriends. Did that mean Jeff was the one God intended for her? If so, why did doubt plague her? She was so confused.

"You might want to take it slow if you think he's hesitant," Salina said. "You won't want to appear too eager and scare him away."

"I agree," Leanna said. "You don't want him to break your heart if he's not ready for another relationship."

"*Ya,* that's true." Bethany smiled. "Concentrate on being his *freind* for now. Get to know him better. But if he is ready, then I think you should go for it. See where the

275

Lord leads you and Jeff together." Then she turned to Salina. "What about you and Josiah Yoder?"

"*Ya.*" Leanna nudged Salina's arm. "I saw you and Josiah talking after church earlier today."

Salina shrugged and picked at the hem of her apron. "He's nice. We've always been *gut freinden.*"

"And . . ." Christiana was grateful the focus had moved from her to someone else.

"And I don't know." Salina gave a little smile. "He's handsome and he's kind. I would go out with him if he asked."

"Ooh!" Bethany clapped. "Maybe both of you will have boyfriends soon."

"There they are!" *Mammi* stepped out onto the porch and smiled. "I knew I'd find you four together. How are you all?"

Christiana smiled as her grandmother sat down on a rocking chair next to her. She always enjoyed spending time with her grandmother. At the age of eighty, *Mammi* had gray hair, and wrinkles outlined the same warm blue eyes she'd given to Christiana's mother. She stood about three inches shorter than Christiana and walked with a slight limp because of pain in her knee. Christiana adored how her grandmother always made time to talk to her and her cousins. She was more than their grandmother; she was their sweet and special second mother who offered an ear when they needed someone to listen and sage advice when they craved it.

"How are things at the marketplace?" *Mammi* asked.

"They're *gut, Mammi,*" Salina said. "Christiana's business is booming, and we're so *froh* she joined us."

"Is that right?" *Mammi* looked at Christiana. "You're selling quite a lot of baked goods?"

"*Ya.* I am."

"And she's made a new *freind* too," Bethany said, chiming in.

"Oh?" *Mammi* leaned toward Christiana and lowered her voice. "Is he handsome?"

Leanna and Salina laughed as Christiana blushed.

"How did you know it was a man, *Mammi*?" Leanna asked with a chuckle.

"Because you wouldn't have mentioned her *freind* if he was a *maedel,* right?" They all laughed again. How Christiana loved her grandmother's sense of humor!

"He is handsome," Christiana said. "But he's only *mei freind.*"

"That's a *gut* way to start," *Mammi* said. "Your *daadi* and I started out as *freinden.*"

She gave Christiana's hand a little squeeze. "Take your time, sweetie. You're young."

Christiana nodded.

Mammi turned to Leanna. "How is your Jam and Jelly Nook? I need to get some more strawberry jam from you."

As *Mammi* continued to talk to the others, Christiana thought about her relationship with Jeff. Had God led them to each other? Did Jeff feel the Lord's blessing on their friendship?

Her grandmother and cousins were right. She shouldn't expect this relationship to move too fast — for her sake as well as for Jeff's. She needed to trust God's timing.

18

Jeff sat at the high-top table in the Coffee Corner on Friday morning a month later. He smiled as Christiana and her cousins laughed. A customer had asked Leanna if she bought her jams and jellies from a store and then put her own labels on the jars.

"Why would I put up a sign saying home-made jams and jellies if I only sold store-bought jams and jellies?" Leanna tilted her head. "Don't you think someone would report me for false advertising?"

"I think so." Christiana turned her bright smile on Jeff, and his heart seemed to turn over in his chest.

He was falling for her, and though it had taken some time, he felt ready to take their relationship to the next level. For several weeks, he and Christiana had enjoyed lunch together every day they were at the market. They had a routine. They met at the Coffee Corner in the morning, and then at one thirty they ate together at the picnic tables, taking turns bringing lunch. In the evenings, he walked her out to the parking lot and helped her load her racks and supplies into her driver's van.

Their lunchtime talks had grown more intimate, and he felt safe sharing his feelings with her. Christiana had become his friend, a dear friend, but he wanted more. He wanted to be her boyfriend, but he needed to meet her family and invite her to meet his.

"What *gegisch* questions have customers asked you?" Leanna asked Christiana.

"Well . . ." Christiana tapped her chin. "One woman asked me if I cooked on a fire pit in my backyard."

Her cousins hooted and cackled as Jeff chuckled.

"You can't be serious," Bethany said as she wiped her eyes.

"Unfortunately, I am serious." Christiana nodded.

"What did you tell her?" Leanna asked.

"First I tried not to laugh." Christiana chuckled. "Then I politely told her that we have propane-powered stoves and refrigerators. She looked confused, but she didn't ask any more questions."

"That's hilarious," Salina said. "Some

people just don't understand our culture."

"No, they sure don't." Bethany turned to Jeff. "You're awfully quiet this morning. Are you feeling okay?"

Jeff lifted his cup. "I'm just enjoying your fantastic *kaffi*. I love this vanilla caramel."

"Do you?" Bethany grinned. "I thought I'd try something different."

"She's a genius," Leanna said.

Bethany smiled at the floor. "*Gude mariye,* Daisy. Do you want your breakfast?"

Daisy meowed and followed Bethany to the counter, where Bethany pulled out a bowl and a bag of food for the gray tabby.

"I'm convinced Daisy spends the day going booth to booth just for food," Jeff quipped.

Salina laughed. "I agree. Have you noticed how round she's become?"

"Oh no." Christiana looked at Bethany's clock. "We need to get going. The market opens in ten minutes." She hopped down from the stool and looked at Jeff. "Are you ready?"

"I am." Jeff stood beside her and looked at her cousins. "Have a *gut* morning."

"You too," Bethany sang out.

Jeff nodded and then followed Christiana.

"You *have* been quiet all morning," Christiana said as they walked down the aisle toward their booths. "Is something on your mind?"

He nodded. "*Ya,* I suppose it is."

She stopped and looked up at him with some hesitation. "Do you want to talk about it?"

He took a deep breath. "We've been *freinden* for about a month now, right?"

"*Ya.* I think a little longer, actually. Why?" Her eyes seemed to search his.

"Maybe it's time we each met the other's family." His chest constricted as he awaited her response.

"Really?" Her face lit up. "That would be so nice."

"*Gut.*" Relief whipped through him. "Would you like to go to church with me on Sunday? I could come to your *haus* and meet your family, and then I could take you to *mei haus* to visit with my family after church — if your *dat* says it's okay, of course."

"I would love to do that. Let me ask *mei dat,* and then I'll let you know."

"*Gut.*" He took her hand in his, and heat sizzled up his arm, sending his senses spinning. "I really hope he agrees."

"How was your day at the market?" *Mamm* asked as the family sat down for supper later that evening.

"It was *gut.*" Christiana took a bowl of mashed potatoes from Phoebe and scooped a pile onto her plate. "I sold out of German chocolate *kuchen* today. I was surprised. Last week it was carrot *kuchen.*"

"That's interesting how different baked goods are popular each weekend," Phoebe said.

"*Ya.*" Christiana peeked at her father and found him looking down as he cut his steak. She took in his pleasant expression. He'd seemed to be in a good mood when he arrived home from work, smiling as he talked about the house he and his crew had finished today. She longed to ask him if she could go to church with Jeff on Sunday, but she worried he might say no.

"Did you hear what I said?"

"What?" Christiana turned toward Phoebe. "I'm sorry. I didn't hear you."

Phoebe's eyes narrowed for a split second as if she were analyzing her. Then she smiled. "I said *Mamm* and I finished the lone star quilt we were working on. The customer came to pick it up, and she was pleased with it."

"I'm sure she was." Christiana cut her steak as she spoke. "It was such a *schee* quilt."

283

"I agree," *Dat* said, chiming in. "I'm not surprised that the customer was *froh* with it. I think it was your best work."

"*Danki,* Freeman." *Mamm* beamed at him.

"*Gern gschehne.*" *Dat* winked at *Mamm* as he lifted his glass of water. "You and Phoebe are the best quilters I know."

Christiana grinned. *Dat* was in a *very* good mood. Now was the time to get his permission. "*Dat,*" she began, "I want to ask you something."

Dat turned his attention toward her as he chewed.

"You've heard me talk about *mei freind* Jeff at the market," she said, and he nodded. "He asked me to go to church with him and his family on Sunday. So I want to ask your permission to go." She held her breath as she awaited his response.

Out of the corner of her eye, she saw Phoebe's expression brighten, and she hoped her sister would keep her excitement to herself. Now was not the time for one of her outbursts.

"Why does he want you to go to church with him?" *Dat* asked.

"We've been getting to know each other for more than a month now, and he'd like me to meet his family." She added quickly, "He'd like to meet you as well, *Dat.* If he picks me up, he can do that before we leave for the service."

Dat glanced at *Mamm,* and when she gave him a slight nod, Christiana's pulse skittered with excitement.

"*Ya,* you have my permission." *Dat* held up his finger. "But your *freind* must come into our *haus* and meet me before you leave. Giving my permission for this visit is not the same as giving you permission to date him."

"I understand. *Danki, Dat.* I'm sure you'll like him."

"You will," Phoebe said. "He's a nice man."

"*Gut.*" *Dat* turned to *Mamm.* "Do you have any new orders for quilts?"

"I do. Now that we're almost into August, people are starting to order for Christmas presents. I think Phoebe and I will stay busy this fall."

Christiana looked down at her plate as excitement buzzed through her.

Dat *said* ya!

She was going to church with Jeff, and she was going to meet his family. She had to wear her favorite teal dress.

She bit her lower lip as she imagined meeting his mother and father. What if they didn't like her? She tried not to get too nervous at the thought.

"Christiana?"

"Ya?" She looked up and found her family staring at her.

"Would you like more mashed potatoes?" *Mamm* asked, looking curious about more than second helpings.

Christiana shook her head. "No, *danki.*"

"Then I think we're ready to clean up," *Mamm* said.

Christiana gathered up the plates and utensils and then carried them to the counter.

"I'm going out to the barn." *Dat* kissed *Mamm*'s cheek.

Christiana hugged her arms to her chest. Her parents' rare public displays of affection always took her by surprise. She found herself imagining her own future marriage. Would her husband kiss her cheek like that? Would he tell her he loved her even when relatives or friends surrounded them?

Would he be Jeff?

She swallowed back a sigh. Why was she imagining Jeff as her future when she hadn't even met his parents? When he hadn't even told her that he cared about her as more than a close friend? She needed to keep taking Salina's advice and set her heart on an even course.

Dat disappeared through the mudroom, and the sound of the screen door clicking shut came through to the kitchen.

"You're going to meet Jeff's family on Sunday," *Mamm* said. "That's a big step."

"*Ya,* it sure is," Phoebe said.

Christiana nodded as she brought the glasses to the counter.

"Aren't you excited?" *Mamm* turned on the faucet to fill the sink.

"I am." Christiana did her best to keep her voice even as she turned to collect the serving bowls and platters.

"Why don't you sound like it?" Phoebe stood at the table, ready to wipe it down.

"I'm *naerfich.*" The words burst from Christiana's lips. "What if his family doesn't like me?"

"Oh, Christiana." *Mamm* turned toward her and touched her cheek. "They'll love you. You're sweet and *schee.* You're everything a parent would want for a daughter-in-law."

"Daughter-in-law?" Christiana shook her head. "No, no, no. I don't think Jeff is ready for that."

"He might not be now, but I have a feeling he will be sometime soon." *Mamm* turned back to the sink and added dish-washing soap as she turned off the running

287

water. "Didn't you say he's twenty-eight?"

"He is, but he hasn't even mentioned dating me," Christiana said. "We're really only *freinden.*"

"Taking you to meet his family and to his church is a step toward dating," Phoebe said. "Shouldn't you know that? You're a lot older than I am, Christiana."

Mamm chuckled as she washed the first plate and then placed it in the drying rack. Christiana picked it up and began to wipe it dry with a towel.

"He's taking things slowly, and so am I," Christiana said.

"Just wait and see," *Mamm* said with a warm smile. "I think the Lord has a *wunderbaar* plan for you and Jeff."

"Mei dat said *ya,"* Christiana told Jeff the following afternoon as they sat at a picnic table outside the market. "You can take me to church tomorrow."

Jeff had overslept and arrived at the market just as it was opening this morning, so he'd had to anxiously wait for lunchtime to find out what her father said.

"That's great." He grinned across the table at her. "I'm so relieved."

"I am too." She picked up her bottle of water. "You can pick me up tomorrow

288

morning, but *Dat* does expect you to come inside to meet him before we leave. You've already met *mei mamm* and *schweschder,* but they're excited to see you."

"Okay." He felt his smile falter.

"Are you okay?" she asked.

"Ya." He pushed his hand through his thick hair. "I'm just concerned about meeting your *dat.* You said he's very strict. Is there anything I should say or do to impress him?"

Her expression told him she was amused. "Just be yourself, and you'll do fine. He's strict, but he has a *gut* heart. He'll probably ask you about your business and your parents. You'll be great."

Dread made him feel a little queasy. What if he said the wrong thing and her father disapproved? Then he'd have to ride to church alone and try to explain to his family what he'd done to ruin his chances with Christiana. He grimaced.

"Jeff?" She leaned forward. "You look like you might be *krank.* Is your ham salad okay?"

"The sandwich is great." He sat up straighter. "I'm not *krank.* I'm just *naerfich.* I'm worried that I'm going to say something wrong, and then your *dat* won't let you go to church with me."

"I'll say it again. You're going to be just fine." Her smile wobbled. "But do you think your family will approve of *me*?"

He laughed. "You don't have anything to worry about. They can't wait to meet you."

"Gut." She smiled. "Tomorrow will be *wunderbaar.*"

"*Ya*, it will." He smiled as he imagined Christiana meeting his parents. He just hoped her father was as open to meeting him as Jeff was anxious.

19

Jeff stood on Christiana's back porch the following morning and wiped his sweaty palms on his trouser legs. He knocked on the door and then released a quaking breath.

The door swung open, revealing Christiana clad in a bluish-green dress that complemented her fiery-red hair.

"Gude mariye," she said, and when her smile widened, his pulse zipped through his veins.

"Gude mariye."

"Come in." Christiana beckoned him to follow her into the house. "My family is looking forward to seeing you."

He followed her through the mudroom into a spacious kitchen, where her parents and Phoebe all stood.

"Jeff, you remember *mei mamm,* Lynn. You met the day I moved into the booth." Christiana pointed to her mother. "And you've met Phoebe a few times when she's

291

helped me at the market."

"It's nice to see you again." He shook her mother's hand.

"You too," Lynn said.

"And this is *mei dat,* Freeman." Christiana made a sweeping gesture toward him.

Jeff quickly took in her father's appearance. Freeman was slightly taller than Jeff, and he had graying light-brown hair and a matching beard. His eyes were light blue, not blue-green like Christiana's.

He gave Jeff a stern nod and held out his hand.

"It's a pleasure to meet you," Jeff said as he shook his hand.

"You too." Freeman seemed to study him. "What is your intention with *mei dochder?*"

Jeff faltered and turned to Christiana, who bit her lower lip. He swiveled back to her father and cleared his throat. "I think a lot of Christiana. She's already a dear *freind,* and I'm enjoying getting to know her."

"Gut." Freeman nodded. "Just be careful on your way to church and on your way back. You know how traffic can get sometimes. These tourists don't know how to drive with buggies around."

"Of course. And if it's okay with you, after church I'd like to take her to my parents' *haus* to visit. I'll be sure to have her home

292

by suppertime."

"That will be fine."

"Danki." Jeff turned to Christiana. "We need to leave now if we want to have a few minutes to socialize before the church service starts. Are you ready to go?"

"*Ya,* I am." Christiana gave her mother a hug. "I'll see you later." She waved to her father and sister.

"Be safe," Lynn called.

Jeff walked with her out to the buggy. "Do you think it went okay?"

"It went great." Christiana gave his hand a squeeze before climbing into the buggy.

He hurried around to the other side and hopped in. When he turned toward her, she seemed to squirm under his stare.

"What is it?" She reached up and smoothed a hand over her prayer covering. "Do I have egg on my face or something?"

"No." He cupped his hand to her cheek. "I was just thinking about how *schee* you are."

"Danki," she whispered, and the air around them felt electrified.

She sucked in a breath as he started to lean toward her. Then he stilled. It was too soon to kiss her. What if her father looked out the back door and saw them? Surely then he'd forbid them from seeing each other. He couldn't risk his opportunity like that.

"We should go," Jeff muttered as he turned toward the windshield. He picked up the reins and guided the horse toward the road while trying to calm his racing heart.

"This is the Blank family's farm," Jeff said as he halted the horse by a large barn. "This is where Lewis's family lives."

"Really?" Christiana peered out the buggy windshield at the large white clapboard house and the large red barn. "His *dat* owns a lawn ornament store, right?"

"That's right." Jeff turned toward her. "Are you ready to meet my family?"

"Ya." She still felt nervous.

"Don't worry." He touched her arm. "They're going to love you."

"I hope so."

She climbed out of the buggy and met him by a path that led to the house. He waved at two couples, one about her parents' age and the other about hers, who stood by a pasture fence. She took in the older woman's warm smile and dark eyes and was certain she was Jeff's mother. The older man was stocky and had dark hair, and his nose resembled Jeff's. The young man was tall, and unlike Jeff, his hair was straight. But he had Jeff's warm smile and similar facial features. That had to be Nick.

"Mamm, Dat," Jeff began, "this is Christiana."

"We're so *froh* to meet you, Christiana," the older woman said. "I'm Joyce, and this is Merle."

"How are you?" Christiana asked, her stomach fluttering as she shook Joyce's hand.

"We're delighted to finally meet you." Merle shook her hand as well. "We've heard so much about you."

"Dat . . . ," Jeff said, and everyone laughed. "Christiana, this is *mei bruder,* Nick, and his fiancée, Kathy."

"Gude mariye." Christiana shook their hands.

"I'm so glad Jeff met you." Nick's smile was wide. "You're just what he needs."

"Danki," Christiana said.

"We're so pleased that you joined us this morning," Kathy said. "Would you like to come into the kitchen with Joyce and me to meet the other women in the congregation?"

"That would be nice." Christiana nodded and then turned to Jeff. "I'll see you after the service."

"I can't wait," he whispered as he leaned close to her ear. Then he, his father, and Nick started toward the group of men who stood near the barn.

Christiana, Joyce, and Kathy stepped into the house's large kitchen where women of the congregation stood greeting one another. Christiana smiled and shook hands as Joyce introduced her to several of them.

When a woman who looked to be around her age approached, Kathy touched Christiana's hand.

"Christiana, this is Renae Detweiler. She's engaged to Lewis Blank, Jeff's best *freind*. Renae, this is Christiana Kurtz. She's Jeff's *freind*."

"Hi, Renae," Christiana said as she shook the hand of this blonde with blue eyes.

"I've heard so much about you from Lewis." Renae's smile was warm. "I'm so glad Jeff met you. Lewis said you're just what he needs."

"That's exactly what Nick just said to me."

Kathy leaned in close. "Jeff had such a rough time when Ella left him. Nick said he was worried Jeff had given up on love."

Love? The word rolled around in Christiana's head. Wasn't it too soon to talk about love?

Yet she was certain Jeff had almost kissed

her in the buggy before they left her house this morning. Maybe he did care for her as more than a friend, but she didn't know for sure. She had to keep her emotions in check.

"Ella is here," Renae whispered as she nodded toward the corner of the kitchen. "You should keep your voice down."

"Where?" Kathy looked over her shoulder. "Oh. I see her." She discreetly gestured to the corner where the same petite blonde Christiana had seen that day in Sara Ann's quilt shop spoke to a brunette. "She's over there. The one wearing a purple dress. She must be visiting her parents today. She normally attends church in her husband's district."

Ella was strikingly beautiful. Christiana imagined her and Jeff together — talking, laughing, kissing — and her stomach soured. Why was she jealous of a woman who had left Jeff and married someone else?

Joyce approached them with a smile. "What are you three conspiring about? It looks like you have a juicy secret."

"We pointed out Ella," Kathy said, keeping her voice low.

"Oh." Joyce's smile flattened. "*Ya,* I saw her earlier. I was surprised to see her here." She shook her head. "I've forgiven her, but I'll never forget how she hurt *mei sohn.*"

Christiana tried to imagine how Jeff felt the day Ella broke his heart, and she silently vowed to never hurt him that way.

"Let me introduce you to *mei mamm,*" Kathy said as she took Christiana's hand and led her toward a group of middle-aged women.

Plastering a smile on her face, Christiana prepared to meet more women in Jeff's church district. But she couldn't get past the feeling that Jeff would be hurt when he saw Ella again — just like that day at the market.

Soon it was almost nine, time to focus on the Lord and not worry about remembering the names of all the women Joyce had introduced to her.

"You'll sit with Renae and me, right?" Kathy asked, her expression hopeful as they walked to the barn.

"Of course I will." Christiana walked with them into the barn and toward the other unmarried young women.

She sank onto the backless bench between her two new friends and then greeted other young women as Kathy introduced her as Jeff's friend. They all seemed happy to meet her, but they did eye her curiously.

When Kathy and Renae each became engrossed in conversations with women sitting close by, Christiana turned toward the rows of young, unmarried men and found Jeff sitting between his brother and Lewis. Delighted, she took a moment to enjoy his handsome face. He was even more attractive than usual dressed in his Sunday clothes — black trousers, a crisp white shirt, and a black vest. Christiana could watch him for hours, but she pulled her attention away and looked down at her apron. She had to remove these thoughts from her mind and focus on the service ahead.

She looked over at the married women section and quickly found Ella, who was talking to the same brunette woman she spoke to in the kitchen earlier. Christiana tried to imagine why Ella would leave Jeff when he was such a kind and gentle man. He also seemed like a hard worker who would make sure he provided well for his family. After all, he'd built her a house.

"Was iss letz?" Kathy whispered in her ear.

"What do you mean?" Christiana glanced over at her.

"You look upset. Is something bothering you?"

"No." Christiana looked over at Ella once again. "I was just thinking about Ella and wondering why she left Jeff."

Kathy clicked her tongue. "Nick has asked

me the same question many times. I don't understand it either. That's why I'm so *froh* he found you. Nick told me you made his *bruder* smile again."

"Is that true?" Christiana asked.

"Ya." Kathy nodded. "We're so grateful for you."

Christiana felt heat crawl up her neck to her cheeks.

"What did I miss?" Renae turned toward Christiana.

"I was just telling Christiana that Nick says she's helped Jeff smile again," Kathy told her.

"Ya," Renae said. "Lewis has told me the same thing."

"Maybe they'll be the next to get engaged," Kathy said.

Christiana shook her head. "But we're not even officially dating."

"I'm sure that will come soon," Kathy said, and Renae nodded.

Christiana's thoughts spun. Could Kathy and Renae be correct? Would Jeff ask her father for permission to date her soon?

Her cheeks felt as if they might blaze with fire. She wanted to stare at Jeff as if she could read his mind if she did, but she knew looking at him was too risky. If he saw her blushing, he might later ask her why. Yet how could she share the conversation she'd just had with Kathy and Renae when it would most likely embarrass him as well?

Kathy and Renae were once again pulled into different conversations, and Christiana breathed a sigh of relief. She stole one last glance at Jeff and found him talking to Lewis. *Thank goodness he hasn't seen me watching him!*

She studied her hymnal to avoid his gaze, but her mind still whirled with Kathy and Renae's words. Was she really a blessing to Jeff? She'd wanted to be.

The service began with a hymn, and Christiana redirected her thoughts to the present. She joined in as the congregation slowly sang the opening hymn, "Loblied," a hymn of praise. A young man sitting across the barn served as the song leader. He began the first syllable of each line, and then the rest of the congregation joined in to finish the verse.

While the ministers met in another room for thirty minutes to choose who would preach that day, the congregation continued to sing. During the last verse of the second hymn, Christiana's gaze moved to the back of the barn just as the ministers returned. They placed their hats on two hay bales, indicating that the sermon was about to begin.

The chosen minister began the first sermon, and Christiana tried her best to concentrate on his holy words. She folded her hands in her lap and studied them, but her thoughts turned to Jeff. She tried her best to keep her focus on the minister, but her stare moved toward the young men across the aisle. She contemplated Jeff, who sat with his head bowed.

What was he thinking about? Was he thinking about her? Was he thinking about what their future could hold if they started dating?

While the minister continued to talk in German, Christiana lost herself in thought. She had enjoyed her time with Jeff these past couple of months. How she'd loved eating lunch together, laughing together with her cousins in the Coffee Corner, and walking in the park.

She hoped they would continue spending time together not only at the market but also outside of the market. Perhaps after today they would start spending time together with their families. Maybe he would invite her over to visit with his family again. Maybe she could have him over for supper.

She glanced at Jeff and found him watching her, his dark eyes intense. A shiver of awareness danced up her spine as her gaze locked with his. Her breathing came in short bursts. Then a smile broke out on his face, and she smiled in return before looking down at her lap.

The first sermon ended, and Christiana knelt in silent prayer between Kathy and Renae.

Relief flooded her when the fifteen-minute kneeling prayer was over following the second sermon. The congregation stood for the benediction and sang the closing hymn.

As she looked once more toward Jeff, she had to admit the truth. If God had something more in store for them, she hoped today would be the day Jeff would tell her how he felt about her, that he wanted more than friendship.

Kathy touched Renae and Christiana's hands. "Let's go help serve the meal."

20

"I approve," Nick said as he sat across from Jeff during lunch.

After the service had ended, Jeff and Nick helped the other men in the congregation convert the benches into tables for the noon meal. Then Jeff sat down with Nick, Lewis, and *Dat* and waited for the women to serve the meal.

"You approve of what?" Jeff asked.

"Are you joking?" Nick asked. "I approve of her, of course."

"I do too," *Dat* said with a smile. "She's lovely."

"She sure is," Lewis said. "*Gut* for you."

Jeff had found himself distracted during most of the service. His eyes kept drifting over to study Christiana. At one point she looked at him as if she felt the weight of his stare. When their eyes locked, his breath stalled in his chest. And then it hit him — he cared more for Christiana than he ever cared for Ella. Christiana had captured his heart in a way Ella never had.

Did Christiana feel the tremendous attraction he was sure had been growing between them?

"Here are some pretzels." Kathy smiled at Nick as she set a bowl on the table. "Enjoy."

"Danki, mei liewe." Nick winked at her, and her smile broadened as she stepped down the line.

"When are you going to ask her out?" Lewis asked as he picked up a pretzel and popped it into his mouth.

"I have to get her *daed*'s permission first."

"What are you waiting for?" Nick asked. "Talk to him when you take her home tonight."

Jeff cleared his throat and glanced toward the other side of the barn where Christiana was filling coffee cups. She looked gorgeous in the dress she wore today. He couldn't wait to be alone with her in the buggy on the way to his parents' house. He longed to talk to her — and possibly hold her hand. Maybe even kiss her cheek.

What was wrong with him? He had no right to think about kissing her until he'd requested her father's blessing.

Lewis leaned toward him. "You haven't answered my question. Why not ask her *dat*'s permission tonight? What are you waiting for?"

"It might be too soon." Jeff picked up a pretzel from the bowl. "I don't want to move too fast and scare her away."

"Move too fast?" Nick snorted. "Haven't you been *freinden* with her for a couple of months now?"

"*Ya,* but we've been getting to know each other. You knew Kathy for a few years before you asked her out."

"Take your time, *sohn.*" *Dat*'s words were gentle. "No one can tell you how fast to move with your relationship. You need to do what feels right to you."

"True, but if he waits too much longer," Nick said, "someone else might ask her out."

A muscle in Jeff's neck stiffened at the thought of someone else asking Christiana to be his girlfriend. No, he couldn't allow that to happen.

"Kaffi?"

Jeff glanced over his shoulder as Christiana appeared with her pitcher of coffee. Her blue-green eyes focused on him.

For a moment it felt as if the rest of the congregation had faded away and they were the only two people in the barn. His heart hammered. What was happening to him?

"Would you like some *kaffi*?" she repeated,

breaking their connection.

"Ya, danki." He handed her his cup, and she filled it.

After she filled the cups of all the men surrounding him, Jeff angled his body and watched her move down the line. He studied her beautiful profile and admired how her eyes sparkled and her rosy lips curved up as she worked her way to the end of the table.

When he realized he'd been staring at her too long, Jeff swiveled around and picked up his coffee cup. He glanced beside him and found Lewis watching him. His eyebrows were lifted, and his expression flickered with amusement.

As he sipped his coffee, Jeff braced himself for Lewis to make a biting comment, but his friend remained silent.

"Are you sure you're not in a hurry to date her? Because that sure looked like attraction to me." Nick picked up another pretzel and took a bite.

Jeff shook his head. "I don't want to make the same mistake twice. I care about Christiana, but I'm not prepared for another heartache."

"Please, Jeff," Nick said. "Christiana is nothing like Ella."

Jeff pressed his lips together. He'd seen Ella at the service today, but for the first time in more than a year, his stomach hadn't soured at the sight of her. He didn't feel the overwhelming embarrassment that normally accompanied seeing her face. Was he finally getting over her?

"That's the truth," *Dat* said, chiming in.

"What?" Jeff asked him.

Dat picked up his cup. "Christiana and Ella are different. Christiana has a sweetness about her that Ella never seemed to have. I think she's more tenderhearted."

Jeff studied his father as he drank from his cup. *Dat* could sense that much about Christiana after meeting her only once and so briefly?

"I agree," Nick said.

"I do too," Lewis added.

"Huh." Jeff considered the observation as he again sipped his coffee. His eyes moved to the far end of the barn, where Ella placed plates of peanut butter spread on the tables. He waited for the anger and grief to bubble up inside of him, but it never appeared. Instead, a mixture of relief and happiness coiled through him.

He was truly over her, and the realization sent elation coursing through him. Ella no longer had a hold on his heart or his memories. She was only part of his past.

"So, Lewis," *Dat* began, "how are things

at your store?"

"They're *gut,*" Lewis told him. "We've stayed busy all summer. I think it's going to be a profitable season for us this year."

"Gut, gut," Dat said.

Jeff glanced at his brother as his father and Lewis continued to chat.

"Make it official," Nick said. "You'll be glad you did."

Jeff nodded, and excitement filled him. Maybe it *was* time to ask Christiana to be his girlfriend. He just had to find the courage to ask her father's permission.

Jeff leaned against his buggy and looked toward the Blanks' back porch, where Christiana stood talking to Kathy and Renae. He smiled as she interacted with her two new friends. He was so grateful that she seemed to not only fit in with his church district but also with his family.

"Jeff?"

He turned as Ella walked toward him with a tentative smile on her face. To his surprise, his stomach still didn't lurch as she approached. He felt nothing — no anger, no grief, just nothing.

"Hi, Ella." He folded his arms over his chest.

She bit her lower lip and then cleared her

throat. "How are you?"

"I'm all right." He shrugged.

"I know you have a booth at the market-place now, selling your wood and leather goods."

How did she know? Had Sara Ann told her?

"*Ya*. It's going well." He tilted his head. "What's new with you?"

"We finally got moved into our new *haus*. John's construction business has been busy . . ." Her expression clouded even more. "I, uh . . . I want to apologize to you."

"Apologize for what?" he asked as suspicion crept into his thoughts. Had she done something to him he didn't even know about?

"I'm sorry for hurting you the way I did." She looked down at the ground and then back up at him, her eyes bright with unshed tears. "I went about the breakup the wrong way. I was immature and selfish. You're a *wunderbaar* man, and you'll always have a special place in my heart. I cherish the time we had together."

His jaw went slack as he stared at her, unsure how to respond.

"Jeff, you did nothing wrong." She sniffed. "My heart . . . changed."

"What do you mean?"

310

She took a deep breath and continued. "I'd had doubts long before our wedding day. I met John a few months before you and I were supposed to get married. I wasn't unfaithful to you, but I felt a connection with him that you and I didn't have." She wiped at her eyes. "You have to admit that you felt we were growing apart too. I know it wasn't just me. We didn't talk like we used to."

He swallowed as he nodded, realizing what she said was true. How had he failed to acknowledge that?

"I knew I was falling in love with John, but I was afraid to tell you. I should have the moment the doubt started creeping in. That was my mistake. Waiting until the last minute was cruel, and I feel terrible, but I felt like I had to go through with our marriage because everyone expected it of me. I'm sorry I wasn't honest with you sooner. I embarrassed us both."

He shook his head. "Wow. I never expected to hear you say this."

"I should have months ago, but I was a coward." She took another deep breath. "Sara Ann invited me to visit her quilt booth at the market, but she didn't mention you had a booth. Then when John and I were there, she pointed it out, telling us

311

you're very successful. We both turned and saw you there, your back to us." Her lower lip trembled. "I made excuses to Sara Ann, and we hurriedly left. Later John encouraged me to talk to you, to make things as right as I could. I finally got up the courage this week, and that's the real reason we're here today."

Her shoulders shuddered. "Can you forgive me?"

He didn't even have to think about it. "Of course I forgive you, Ella."

"*Danki.* You deserve happiness, and if you don't have it yet, I hope you find it soon." She smiled at him and then looked over her shoulder. "I need to go. Take care, Jeff."

"You too." Jeff nodded, and she walked away.

He glanced toward the house where Christiana still stood talking to Kathy, and he smiled. He did deserve happiness, and he was almost certain he'd found it in Christiana.

Christiana sat in a rocking chair on Jeff's parents' porch later that afternoon. A gentle breeze sent the colorful flowers in his mother's garden swaying as if moving to music only they could hear. She took in the brilliant colors of the daffodils, peonies, zinnias, daylilies, and gaillardias and silently marveled at God's glorious creation of this beautiful summer day.

She smiled as she lifted a mug of root beer and looked out toward Jeff's house sitting across the field. She studied the two-story, whitewashed home with its welcoming wraparound porch and large windows. She tried to imagine Jeff living there all alone. The house seemed to call for a family, to beg for one.

"Have you had a *gut* day?" Jeff asked as he rocked beside her.

She turned her attention toward him and nodded. "I have. Your family is *wunderbaar.*"

She smiled as she recalled eating lunch with Kathy, Renae, and Joyce and then visiting with Jeff's family and Kathy again when they arrived here. The afternoon had been perfect. She talked about recipes with Joyce and Kathy, and then she'd laughed as Merle and Nick shared funny stories about Jeff's childhood.

Christiana felt so comfortable with Jeff's family. It was as if she belonged there.

"*Ya,* they're okay," Jeff said, joking. "I can tell they like you too."

"I'm so glad." She looked over at his house again. "Your *haus* is so *schee.* I love the porch."

"Danki." He smiled, and his smile was warm and sweet.

Christiana longed to tell him that she'd seen Ella and that Joyce had pointed out John while they were delivering the noon meal, but she was concerned that bringing up his ex-fiancée might dampen the mood.

"Ella and John were at the service today," Jeff said before taking a drink of his root beer.

Christiana spun toward him. "You saw them?"

He nodded. "I did."

"Kathy and your *mamm* pointed them out to me."

"Oh." He set his mug on the small table between them. "It was actually *gut* to see them."

"Why?" She waited for his pleasant expression to morph into a frown. But to her surprise, it never clouded.

"For the first time, I didn't get upset when I saw Ella. I realized today that I'm truly over her."

"Really?" Christiana asked, and he nodded. "I'm so glad to hear that."

"Ella surprised me."

"What do you mean?"

"When I was waiting for you at my buggy, she came over and apologized for hurting me. She said she should have told me months sooner that she was having doubts. She told me I was a *gut* man and deserved happiness, and she begged me to forgive her."

"What did you say?"

"I said I forgive her." He set his mug on one arm of the rocking chair. "I wasn't expecting an apology from her, but I'm ready to move on."

"That's *wunderbaar*. I'm so glad to hear it." She pointed across the field. "And I'm glad you didn't give your *haus* away."

"I am too." He threaded his fingers with hers, sending heat roaring up her arm. "It's nice to have you here today."

Their eyes met, and her heartbeat stuttered. She could see a future together. Could he see one too?

"This was a perfect day," Christiana said when Jeff halted the horse by her back porch later. "*Danki* for asking me to spend it with you and your family."

He looked over at her, taking in her beautiful profile. "We'll have to do this again soon."

"*Ya.* Would you like to come to church with me next time? Then you can meet more of my family too."

315

"That would be fantastic."

He reached over and ran his fingertip down her cheek, and she shivered under his touch. "*Danki,* Christy," he began, his voice husky, "for all you've done for me."

"What have I done?" she whispered, her eyes wide.

"You've shown me that I'm worthy of finding someone new. You've shown me that I don't have to give up on the dream of filling *mei haus* with love and laughter." He moved his fingers down to her neck. "And you've shown me that my breakup with Ella doesn't have to define me. I don't have to hold on to that grief for the rest of my life. You inspired me to forgive her today. *Danki* for showing me that I'm strong enough to move on."

"Of course you are. It's not your fault that she chose John. Instead, it gave you the opportunity to choose a different path. I'm certain God is guiding you down the road he's chosen for you."

"I believe that now, and I owe that to you. I'm grateful God led you to open your booth, grateful he led you to me." He grinned. "And I'm glad you spilled that *kaffi* on me too."

She chuckled.

"I'm so thankful for you, Christy. I can't

tell you how much."

"I'm thankful for you, too, Jeff."

"Promise me that you'll give our relation-ship a chance to keep growing."

"I promise."

"I'm ready to be more than your *freind,* if you're ready."

She nodded. "I am. Are you ready to talk to *mei dat*?"

"*Ya.* You let me know when you think the time is right."

"What if I ask him if you can bring me home after the market closes one evening? Then you can talk to him and stay for sup-per. What do you think?"

"I love that idea." *And I think I love you.* And then without thinking, he leaned down and brushed his lips across her cheek. She sucked in a breath at his touch.

He turned her face and placed a hand on her shoulder, and then he kissed her. The contact sent liquid heat shooting from his head to his toes.

"I can't wait to see you again," he whis-pered against her cheek.

"I can't wait either." Her voice trembled.

He gently pulled away. *"Gut nacht."*

"Gut nacht."

She climbed out of the buggy and hurried up the porch steps, turning to wave before disappearing into the house.

As Jeff guided the horse toward the road, he smiled. Soon Christiana would be his girlfriend, and before long they could be planning their future together.

21

"What a nice surprise," Christiana announced as her parents and Phoebe stepped into the Bake Shop Thursday afternoon just as the last customer was leaving following a rush. "What brings you to the market today?"

"Your *dat* finished a job early, so he thought we could come by and visit you." *Mamm* walked around the booth, taking in all of her selections. "Everything looks so nice."

"*Ya,* it does." *Dat* scanned the booth. "You did a *gut* job setting it up."

"*Danki.*" Christiana smiled as Daisy sauntered into her booth. "Have you ever met the market's resident cat?"

Mamm laughed. "Who is this?"

"This is Daisy," Phoebe said. "Most of the vendors keep food for her." She looked down. "Would you like something to eat, Daisy?" She beckoned for the purring creature to follow her to the counter.

Daisy meowed and then skipped along behind Phoebe.

Christiana walked to the cookie shelves. *"Dat."* She waved him over. "Would you like some of your favorites — oatmeal raisin?"

"Ya, that sounds *appeditlich."* He pulled out his wallet. "How much?"

"Oh stop." She waved off his money and handed him a bag of cookies. "Enjoy."

"Danki." He took the bag and then looked up at the ceiling as he sniffed. "Is something burning?"

"No, I just put a sheet of chocolate chip *kichlin* in the oven, but they're not burning." Christiana snapped her fingers. "Oh wait. That's Jeff's burnishing machine next door. He uses it to cut leather for the leather goods he sells."

"His machine smells so strongly that you can smell it here?" *Dat* asked, his expression serious.

"Ya. You can even smell it down at the Coffee Corner sometimes."

"Doesn't it bother you?" *Dat* asked, concern filling his eyes.

"Nope." Christiana shook her head. "When I first met him, I thought maybe the market was on fire, but now I know it's just his machine."

"Huh." *Dat* rubbed his beard and looked toward her booth exit. "That would concern me very much. I'm surprised no one has reported it to the fire department."

"We all know it's just Jeff's machine."

She decided this might be a good time to ask her father about the next step she and Jeff wanted to take. She already knew Jeff had no plans tonight. "By the way, *Dat,* could he give me a ride home today and stay for supper?"

"I want to talk to him before I agree to that."

"Sure, but why?" Christiana wondered why her father's expression looked so grim. He'd seemed to accept Jeff when they met last Sunday.

"I want to learn more about this machine that smells like it's on fire. It concerns me that it's located next to your booth." *Dat* turned as a group of six older *English* ladies came into the Bake Shop.

"Hello." Christiana plastered a smile on her face. "How are you today?"

"We're great," one lady announced.

"We're on a mission for whoopie pies," another lady called.

"You got that right, Norma," another one said before turning to Christiana. "The young lady at the Coffee Corner said you

321

have the best whoopie pies in Lancaster County."

"That's a nice compliment to receive." Christiana led the women to the whoopie pie section of her booth. "Which flavors are you looking for?"

"Oh, I haven't met one I didn't like," the first lady said. "Right, Wilma?"

"Right, Clarice."

The women laughed, and Christiana looked up as her mother and Phoebe followed her father out of her booth and toward Jeff's. Her stomach twisted. She hoped Jeff would say the right things and give her father whatever answers he was looking for regarding his machine. If only she could ride home with Jeff, he could ask her father for the permission they needed to date.

If everything went as planned, by tomorrow she'd be Jeff's girlfriend. A smile turned up her lips as excitement skittered through her.

"Which flavors do you recommend?" Norma asked her.

"Vanilla is my favorite, but my customers seem to prefer the red velvet." Christiana pointed to the boxes. "But if you don't want to choose one kind, I have a sampler over here."

"Perfect!" Wilma clapped her hands.

Jeff looked up from the burnishing machine as Freeman, Lynn, and Phoebe stepped into the booth. "Hello there. *Wie geht's?*"

"We're well. How are you?" Lynn asked.

"Great." Jeff removed his safety glasses and then wiped his hands on a red rag as he walked over to them. He held out his hand to Freeman. "How are you, Freeman?"

Freeman shook his hand but pointed to his worktable with his other hand. "It smells like your booth is on fire."

"Oh. That's just my burnishing machine. I use it to cut leather for my gifts."

"Look at the gifts he sells, *Dat.*" Phoebe tapped her father on the arm and pointed. "See? He makes leather bracelets, wallets, and key chains. He also has journal covers. He personalizes them too. And look at his wooden gifts." She pointed to the alphabet trains. "Look at these cute little trains. Christiana says a lot of people buy them as toys for *bopplin.*"

Freeman scanned the booth and nodded before turning his furrowed brow back toward the worktable. "How do you power that burnishing machine?"

323

"I, uh . . . You want to know how I power it?" Jeff swallowed nervously as he studied Freeman's expression and narrowed eyes.

"*Ya.*" Freeman walked toward the worktable. "It's a simple question. Do you use a power inverter, an air compressor, or a car battery?"

Jeff hesitated as dread gripped his shoulders. "I use electricity."

"What?" Freeman's voice rose.

"I do." Jeff swallowed as his body began to tremble.

"You're Old Order Amish, right?" Freeman's tone challenged him. Thank goodness his voice hadn't risen again, but he had grown more intense.

"I am."

"Then how do you justify using electricity to make items to sell?" Freeman gestured around the booth. "I imagine you make a decent living selling these fancy gifts to *Englishers.*"

"My gifts are not fancy. They're simple and handmade." Jeff worked to keep his tone even as his temper flared. He couldn't afford to argue with Christiana's father, no matter what he said.

"Do you make a *gut* profit?" Freeman stood tall in front of Jeff.

"I do okay."

"But you use electricity to make them." He pointed at the machine. "Does your bishop know you use electricity to make these items?"

"He does. And this market is owned by an *Englisher,* Freeman. I don't own it."

"What difference does that make?"

"These are electric lights." Jeff pointed above him. "The market also has smoke detectors, a sprinkler system, and electric doors. This is not an Amish business." He pointed to the booth exit. "Bethany uses electricity to power her coffeepots, her oven, and her cash register."

"Bethany is not *mei dochder,*" Freeman said.

"And I'm not your *sohn.*" Jeff pinched the bridge of his nose when he realized what he'd said. He'd just disrespected the father of the woman for whom he cared. Why did he so often manage to say the wrong words! "Look, Freeman, I'm using electricity here only to make my job easier and faster. I don't use it at home. I use a power inverter at home."

"It's wrong." Freeman turned toward Lynn and Phoebe, who looked on with their eyes wide. "I've seen enough. Let's go."

"Freeman, wait!" Jeff rushed after him. "I'm Amish. I'm not committing any sin."

Freeman faced him. "That's your business, but you will not involve *mei dochder* in your *Englisher* ways." Then he marched toward Christiana's booth.

"Please don't say that." Jeff started after him as his veins froze in fear.

Phoebe walked over to him and held up her hand. "Wait, Jeff."

"I think I just lost my chance with your *schweschder.*" Jeff groaned and cupped his hand to his head. "I can't believe I did that. I was planning on asking for his permission to date her. What am I going to do now?"

"Don't worry about it." Phoebe peeked over her shoulder and then looked back at him, lowering her voice. "I'll ask if I can stay and help Christiana. After my parents leave, we'll work out a plan for her to win *Dat* over. Don't worry."

"All right, if you say so. Please tell her I'm sorry."

"I will." Phoebe gave him a weak smile. "Don't lose hope."

"Danki."

But as Phoebe walked away, Jeff felt his heart crumbling. He was going to lose Christiana before he even had a chance to date her, to call her his girlfriend. He needed help, and only God could provide that help. He closed his eyes and sent up a silent prayer.

Please, God. Soften Freeman's heart toward me. I can't lose Christiana. I need her in my life. Please pave the way for us.

Christiana's smile faltered as her parents walked back into her booth with frowns lining their faces. Their bleak expressions sent a mixture of trepidation and anguish through her, and as the group of ladies left, she was glad the market seemed unusually quiet.

"Did you sell a lot of whoopie pies?" *Mamm*'s smile looked forced.

"I sold five sampler boxes." Christiana divided a look between her parents, taking in her father's frown and her mother's wobbling smile. "Did you talk to Jeff?"

"I did." *Dat* crossed his arms over his chest. "You will not be riding home with him tonight."

Christiana felt tears pricking the corners of her eyes. "Why not, *Dat*?"

"We'll discuss it later." *Dat* turned to *Mamm*. "Let's go, Lynn."

"Wait." Christiana grabbed her father's arm. "Please tell me. Why am I not allowed to get a ride from him? You approved of him on Sunday." She glanced at her mother for support, but *Mamm* looked down at the

327

floor. "Why did you change your mind, *Dat*? I don't understand."

"I said we'll discuss this later, in private." *Dat* enunciated each word as if Christiana were four years old. "We're going home now." He looked over his shoulder. "Phoebe, we're leaving."

Phoebe came to stand beside Christiana, looking determined. "I'd like to stay and help Christiana."

Dat studied her. "Why?"

"Because I enjoy helping *mei schweschder* when the shop's busy." Phoebe's smile was too bright as she touched Christiana's arm, and she hoped her father didn't realize the booth was devoid of customers for a change. "I'll come home with her, okay?"

"Let her stay, Freeman," *Mamm*'s voice pleaded. "Please."

Christiana looked at each of her family members, taking in their strained expressions. Her heart sank. Something had happened in Jeff's booth, and she was determined to find out what before she went home. She balled her hands into fists as she awaited her father's verdict on whether her sister could stay.

Just then a young couple who looked like tourists stepped into her booth.

Christiana turned toward them and forced

her lips into a smile. "Hello. How are you?" Her voice squeaked with anxiety. "May I help you find something?"

"Hello," the woman said. "We're looking for shoofly pies."

"The pies are over there." Christiana pointed toward the other side of the booth. "I'll be right there to help you."

"Thank you," the woman said.

"Let Phoebe stay, Freeman," *Mamm* repeated, her voice low and determined.

"Fine." *Dat* pointed his fierce expression at Christiana. "You come right home when the market closes tonight. You have my driver bring you home. We'll talk then."

"Ya, Dat." Christiana's shoulders sagged.

With a curt nod, her father walked out of the booth. *Mamm* gave Christiana a sad look and then trailed after him.

Christiana turned to her sister and whispered, "What on earth happened in Jeff's booth?"

Phoebe placed her hand on Christiana's forearm and leaned in close. "I'll tell you everything after these people leave." She nodded toward the customers who were looking over the pies. "Go help them."

Christiana rubbed at a tense muscle in her neck as she sat on a stool at her counter.

The couple was gone, buying nearly all of her shoofly pies plus a raspberry angel food cake. "So *Dat* is upset because Jeff uses electricity to make his leather gifts? That's why he won't let me ride home with him?"

Phoebe gave her a solemn nod. "He was outraged, Christiana. I was stunned. Jeff tried to justify it by saying that the market is owned by an *Englisher* and that Bethany uses electricity in her booth."

"But that didn't help?"

"No, it didn't." Jeff appeared behind Phoebe, his handsome face twisted with a deep frown. "I'm so sorry, Christy. I tried to smooth it over, but everything I said was wrong."

"Christy?" Phoebe divided a look between them. "He calls you Christy?"

Christiana shook her head, ignoring her sister's question. "*Mei dat* was determined that I not use electricity when I moved my business here, but I never realized he would care that the man I liked used it." She looked at Phoebe. "Did you stay to warn me?"

"*Ya.* And I wanted to help you come up with a plan to change *Dat*'s mind."

Christiana looked at Jeff. "Can you convert your machine to operate with an air compressor or maybe a power inverter?"

"Ya." Jeff nodded. "Would that help?"

"Maybe." Christiana looked at Phoebe. "Do you have any other suggestions for how to convince *Dat*?"

Phoebe shrugged. "Tell him how you feel. Convince him that Jeff is the one and maybe he'll listen."

"What if I take you home tonight?" Jeff offered. "I could apologize and tell him that I'll do anything to win back his confidence."

"No," Christiana and Phoebe said in unison, and Jeff winced.

"I'm sorry, but he specifically told me that I can't accept a ride from you," Christiana said. "He doesn't want me to bring you to the *haus.*"

"I'll be there when you talk to *Dat,*" Phoebe said.

"But if you try to defend me, you'll be in trouble too. You know how he gets when he's made a decision." Christiana rubbed her temple where a headache began to throb. "*Mamm* doesn't even go against him, so it's not a *gut* idea for you to try." She smiled at her younger sister. "But I appreciate how you support me. It means a lot."

"I'm rooting for you two." Phoebe gave them a bleak smile. "I want to see you together."

Christiana looked at Jeff as her dream of

being his girlfriend started to dissolve. In the back of her mind, she worried that she'd lost him before they even had a chance.

22

Christiana's body shook like a leaf in a hurricane as she and Phoebe pushed the baker's racks up the ramp her father had built off the back porch. She halted by the back door.

"Everything will be fine," Phoebe insisted for the twentieth time since they'd left the market, but Christiana was certain her sister was wrong. Nothing would be okay, because *Dat* was going to forbid her from seeing Jeff ever again. She knew her father too well to believe otherwise. Once *Dat* made up his mind, there was no discussing the subject any further.

"Just tell *Dat* that Jeff already said he'd stop using electricity," Phoebe continued. "I'll back you up."

"That's as *gut* a plan as any," Christiana said. She squared her shoulders and walked through the mudroom to the kitchen, where her father and mother already sat at the table.

Christiana took a deep breath before addressing her parents. "What do you want to discuss, *Dat?*" She tried to mask the tremble in her voice.

"I assume your *schweschder* already told you."

Christiana looked at Phoebe, who gave her a reassuring nod, and then turned back to *Dat.* "Phoebe told me you were upset because Jeff uses electricity in his booth."

"That's putting it mildly." *Dat*'s voice rose. "I'm furious you would be interested in a man who uses electricity at all. You know it's forbidden in our culture."

"*Ya,* but he uses it only at the market." Christiana pointed to her chest as frustration gripped her. "I work there, too, and I use the electric lights to see when I'm working." She pointed to her sister. "Phoebe has *freinden* who work at a bakery that's owned by an *Englisher.* They use the ovens and the electric cash register to do their jobs. They even have air-conditioning in the summer. How is that different?"

"It's very different." *Dat* stood. "Jeff uses electricity to make goods to sell. He's using the *Englisher* ways to make a profit. That's the start of a dangerous road." He began counting off a list on his fingers. "Soon he'll install electricity in his home, and then he'll wear fancy clothes. Then he'll get a driver's license and drive a car. I can't risk allowing *mei dochder* to be exposed to that."

"Are you kidding?" Christiana searched her father's eyes for any sign of a joke. "You can't be serious."

"I'm very serious."

"Bethany uses electricity to run her coffeepots, and she doesn't dress *English* or drive a car. She's just as Amish as we are." Christiana's voice rose as her body shook. "Why aren't you accusing Bethany of being too *English*?"

Dat wagged a finger at her. "Bethany has nothing to do with this. I'm concerned only about you, and you are not to see this man again."

"But he's Amish just like us." She gestured around the kitchen as anger thickened her voice. "He lives in an Amish home he built himself. He doesn't have electricity or fancy items. His *haus* looks just like ours, only it isn't brick."

"You've been in his *haus*?" *Dat*'s voice boomed. "Alone?"

"No. When I was at his parents' *haus* after church on Sunday, I could see his from their back porch. He comes from a traditional Amish home. He's never given me any indication he's unhappy with his life or that

335

he wants to leave the church."

"Trust me," *Dat* said. "This is only the beginning. Now that he's had a taste of the *Englisher* life, he *will* eventually leave the church. If I allow you to see him, he'll try to take you with him."

"No, *Dat.*" She nearly yelled the words. "I know Jeff, and he isn't interested in leaving the faith. We've spent a lot of time together during the past couple of months. We've eaten lunch together, and we talk about everything from our families to our hopes and dreams. I feel like I know him well."

Christiana spoke quickly, her words tripping over one another. "He wants to stay Amish. In fact, he wants to date me. We care about each other, and we both want to be Amish. We both are faithful to the church, and we wouldn't risk our beliefs for anything."

"You will *not* date him." *Dat* pointed toward the back door, as if Jeff were on the back porch, waiting to whisk her away.

"But I want to," she insisted, her voice growing thin. "I care about him, and he cares about me. You can't forbid me from seeing him."

"*Ya,* I can, and you will not defy me." *Dat*'s voice rose again. "You are to stay away from him. No more lunches together. No visits at all. Your relationship with him is over as of right now. Do you understand?"

"Please, no." Christiana shook her head as her eyes filled with furious tears. "You have to listen to me." She folded her hands as in a plea. "Jeff understands that you disapprove of his use of electricity. He told Phoebe and me that he'll stop using it to win your favor. Right, Phoebe?" She turned to her sister, who nodded with such vigor that the ties from her prayer covering bounced off her shoulders. "He'll convert to a power inverter or even use an air compressor at the market."

"No." *Dat* shook his head. "Jeff has already exposed himself to another way. It's too late."

"Please be reasonable, *Dat.*" Christiana held out her hands as tears spilled down her cheeks. "Why don't you give him a chance to prove himself? Let him convert to another method of powering his machine and then let him visit us. He can come to church with us next Sunday and then visit our home. He can spend the afternoon here, and you can talk to him more. If you get to know him, *Dat,* you'll really like him. *Mamm* already likes him. She was there when he helped us set up my booth on the first day. He even caught Chester before he fell when he was trying to hang a sign. Then he taught Chester how to fix the shelves in my booth. He's a *gut,* solid Christian man."

Christiana looked to her mother for help. "Right, *Mamm?* You like him. Won't *Dat* like him?"

Mamm's eyes widened, and she shook her head as if warning Christiana to not push her father any further.

"Christiana!" *Dat*'s voice echoed in the large kitchen, and she jumped. "I already told you. You will *not* see him. No more discussion."

A sob broke free from Christiana's throat. Her hands trembled as she held them up. "Please, *Dat.* I care for him. I think I may even be falling in love with him."

Mamm covered her face with her hands, and Phoebe rubbed Christiana's shoulder.

"You can't do this to me," Christiana said, pleading. "I've finally found a man who cares about me. I can see myself building a future with him. I care deeply for him. I feel as if God sent me to the market to meet him. I don't know if *Mamm* told you about Jeff losing his fiancée, but I've helped him deal with that. He's made me realize that I'm worthy of a future too. You can't just tell me —"

"*Ya,* I *can* tell you what to do, and I *am*

telling you what to do." *Dat* seemed to growl. "You are *mei dochder,* and it's my job to protect you from the *English* world. This is why I didn't want you to go to the market in the first place! I wanted to shield you from members of our community who say they're Amish and then fall into the ways of the world."

"He *is* Amish." She heard a meekness in her voice as she wiped away her tears.

"He's not a real Amish man! Real Amish men do not use electricity!" *Dat* bellowed.

"That's not true." Christiana shook her head. "*Onkel* Lamar is our bishop, and he has never told Salina that she can't have a booth at the market. He allows his *dochder* to be there, just like he allows Leanna and Bethany to keep their booths there."

"Christiana, this discussion is over," *Dat* said.

"But it can't be," Christiana said, fighting a sob.

Phoebe handed Christiana a paper napkin, and Christiana wiped her eyes and nose as she tried to control her emotions.

"You will not see Jeff again. If you do, I will forbid you from going to the market at all. Is that clear?"

"*Ya, Dat,*" Christiana nearly whispered.

"*Gut.*" *Dat* turned to *Mamm.* "Let's eat. I

339

have work to do in the barn tonight."

Christiana's heart crumbled as she helped her mother and sister deliver fried chicken, noodles, and green beans to the table. With her stomach in knots, she forced herself to eat a few bites as her parents talked about mundane events of the day. She couldn't understand how her *dat* could carry on as though he hadn't just ruined the only chance at love she'd ever had.

When the meal was over, *Dat* disappeared outside. Christiana's head pounded as she helped clear the table and then started washing dishes. As her sister wiped down the table and her mother swept the floor, the large kitchen was quiet except for the familiar sounds of their work.

Mamm finally broke through the silence as Christiana washed the last serving platter. "Your *daed* only wants what's best for you. He has your best interest in mind."

Christiana dropped a dish back into the sink and spun to face her mother. "But he's breaking my heart. I'm falling in love with Jeff. He's a *gut,* Christian man, and he cares about me. He's not breaking any rules by using electricity at the market. Just like I'm not breaking any rules working there. Why can't *Dat* see that?" She tossed the green pad she'd held into the hot water and even with wet hands hugged her arms to her chest as if to shield her aching heart.

"Your *dat* has his reasons," *Mamm* said.

"What are they?" Christiana asked, demanding an answer. "None of this makes sense! Bethany uses electricity in her booth, but *Dat* refused to answer me when I mentioned it."

"He's not worried about Bethany." *Mamm* pointed at Christiana. "He's worried about you."

"But you know me. I've never done anything that would put me in jeopardy of being shunned or embarrassing you and *Dat*. Why doesn't he trust me?"

Mamm shook her head. "You know I can't go against your *dat*. My hands are tied."

"What am I going to do?" Christiana covered her face with her hands as fresh tears flowed down her cheeks.

"Shh," *Mamm* whispered as she pulled Christiana into a hug. "*Ach, mei liewe.* Everything will be okay. Your heart will repair itself. You'll meet someone new and forget all about Jeff. God has the perfect plan for each of us, and if he intends for you to marry — and I believe he does — he'll lead you to your future husband."

"How do you know it's not Jeff?" Christiana stepped out of her mother's embrace.

"How do you know Jeff isn't the one and *Dat* is making a big mistake?"

"You can't doubt your *dat*. He takes *gut* care of us." *Mamm* returned to sweeping the floor. "He's never led us astray, so you need to accept his decision."

Christiana gritted her teeth. If *Dat* knew what was best for her, why did she feel like she was drowning in grief?

Letting go of Jeff wouldn't hurt so much if it were the right thing to do.

Later that evening, Christiana sat on her bed and tried to read the Christian novel she'd started last week. But after reading the same paragraph several times, she still couldn't comprehend the meaning.

Her thoughts were tangled, and her grief nearly choked her. How could she say good-bye to Jeff? How could she even consider finding someone new when he had carved out a piece of her heart?

"How are you feeling?"

Christiana looked up at her sister, who stood in the doorway clad in a pink night-gown. Her thick, light-brown hair hung in waves to her small waist.

"I don't know." Christiana's voice was hoarse from crying. She'd taken a shower and then curled up on her bed and cried until she'd run out of tears. "I'm so angry and *bedauerlich* and distraught. I don't know how I'm going to say good-bye to Jeff tomorrow. He's important to me." She looked down at the cover of the book. "I care for him more than I've cared for any other man."

Phoebe stepped into the room and perched on the edge of Christiana's bed. "Did you mean it when you said you think you love him?"

"*Ya,* of course. I wouldn't lie about that." New tears burned at the back of her eyes.

Phoebe looked toward the doorway and then back at Christiana. "Remember last night when *Dat* read from the book of Isaiah during devotionals?"

Christiana nodded. *"Ya."*

"I keep thinking about that one verse. I think it went, 'The Lord will guide you always; he will satisfy your needs in a sun-scorched land and will strengthen your frame. You will be like a well-watered garden, like a spring whose waters never fail.' "

Phoebe took Christiana's hand in hers. "God will take care of your broken heart. Just ask him to help you through this. He will, and I will too."

Christiana sniffed and then rested her

cheek on Phoebe's slight shoulder for a moment. "How did I wind up with such an amazing little *schweschder*?" she asked as she straightened.

Phoebe shrugged as her lips twitched. "Well, I think you're just very blessed."

Christiana chuckled despite her broken heart. She had lost Jeff, but she still had her precious Phoebe. If only their relationship could be enough to sustain her for a lifetime.

Bethany's eyes widened as Christiana sat with her cousins in the Coffee Corner the following morning. "I had no idea your *dat* was that strict."

Salina turned toward Christiana. "I'm so sorry that he forbade you from seeing Jeff." She touched her chin. "Do you think it would help if *mei dat* talked to him? After all, he's the bishop."

"*Danki,* but no." Christiana shook her head. "He said the discussion is over. And when he says it's over, he means it."

"Why is he so afraid you'll leave the faith?" Leanna asked. "You've never been rebellious. You didn't even want to go camping with your youth group back when you were eighteen."

"And you missed a super-fun weekend," Salina said, reminding her. "Seriously, that would be so out of character for you. None of us has ever said we wanted to leave the faith. We were all baptized with our youth group. We never second-guessed the church."

"I know." Christiana stared down at her coffee as her lips trembled. She had to control her emotions. She would not cry again today.

"If only Jeff could do something to prove that he's not going to corrupt you." Bethany tapped her finger against her lower lip. "It really wasn't *gut* enough that he offered to stop using electricity?"

"No." Christiana shook her head. "*Dat* said since Jeff has had even that little taste of the world, he'll move on to other things, like fancy clothes and cars."

"That's ridiculous." Leanna shook her head. "So many Amish work in stores with electricity, and they don't leave the faith."

"That's what I said, but he told me I had to stay away from Jeff and abide by his rules. If I don't, he'll make me leave the market and go back to my bake stand at the *haus.* I can't lose my booth. It means too much to me." Christiana sniffed. "I just don't know how I'm going to say good-bye to Jeff."

"*Ach,* I'm so sorry." Salina rubbed Christiana's back. "I know you care about him. If only there was something we could do to change his mind."

"But what?" Leanna looked up at the ceiling as if it held the answer to Christiana's problems. "What if Jeff went by the *haus* to talk to him?"

"No." Christiana shook her head. "He's not welcome there. *Dat* made that clear. He wants me to meet someone else, but I only want to be with Jeff."

"You don't just care about him," Bethany said. "You care about him *a lot.*"

"Ya." Christiana gave her a watery smile. "I'm falling in love with him."

Her cousins gasped in unison, and Christiana looked down at the table as she wiped her eyes. Sadness squeezed at her lungs.

"Hey. Christiana." Salina tapped her shoulder. "Someone is here to see you."

Christiana looked up as Jeff stepped into the Coffee Corner. Her stomach seemed to sink and fresh tears threatened as his eyes searched hers.

"Christy," he said as he approached the table. "Can we go somewhere private to talk?"

"Ya." Christiana picked up her cup of coffee and divided a look among her cousins. "I need to go."

"Be strong," Salina whispered as Christiana followed Jeff out of the booth.

23

Panic crashed through Jeff as he led Christiana out to the far end of the parking lot under a large oak tree. The tears now streaming down her beautiful face were breaking his heart.

"Please tell me what happened when you got home last night." He worked to keep his voice even despite the worry that made him feel ill.

"I can't see you anymore." Her voice had thickened. "*Mei dat* has forbidden it. I can't be your *freind,* and it's killing me." She sniffed and wiped at her eyes with the back of her hand.

"I don't understand. He won't even let us be *freinden?*" Jeff took a step toward her, but she backed away.

"Please don't make this harder. *Mei dat* was furious when I got home." She explained what he'd said.

"But I'd never leave the faith! Didn't you

tell him I'll stop using the electricity immediately?" He searched her eyes for any trace of hope, but he found none. His chest constricted as if someone were tightening a rubber band around it.

"I did, but he said it was too late. He said if someone has already experienced the *English* ways, there's no going back." She told him how she used the example of other Amish working for *Englisher* businesses, but nothing convinced her father that Jeff wouldn't leave the church. "I tried, Jeff. I truly did. I asked him if you could go to church with us and then come visit. I told him he would approve of you if he gave you a chance and spent time with you."

"And he still wouldn't give an inch?"

"No." She sniffed. "He said I have to stay away from you and that I'll meet another man."

Jeff gritted his teeth as jealousy walked up his spine as if on spider legs.

She took a deep, shuddering breath. "And I told him . . . I told him . . ." More tears fell.

"What, Christy?" He wiped away her tears with the tips of his fingers. "What did you tell him?"

"I told him I'm falling in love with you,

but he wouldn't listen to me. It didn't matter."

Jeff froze at her words. *She loves me. She loves me. She loves me!*

"I can't do this." She took a step back. "I have to go. I'm so sorry, Jeff. I'll miss you."

Before Jeff could respond, Christiana took off, running across the parking lot, the ties from her prayer covering fluttering behind her. He stared after her as what she'd said echoed in his mind. Christiana loved him, but the door to their future had closed — now, after his heart had finally begun to heal. How would he ever recover?

I'm falling in love with you too.

Jeff knocked on the front door of the two-bedroom *daadihaus* on Lewis's father's property later that evening. He jammed his hands into his pockets and rocked back on his heels as he waited.

The screen door wrenched open, and Lewis's dark eyes widened as he peered out.

"Jeff, hi." His brow furrowed. "I wasn't expecting to see you this evening."

"I'm sorry for just stopping by. Are you alone?"

"Ya." Lewis opened the door wide. "Come in. What's going on?"

"I have a problem. I need your advice."

Lewis frowned. "It sounds serious." He pointed toward the table. "Have a seat."

"*Danki.* It is serious."

"Do you like chicken potpie?"

"I love it. I didn't know you cooked." Jeff sat down at the table.

"I don't, but *mei mamm* loves me." Lewis gave Jeff his signature grin as he opened the oven and took out two chicken potpies on a cookie sheet. "*Mei mamm* makes them ahead of time and freezes them. I was feeling hungry tonight, so I made two. I'm also feeling generous, though. I'll let you have one."

"*Danki.*"

Lewis brought the potpies to the table, and after a silent prayer, they began to eat.

"Tell me what's going on," Lewis said.

Jeff told his best friend about the last two days, hoping a brilliant idea for how to improve his situation would come to mind as he recounted them. But nothing new occurred to him.

Lewis put down his fork, and his lips pressed together in a flat line as he listened.

"So today I learned that Christiana loves me, but she's forbidden from seeing me," Jeff concluded. "I can't even be her *freind.* I tried to talk to her again before we left for the evening, but she told me to have a nice night and hurried off. I can't believe that the day I find out she loves me is also the day I find out I can't even have conversation with her anymore."

Lewis clicked his tongue and shook his head.

"Please say something," Jeff said, begging him. "I feel like I'm going out of my mind."

"I'm stunned, and I don't understand Freeman's view at all. Renae's *schweschder* works at a store that has electricity, and she's still Amish. The bishop approves because the business is owned by an *Englisher.* That's how it is." Lewis picked up his fork and dug into the potpie's flaky crust. "I think Freeman is completely wrong." He took a bite and chewed.

"I agree." Jeff leaned forward, desperation boiling in his gut. "How can I fix this? Please tell me what to do. Give me some advice that can help me get Christiana back."

"That's a tough one." Lewis picked up his glass of water and took a drink. "Freeman is determined to keep you two apart, so I honestly don't know how to help."

Jeff groaned as he looked down at his uneaten potpie. His appetite had dissolved as he told his story.

"You should eat that," Lewis said. "I

promise you won't find a better potpie in all of Lancaster County."

Jeff stared at the pie as his thoughts spun with the memory of Christiana's sad face. "I don't know how to go on without her."

"You love her."

"Ya." Jeff looked over at Lewis, who smiled. "Why are you smiling?"

"I'm *froh* that you finally got over Ella and found someone else. That's a big step forward for you."

"But now I'm heartbroken because I can't be with the *maedel* I love." Jeff held up his hand. "Help me fix this."

"Well . . ." Lewis wiped his mouth with a paper napkin. "Stop using electricity at the market, let things settle down for a month or so, and then go see her *daed.* Try to explain that your intentions are *gut* and genuine. Promise him that you'll stay Amish. Tell him you love his *dochder* and you'd never hurt her."

Jeff nodded as he considered the idea. "That sounds *gut,* but how do I stay away from her for that long?" Trepidation pressed down on his shoulders.

"You don't have a choice." Lewis pointed his fork at Jeff. "We just have to figure out how to convince her *dat* to let you back into her life."

353

Jeff stared out a window as anguish punched him in his gut, sending an ache throughout his body. He had no idea how he would carry on at the market every day without Christiana's friendship, but worse, how was he going to convince Freeman to give him another shot?

"Hey, Jeff!"

Jeff stopped climbing his back steps and turned as Nick hurried up the path to his house. "What are you doing here?"

"I was looking for you." Nick pointed toward their parents' house. "*Mamm* thought you were going to join us for supper tonight. She was worried about you. We all were."

"I went to see Lewis after I left the market." Jeff unlocked his back door and pushed it open.

Nick ascended the steps. "You look upset. Is something wrong?"

Jeff snorted. "You could say that."

"Did something happen with Christiana?"

"*Ya.* It sure did. In fact, a lot happened." Jeff sighed as he stepped into the mudroom and hung his straw hat on the peg by the door.

"Did you break up?"

"Not exactly. I never even got an opportunity to date her."

"Uh, I'm confused. Didn't you get the chance to talk with her *daed*?" Nick followed him into the kitchen.

Jeff set his lantern on the table and then leaned back against the counter. "No. He's forbidden her to see me."

"Why?" Nick took a step back as he put his hands on his hips. "What could you have possibly done to make him do that?"

"I used electricity at work." As Jeff explained what happened, his brother listened wide-eyed. "I went to see Lewis when I left the market to get his advice."

"What did he say?"

Jeff ran his hand down the stubble on his chin. "He suggested I convert to a power inverter at the market, wait a month or so, and then go see Christiana's *daed* and ask for another chance."

"Do you think that will work?"

"I doubt it." Jeff crossed his arms over his chest. "I have no idea what to do." He paused and looked down at the floor. "She told me she loves me today. I love her too. But now I'm stuck. I can't see her, and it's killing me." He looked at his brother's shocked expression. "Can you offer me any advice?"

"Wow." Nick sank down onto a kitchen

chair. "I'm just stunned."

"Because of what happened? Or because I admitted I love her? Never mind. Either way, that makes two of us. Yesterday I was planning to visit her *daed* to ask his permission to date her. Now I'm not welcome in his *haus.*"

"This is so ridiculous," Nick said. "Did she tell him our bishop approves of your working at the market and using electricity?"

"I think so."

"That's what you can tell him." Nick stood again. "You can take Lewis's advice and then go see him. Tell him you converted to using a power inverter. When he says you're already a sinner, tell him our bishop approves of using some electricity when working for *Englishers.* If he's a reasonable man, he'll allow you to date Christiana." His expression relaxed. "Just give him some time to calm down."

"I don't know. Christiana says his mind is made up. I doubt he even cares that some bishops allow the use of electricity at *English* businesses, including his own brother-in-law. She told me her *daed* was strict, but now I see he's more than strict. He's set in his ways and unbending."

"But doesn't he want his *kinner* to be

froh?" Nick asked. "*Mamm* and *Dat* always told us to work hard, stay in the church, and be *froh*. Why would Freeman deny his *dochder* happiness? You're both baptized into the church. You're both living the Plain life. Isn't that what our parents pray for us to do?"

"I thought so." Jeff detected a thread of desperation in his voice. "I've been trying to figure this out all day." He rubbed at an ache in his chest. "I don't understand why God would lead me to Christiana and then take her away. It doesn't make any sense." His eyes burned, and he struggled to keep his emotions under control. "I feel like I've lost her forever, and it scares me."

"Don't give up." Nick patted his arm. "Trust God. Pray that Freeman will realize he's made a mistake."

"I will." Jeff would send up the most fervent prayers he'd ever prayed, begging the Lord to bring Christiana back to him.

"Did you talk to your *dat* about Jeff again last night?" Salina's question was gentle as Christiana sat with her cousins in the Coffee Corner the following morning.

"No." Christiana's voice was soft as she absently folded a napkin over and over until it was a small square. "He made it clear that

357

there's no room for debate, so I said very little to him."

"Did your *mamm* say anything?" Bethany asked. "*Aenti* Lynn is so sweet and supportive. Did she offer to talk to your *dat* for you?"

"No." Christiana tried to clear her thickening throat. "She always says his decisions are final." She pressed her lips together as renewed frustration boiled in her stomach. If only her *mamm* would just once stand up to her *daed*. She sighed. This wasn't *Mamm*'s fault. It was *Dat*'s fault for being so stubborn.

"What happened after you and Jeff left here together yesterday morning?" Leanna asked. "We all wanted to come see you later, but none of us could get away."

Bethany and Salina both nodded.

Christiana unfolded the napkin. "I told him I can't see him anymore. Then I avoided him all day because I don't know what else to do." How it hurt her heart to stay away from Jeff, but she had to obey her father's rules if she wanted to keep her booth at the market. She didn't want to lose the opportunity to at least see Jeff from afar. Just knowing he was there gave her comfort. She also didn't want to give up her time with her cousins. Their talks helped her make it through the day.

She didn't want to lose her precious booth for another reason too. After spending years under her father's strict roof, she considered her booth her one place of freedom, her place of purpose. It was hers, all hers. It was where she connected with the community and shared her special baked goods. She dreaded the thought of going back to her roadside stand after building up this place of solace and happiness.

When she felt something soft rub against her leg, Christiana looked down at Daisy. The gray tabby blinked at her. She smiled at the cat, despite her overwhelming sadness.

"I'm sorry." Salina's expression was kind. "I know Jeff means a lot to you."

"*Ya.*" Christiana gave her a weak smile. "He always will."

She looked toward the entrance to the Coffee Corner just as Jeff walked in, and her breathing paused as she took in the sadness in his eyes. She felt as if her heart was shattering bit by bit as she stared at him. How was she supposed to see him at the market and not be reminded of what she'd lost? It was too much. She had to leave before threatening sobs choked her.

"I need to go," Christiana told her cousins

as she stood up. She headed for the exit, and as she moved past Jeff, she whispered, *"Gude mariye."*

"Christy. Wait." He reached for her arm, but she slipped by him, picking up speed.

Jeff's hope deflated like a balloon quickly losing its air as Christiana moved past him. He'd hoped to have a minute to talk to her, but she'd rushed off without giving him the opportunity to say a word.

He'd spent hours pouring his heart out to God before he fell asleep last night, and he was certain he would carve out a path for them. All Jeff had wanted this morning was to tell Christiana how much he loved her and what he planned to do about her father.

"Hi, Jeff." Bethany gave him a wide smile. "Come sit with us. I'll get your *kaffi* and donut. I made pecan-flavored *kaffi* today. I think you'll like it." If only he could have an ounce of her enthusiasm and positivity. She tapped the table before moving to the counter. "Have a seat right here."

"Okay." Jeff looked over at Salina and Leanna.

Salina waved him over. "We want to talk to you."

Jeff hopped up on the stool Christiana had

been sitting on. If only she were beside him now.

"How are you?" Leanna said in earnest.

"I'm not sure." Jeff rested his elbows on the table. "I'm still in shock."

"Christiana is too." Salina looked grim. "She's heartbroken."

"I just don't understand Freeman," Jeff said. "How is using electricity in a market the same as being shunned? Surely your whole family doesn't believe that" — he pointed toward the counter where Bethany poured coffee — "because Bethany uses electricity here."

"No, our whole family doesn't believe that," Leanna said. "Most of our family members believe it's okay to use electricity if you work for an *Englisher*. And Salina's *dat* is our bishop."

"It's just not okay to use it at home," Salina added.

"Exactly." Jeff pushed his hands through his curls. "I just don't see how Freeman's beliefs are so far afield."

Bethany approached the table and handed him his cup of coffee and a donut. He pulled out his wallet.

"Put that away. It's on the *haus* today." Bethany smiled.

"*Danki.*" He took a sip of the coffee. "I

went by to see my best *freind* after I left here last night, and then I talked to *mei bruder.*" He shared what Lewis suggested to win over Freeman. "Do you think that will work? You all know him better than I do." He searched their faces for any sign of hope.

"It might." Bethany seemed to be forcing her smile. "I think giving him time to cool down is definitely a *gut* plan."

"I do too," Leanna said. "And converting to another kind of power will show him that you're serious."

"But . . ." He divided a look among them. "You're all hesitating. Tell me what you truly think."

Leanna's expression warmed. "I can tell you love Christiana, and she loves you too. I think it's important that neither of you give up."

"Exactly." Bethany nodded vigorously. "Have faith. Ask God to guide *Onkel* Freeman's heart."

Jeff nodded. Only God could close this great chasm between Christiana and him. He knew that for sure.

24

The next week Christiana tried to concentrate on the church service, but her thoughts kept swirling. Her eyes betrayed her and frequently focused on the unmarried men section of the congregation. She imagined Jeff sitting there, smiling at her while they enjoyed the service together.

But Jeff wasn't here with her today at the Bontrager family's farm. He wasn't welcome because of her father. And the last week had been one of the most difficult of her life.

Christiana stared down at her white apron and the skirt of her yellow dress as the minister continued to talk about the book of Mark. She sniffed as anguish filled her chest.

She reached into her apron pocket and fiddled with the key chain Jeff had given her. She had kept it with her every day since he'd placed it in her hand, and she planned to keep it as a reminder of their friendship and her love for him. It was the only piece of him she had left.

"You okay?" Salina's soft voice was next to her ear.

Christiana nodded, afraid her tears would spill if she spoke.

"Everything will be okay. I promise you." Salina touched her back.

Oh, how Christiana wanted to believe her cousin. But how could anything ever be okay again if her father refused to believe Jeff was a good man?

Christiana did her best to concentrate on the remainder of the service. After the last hymn, she walked toward the house to help serve the noon meal with her cousins.

"Christiana!"

Christiana turned as *Mammi* came toward her, limping a little. "Hi, *Mammi.* Is your knee bothering you today?"

"It's a little sore. *Danki* for asking, sweetie, but I'm fine. I'm just worried about you."

"What do you mean?" Christiana's body trembled. What did *Mammi* know about Jeff?

"Would you take a walk with me so we can talk?" *Mammi* nodded toward the Bontragers' pasture. "Why don't we take a stroll along the pasture fence?"

Oh no. Is she going to lecture me? What has Mamm *told her?*

Christiana forced a smile as her hands trembled. She couldn't take another round of accusations about how Jeff would convince her to leave the Amish.

"Of course, *Mammi*," she said. "That sounds nice." She folded her hands and fell into step with her grandmother. "How are you today?"

"I already told you I'm fine. I want to talk about you." When they reached the fence, *Mammi* touched Christiana's arm and turned toward her. "You looked so *bedauerlich* during the service that it almost made me cry." She cupped her hand to Christiana's cheek. "What's going on, *mei liewe*?"

Christiana studied her grandmother's blue eyes, which reminded her of her mother's and sister's. Maybe she didn't know about Jeff and her father's directive to avoid him. "You don't already know?"

"Don't know what, dear?"

"*Mei mamm* didn't tell you about Jeff Stoltzfus?"

"Who's that?" *Mammi* smiled. "Is he the handsome man at the marketplace your cousins told me about? Is he your new boyfriend?"

Christiana shook her head and leaned forward over the split rail fence. She looked out toward the horses frolicking happily in the field. How would it feel to be free like those horses, trotting around without a care in the world?

"Christiana?" *Mammi* touched her shoulder. "Do you want to tell me what's bothering you?"

Christiana turned toward her. "You're right. Jeff is the handsome man I met at the market. We had become *gut freinden,* and I really care about him, but *mei dat* won't let me see him anymore."

"Why?" *Mammi*'s eyes seemed to fill with concern.

"At the market, he uses electricity to run a machine that cuts leather for the leather gifts he makes to sell. *Dat* said I can't see him because Jeff will influence me to leave the church. He thinks he'll go from using electricity at the market to using it at home, driving a car, and leaving the church." Christiana's voice quavered. "It doesn't make any sense. Bethany uses electricity at the market, and *Onkel* Lamar doesn't forbid it. Why does *Dat* believe Jeff would lead me away from the church just because he uses electricity?"

"I'm so sorry." *Mammi*'s expression was sympathetic. "Your *dat* is a little more overprotective than your *onkels* are."

"But he's even more overprotective than

our bishop, *Mammi.* Do you know why?"

Mammi looked past her toward the horses.

Christiana gasped. "You *do* know something. What is it?"

Mammi pressed her lips together. "I'm guessing your parents never told you about your *onkel* Aquilla."

"Who?" Christiana scrunched her nose. Was *Mammi* getting confused in her old age?

"He was your *dat*'s older *bruder.*"

"Dat was an only *kind."* *Mammi was* getting confused.

"No, *mei liewe,* he had a *bruder* who was ten years older than he was."

Christiana's eyes widened. "Then why have I never heard of him? What happened to him?"

"He was a brick mason like your *dat.* He worked with your *daadi,* just as your *dat* did when he was old enough. He got an offer to work for an *Englisher* and make more money. Your *daadi* didn't want him to go, but Aquilla took the job. I think he was about twenty years old. Then Aquilla started abandoning his Amish ways. He started dressing *English* and got involved with an *English* woman."

Christiana gasped. "Did he leave the Amish church?"

"*Ya,* he did." *Mammi* frowned. "Your *daadi*

367

and *mammi* tried to convince him to stay. They reminded him that he was baptized, and that if he left, he would be shunned. They begged him not to go. They offered to build him a *haus.* They tried everything they could to get him to come back to the faith, but he left the community when he was twenty-two or twenty-three."

"And what happened then?" Christiana hung on her *mammi*'s every word.

Mammi's eyes grew sad. "Not long after, he died."

"What?" Christiana cupped her hand to her mouth. "How?"

"He was found with drugs in his system. He overdosed, but they don't know if he took his own life or if it was accidental. Your grandparents were devastated. In fact, they never got over losing him. He was only twenty-five."

"Oh, *Mammi.*" Christiana wiped at her wet eyes with her hand. "I had no idea. I always believed *mei dat* was an only child. I had no idea I had another *onkel.*"

"I think it was too painful for your grand-parents and your *dat* to talk about him. Your *dat* told your *daadi* and me the story one night when he was dating your *mamm.* But he never mentioned it again after that." *Mammi* rubbed Christiana's shoulder. "Do you understand now why your *dat* is so strict with you?"

"I do." Christiana pulled a tissue out of her pocket and wiped her eyes and nose. "Now it makes more sense. I always wondered why he was so leery of *Englishers.* He doesn't want to lose me to the *English* world like he lost his *bruder.*"

"Exactly."

"But I'm not his *bruder,*" Christiana said. "I'm loyal to my church, and Jeff is too. Jeff has never said he's interested in leaving. How can I convince *mei dat* that he's misjudging both Jeff and me? That we aren't in danger of abandoning our faith?"

Mammi shook her head. "I don't know. It's not my place to tell your *dat* what to do."

"But I love Jeff, *Mammi.*" Christiana's voice cracked. "I believe God sent me to the market to minister to him and help him learn to trust again after his fiancée broke his heart last year. We've come such a long way in our friendship. How can I give up on him now?"

Mammi clicked her tongue. "I can pray for you, but I cannot change your *daed*'s mind. You could try talking to your *mamm.*"

Christiana shook her head in disappointment. "*Mamm* never goes against *Dat.* She says he's the head of the household and she'll obey whatever he decides."

"She learned that from me." *Mammi* smiled. "But a *fraa* has a way of talking to her husband and sharing how she feels. If you talk to your *mamm,* maybe she'll be willing to try to soften your *dat*'s heart. He might be more apt to listen to her because she won't seem as disrespectful as he might think you do when you disagree with him."

A tiny glimmer of hope took root in Christiana's soul. *"Danki, Mammi."* She wrapped her arms around her grandmother and hugged her. *"Danki* so much for talking to me today."

"Gern gschehne." Mammi squeezed Christiana's hand. "We'd better get back to the kitchen before your cousins send out a search party."

As Christiana walked with her grandmother toward the house, her mind swirled with thoughts of her father and his older brother, whom she'd never known. She'd rarely considered what her parents experienced before they were married and had children. Her father had a whole life she never knew existed! Now she understood his overprotectiveness, but she needed to convince her mother to help her change his mind. She'd pray for the right words and approach *Mamm* when the time was right.

"*Mamm?*" Christiana tapped on her mother's open bedroom door later that evening. "Do you have a few minutes to talk?" Her heart hammered so hard she was certain *Mamm* could hear it.

She'd waited all day for this perfect opportunity. While *Mamm* relaxed on her bed reading, *Dat* was outside checking on their animals and Phoebe was in the shower. Christiana guessed she had a half hour to talk to her mother alone before anyone interrupted them.

"Of course." *Mamm* set her reading glasses on the bedside table and placed her book beside them. "What's on your mind?"

"I spoke to *Mammi* today, and she told me an interesting story."

"Oh?" *Mamm*'s expression was bright as she pointed to the bed. "Have a seat and tell me."

Christiana sank down on the corner of the bed. "She told me about *Onkel* Aquilla."

Mamm's eyes rounded as she looked at the doorway and then back at Christiana. "Why did she tell you that story?"

"Because I told her how *Dat* feels about Jeff. Why did you never tell me I had an *on-*

kel I'd never met?"

Mamm lowered her voice. "Your *dat* doesn't like to discuss it. It's his story to tell, not mine."

"But *Onkel* Aquilla is the reason *Dat* is so overprotective of Phoebe and me?"

Mamm nodded. "*Ya*, and I don't blame him. We don't want to lose either of you. We don't want you to leave the faith, and we certainly don't want you to experience the world the way Aquilla did." Her expression became grave. "A parent should never have to bury a *kind.*" She clicked her tongue as her blue eyes sparkled with unshed tears.

"I know, but you can trust me. I'm not Aquilla. I'm not interested in dressing like an *Englisher* or dating an *Englisher.* I'd also never abandon the faith. I think I've shown you that I'm trustworthy."

"Now, Christiana" — *Mamm* lifted her chin — "I don't like your tone. I'm not going to go against your *daed.* You know that. If he says you can't date Jeff, it's not my place to go against him. His word is final."

Christiana nodded and took a deep, trembling breath. "I'm only asking you to listen to me. Please." She took one of her mother's hands. "I love Jeff. I'm heartbroken that I can't be with him. I feel in my heart that I belong with him. Didn't you feel that way

372

when you met *Dat*?"

Mamm gave her a solemn nod and withdrew her hand to smooth a wrinkle in her dress. "I did feel that way."

"Then why can't you at least try to talk to *Dat* for me? Tell him that I'm trustworthy and that I would never do anything to deliberately disappoint you or disrespect the church in any way. Tell him he should give Jeff a chance to prove that he's not a bad influence. Remind *Dat* that Jeff isn't Aquilla."

Mamm studied her, and Christiana shifted under her stare. "Did your *mammi* tell you to say that to me?"

"No." Christiana shook her head "*Mammi* suggested that I talk to you, but she didn't tell me what to say."

Mamm shook her head. "Leave it to *mei mutter* and her advice."

"She's a very *schmaert* woman."

"*Ya,* she sure is." *Mamm* touched Christiana's shoulder. "I don't know if I can convince him to give Jeff another chance, but I'll try my best. You must give me time to choose the right moment to talk to him. And you need to understand that my efforts might completely fail. All I can do is try."

"That's all I ask. *Danki.*" As Christiana hugged her mother, she closed her eyes and silently prayed.

Lord, danki *for my family.* Danki *for blessing me with a* wunderbaar mamm *and* mammi. *Please give* Mamm *the right words to convince* Dat *to give Jeff another chance so I can be with him. And please bless Jeff and keep him safe.*

25

"Gude mariye." Christiana gave Jeff a little wave and a sheepish smile as she walked past his booth carrying a cup of coffee that Thursday morning.

"Gude mariye." His pulse sped up as it did every morning when she walked past him in the market. "It's a *schee* day, isn't it?"

"Ya, it is." She tossed the words over her shoulder as she continued to her booth. "It's hot out already. It certainly feels like August."

"It does," he called after her. "Have a *gut* day."

His shoulders slumped as she disappeared into her booth. He'd hoped and prayed she'd come into his booth one morning and announce that her father had agreed to give him a second chance. But for now they were reduced to mundane pleasantries and waves from across the market. How he missed her friendship. He missed their lunchtime talks

375

and the way she gave him a sweet smile that seemed to be meant only for him. He missed her voice, her laugh, her adorable freckles.

As much as it hurt his heart, this morning he'd made his own coffee at home and brought it with him in a thermos. It wasn't nearly as good as Bethany's delicious flavored coffee, but he hoped giving Christiana some space at the Coffee Corner would help her figure out if she wanted to fight for his friendship.

So far, though, the distance had created only more distance, and it was slowly eating away at his soul.

Jeff had kept his promise and converted from using electricity to using a power inverter to run his burnishing machine. And just as Lewis and Nick had suggested, he was going to wait a while before trying to convince Freeman that his love for Christiana was real. He wanted the chance to prove he would love and cherish his daughter and never lead her away from the Amish church.

"Hi, Jeff." Sara Ann stepped into his booth.

"Gude mariye." Jeff worked to keep a smile on his face despite his annoyance. He didn't need her gossip or snide comments today.

"Have you heard anything about a renter for that booth next to yours?" she asked. "I would have thought a new vendor would be in it by now. It's been empty for two weeks."

"No, I haven't."

"Oh." She paused, but only for a second. "Say, I noticed you and Christiana aren't talking much these days, and your lunch dates have stopped. Did you two break up?"

Jeff swallowed a sigh. "We were never officially dating, but we're still *gut freinden.*"

She seemed to study him. "How do you figure that if you don't see each other much?"

"We're both busy." He cleared his throat and gestured toward his workbench. "Speaking of being busy, I have some work to do."

Sara Ann opened her mouth to speak but was cut off by a group of four *English* women chatting loudly as they stood just outside Jeff's booth. When they made eye contact with him, he smiled and nodded.

"Good morning," he said. "Welcome to the Bird-in-Hand market." *Please come interrupt us. Please save me from this awkward conversation!*

"Good morning, son," one of the older women said. Then she turned to her companion and muttered a little too loudly, "Isn't he a handsome young thing?"

"He is," she answered, also loud enough for him to hear.

Jeff felt his cheeks heat, but he continued to smile.

"How are you?" Sara Ann asked the women.

"We're fine," one of the other women said.

"Oh look, girls," the fourth said to her companions. "There's a bake shop. Let's get some whoopie pies."

"You'll have to come to my quilt shop when you leave the bakery," Sara Ann said. "It's right across the aisle."

Sara Ann headed for her booth, and the women started for the Bake Shop. As Jeff watched them, three boys who looked to be around fourteen years old ran into the aisle, nearly knocking into one of the women. As they ran past Jeff, he opened his mouth to warn them, but they were so fast they disappeared around the next corner before he could get out the words. That was all he needed — a customer injured right outside his booth.

Jeff switched on the burnishing machine and began cutting pieces of leather for key chains. Although all his displays were full and he already had extra key chains, the work helped keep his mind off Christiana. At least, that's what he told himself.

Thoughts of her lingered in the back of his mind, haunting him throughout his days and during his dreams at night.

The smell of burning leather filled his lungs, and he relished the familiarity of the scent. This was solace. This was his time to continue praying, asking God to heal his battered soul and bring Christiana back to him.

Please, God. Please convince Freeman I'm gut *enough for his* dochder. *Please bring my precious Christy back into my life.*

"Excuse me," a woman's voice said.

Jeff looked up as a couple about his parents' age stepped into his booth. "Good morning. How may I help you?" He stood.

"We'd like to get a few of your alphabet trains for our grandchildren. Our daughter just had twins a couple of months ago," the woman said as the man beamed beside her.

"What a blessing." Jeff pointed to the shelf with the trains. "What are their names?"

"Your baked goods smell divine," said one of the *English* women who had come into the Bake Shop. After taking in nearly everything Christiana had to offer, she'd finally brought an armful of sampler boxes with cookies to the counter to pay for them. Her friends were still looking.

379

"Thank you." Christiana began to ring up her items.

"Are you baking cookies back there?" The woman pointed to the oven at the back of the booth.

"Yes, I am," Christiana said. "Snicker-doodles."

"They smell divine too." Christiana sensed she was about to say something else. "Say, we saw that handsome young man who runs the booth next door."

"Oh?" Christiana's pulse danced as she recalled Jeff's warm smile this morning.

Oh, how she missed his friendship! She'd found herself itching to pack a big lunch and invite him to join her at the picnic table. She longed to stop by his booth and chat whenever her booth was quiet. She wanted to ask him to give her a ride home.

But she couldn't disobey her father. She couldn't risk losing her booth and the chance to at least see Jeff at the market. So, instead, she relished the few times she was able to see him from afar, wave to him, and memorize his handsome face, attractive smile, and adorable curls.

If only things were different.

"He's quite the looker." The woman's further comment slammed Christiana back to the present.

"He doesn't have a beard, and that means he's single, right?" the woman behind her added.

"*Ya,* that's true." Christiana kept her eyes focused on the cash register to avoid their goofy grins. Most *Englishers* were courteous, but these women's comments were so inappropriate. They looked old enough to be Jeff's mother!

"What's his name?" a third woman asked.

Oh, how Christiana wished she could change the subject! "His name is Jeff."

"Well, if you don't have a boyfriend . . . ," the first woman said, and the other three cackled.

Christiana pushed the ribbons from her prayer covering over her shoulders and tried to ignore her flaming cheeks. Then she gave the first woman her total.

"Do you smell that?" One of the ladies turned around and sniffed the air. "It smells like something's burning."

"Oh, that's just Jeff's burnishing machine." Christiana waved off the comment as she gave the first woman her change. "It smells like that all the time."

"Are you sure?" The woman pointed to the booth exit. "Because I see smoke."

Christiana gasped as she saw smoke in the aisle.

"Jeff!" she screamed as she took off running. "Jeff!"

Her heart pounded against her rib cage as she slid out of her booth and skidded to a halt in front of his. She coughed and coughed, covering her mouth with one hand and fanning the smoke billowing out of his booth with the other. She couldn't see a thing.

"Jeff! Jeff!" she called as icy fear slithered up her spine. "Jeff! Are you there?" Her eyes burned as the smoke swirled around her.

"I'm going to call nine-one-one," she heard someone yell. Christiana turned to see her customers following the crowd heading for the exit.

A fire alarm blared and sprinklers hissed above her, sending cool raindrops spraying down over her prayer covering and face.

"Christiana!" Salina ran up to her and grabbed her arm. "Let's go! We need to get out of here now!"

"No!" Christiana shook her head as her breath came in short bursts. "Jeff could be in there!" She took a step toward his booth, and Salina pulled her back.

"No! We have to get out!" Salina gave Christiana's arm a tug, and Christiana stumbled. "Let's go!"

"I have to find Jeff. I can't leave without

him." Christiana's voice broke as she coughed, and hot tears streamed down her cheeks, dripping onto her apron and dress.

"Come on." Salina pulled Christiana and then stopped when a coughing fit overtook her.

"Go, Salina!" Christiana gave her a nudge. "Get out. I'll come as soon as I find Jeff."

"What are you waiting for?" Sara Ann appeared behind Salina. "Let's go! We need to get out of here before the fire spreads."

"Go with Sara Ann," Christiana told Salina. "I'll be out. I promise."

Salina hesitated, her eyes narrowing. "I won't leave without you."

"You need to get out." Sara Ann started to cough as she walked backward and joined another crowd of customers rushing for the doors, pulling Salina with her.

Voices yelled out, ordering everyone to evacuate as knots of people pushed by.

Christiana hugged her arms to her chest and held back another cough as the smoke cleared just a little. She peeked into the booth, searching for Jeff, but he was nowhere in sight.

Where was he? Was he hurt?

Her body shook as tears stung her eyes. Fear wrapped its fingers around her throat and squeezed as air scraped out of her lungs.

She couldn't lose him!

"Jeff! Jeff!" Her voice sounded too high.

"Christiana!" Jeff appeared beside her, holding a fire extinguisher. "Get out of here!"

"Jeff!" She reached for his arm as a sob escaped her throat. "I thought something had happened to you."

"Go!" He nodded toward the exit. "I'll be fine. Please go."

Christiana spun and rushed out of the market. She weaved through the crowd to the back of the parking lot where her cousins stood huddled together.

"Christiana!" Leanna ran over to her. "Where were you? We were worried sick."

"I was looking for Jeff," Christiana began as a fire engine steered into the parking lot with sirens blasting.

"Did you find him?" Salina asked.

"*Ya.*" Christiana covered her mouth and coughed. "He was getting a fire extinguisher."

"The fire was in his booth?" Leanna asked.

"*Ya.*" Dread filled her. If Jeff had caused the fire, surely that would be the end of his business. She'd never see him again. She leaned against Leanna as more tears filled her eyes.

"Hey." Salina looped her arm over her wet

384

shoulders. "He'll be fine." She pointed toward the back door. "Look! There he is! He's talking to Kent." She put one arm around Christiana's waist. "See? He's okay. We all made it out just fine."

Christiana sniffed. "But if the fire was his fault, he'll have to close his booth, and I'll never see him again."

"Be positive, Christiana," Bethany said. "Have faith that God will work it out."

Jeff was still with Kent. Jeff nodded and pushed his hands through his curls as they both listened to a firefighter. Then Kent gave Jeff a pat on the back before Jeff descended the steps into the parking lot.

Jeff scanned the parking lot, and when his gaze landed on Christiana, her breath caught. He started toward her, and she hugged her arms across her chest.

"He's coming over here," Salina said.

"How about we give them some privacy?" Leanna said. "Come on, Salina and Bethany. Let's go sit at that picnic table."

"Everything will be fine," Salina whispered. She gave Christiana's arm a squeeze as she followed her cousins to the picnic area.

Christiana wiped her eyes with the back of her hand as Jeff approached her.

"Are you okay, Christy?" he asked. "Do

the medics need to check on you?"

She shook her head and squeezed her arms more tightly around her. They were both wet, but she was shivering even under the hot August sun.

"Can we go for a walk?" he said.

"Ya." She followed him to the row of trees that separated the parking lot from the park.

When they reached the trees, he turned to her. "Why didn't you leave the market right away?" His dark eyes seemed to search hers.

"I saw the smoke pouring out of your booth, and I couldn't tell if you were in there. I thought you might be injured, and —" A sob choked off her words. She covered her face with her hands as all the emotions she'd pent up since her father's edict about Jeff came flowing out in shuddering waves.

"Hey. It's okay." He rubbed her arm.

"No, it's not," she managed to say. "I miss you."

"I miss you too." His face clouded with a deep frown. "You have no idea how much." His voice was hoarse, and she knew it wasn't just from the smoke he'd inhaled. "I miss you every second of every day."

He opened his arms to her, and she stepped inside them.

Resting her head on his damp shoulder, she breathed in the scent of wood, leather, and soap despite the odor of burning wood that clung to his clothes. Her eyes filled once again, and then the tears spilled over. He rubbed her back, and she felt safe and secure surrounded by his warmth.

If only she could stay in his arms forever.

"I'm here," he muttered into her prayer covering. "I'm not going anywhere." His voice sent a tremor through her entire body.

She closed her eyes as her tears subsided. "I'm so thankful you're okay."

"I'm thankful you're okay too."

She took a step back as she pulled a tissue from her apron pocket and wiped away her tears. "Did the fire start in your booth?"

"I don't know, but I hope not. I thought I saw flames . . ." His expression changed. "Listen, the fire marshal will investigate, and thanks to the sprinklers in the ceiling and what I was able to do with the extinguisher, the fire didn't spread too far. I think most of the damage was contained to my booth. Everyone else's stock should be all right, depending on any smoke damage, of course. I hope Sara Ann's quilts are all right."

He blew out a deep breath and looked back toward the market. "This could be my fault. I converted to a power inverter a few weeks ago, and it hasn't given me any problems. But I don't think I turned off the burnishing machine when a couple of customers came in not long before —"

"Wait a minute." She held up her hand. "You converted to a power inverter?"

"*Ya.*" He nodded.

"Why?" She took a step toward him as her pulse fluttered.

"Why do you think?" He cupped her face in his hands. "I did it for you. I was going to wait a while and then ask your *dat* to reconsider his decision about me."

He moved his thumbs down her cheeks, sending a thrill zinging over her skin. "*Ich liebe dich,* Christy, and I want to be with you. I've learned so much from you. You've taught me to believe in myself and to have patience with others and myself. You've shown me how to forgive and that love is worth the risk of getting hurt. You're the reason I was able to move past what Ella did and get on with my life.

"But it's more than that. I love you more than I ever loved Ella. I'm certain you're my future. You're the one God has chosen for me, and I'll do anything to prove to your *dat* that I have no intentions of leaving the church and that I'm devoted to our Amish ways."

"I love you too," she whispered as his

precious words wrapped around her heart. "And I've learned from you too. You've shown me that being stubborn and judgmental didn't allow me to give you the chance you deserved. We all make mistakes, and we all need grace. I believe you're the one God intends for me. I'm praying *mei dat* will see how much you mean to me and that our relationship is meant to be."

He brushed his lips across hers, sending her stomach into a wild swirl. She closed her eyes and savored the sensation of his warm mouth on hers.

"I'm sorry this happened." He shook his head. "This is all a big mess, and it's my fault. If I hadn't brought my burnishing machine to the market, your *dat* wouldn't have forbidden you from seeing me. Worse, maybe we wouldn't have had a fire just now."

"Shh." Christiana touched his shoulder. "None of it is your fault. We'll find a way forward."

"Do you think I should visit your *dat*?"

Christiana nodded. "*Ya,* I do. I asked *mei mamm* to talk with him, and she agreed. But I don't know if she's had the opportunity. Let me find out if the time is right. I'll talk to her, and then I'll let you know."

"Sounds *gut*." He squeezed her hand. "I have to go talk to Kent again as well as the fire marshal, if he's arrived. I'll talk to you later."

Christiana's heart took on wings as she returned to her cousins. As soon as she got home, she was going to check with her mother to see if her prayers had been answered.

26

"Christiana!" *Mamm* announced as she stepped into the kitchen. "You're home early."

Phoebe set a bowl of chicken salad on the table in front of *Dat* and then glanced at the clock. "It's only noon. Is everything all right? You look kind of . . . wrinkled?"

Christiana set her tote bag on the floor and started washing her hands. "I'm fine, but we had a fire at the market. Everyone is okay, though. I just got wet when the sprinklers in the ceiling kicked on."

"A fire?" *Dat* asked. "What happened?"

"We're not sure yet, but the fire marshal is investigating. The market is closed until the investigation is complete and some repairs are done, so I'll be home until then." She grabbed four glasses from the cabinet.

"Are you all right?" *Dat* asked as she set the glasses on the table. It occurred to her that he wasn't usually home this time of day on a Thursday, but maybe she just didn't remember he was taking the day off.

"I'm fine. It was a small fire contained to one booth. Everyone got out of the market safely. No one was hurt."

"What a blessing." *Mamm* set a bag of chips in the center of the table as Phoebe placed a basket of rolls there.

"Sit down and we'll eat," *Dat* said.

Christiana took her usual seat across from Phoebe and bowed her head in prayer.

Lord, please bless this food. Please bless my words as I talk to Mamm *about Jeff later today. Please keep Jeff strong during the fire investigation. And please soften* Dat's *heart toward Jeff so we can be together.*

After the prayers, they all began to build their chicken salad sandwiches.

Phoebe scrunched her nose as she picked up the pitcher of water she'd brought to the table. "Phew, Christiana. You smell like smoke. You should go change."

Dat turned his gaze toward Christiana. "Where did you say the fire started?"

Christiana chewed a bite of her sandwich and stared at her father. She was glad he was home. Now was her chance to tell him Jeff no longer used electricity at the market. But would that news start an argument at the table? Was she mentally prepared for that? Despite the comfort Jeff had given her, her nerves were still raw after experiencing the fire.

"Christiana?" *Dat*'s expression filled with concern. "Are you all right?"

"I'm fine." Christiana swallowed and lifted her glass of water. "The fire started near my booth."

"Your booth?" *Dat*'s voice rose. "What do you mean?"

"It might have started in Jeff's booth. We're not sure." Christiana held her breath, waiting for the explosion.

"*Ach* no!" *Mamm* said.

"Is Jeff all right?" Phoebe asked.

"He's fine."

Dat's eyes narrowed. "That man put everyone in the market in jeopardy by using that machine that's powered by electricity." He pointed a finger at her. "I told you he was no *gut*! Not only did he break the church's rules, but he put you in harm's way. You are not going back to that market." He pointed toward the windows. "I'll put your bake stand back out at the road, and you can sell your baked goods there."

"What?" Christiana's stomach seemed to drop. "No, you can't do that. I need to go back to the market. I've built up a customer base, and I enjoy seeing my cousins there.

393

Please don't do this."

"It's too risky for you to be there, and I don't want you to be near that Jeff Stoltzfus." *Dat* picked up his sandwich. "My decision is final." He bit into his sandwich as if he were discussing something as mundane as the weather.

Christiana's body shook as anger exploded in her chest. "You're wrong about him," she said, seething.

"Christiana, don't talk to your *daed* that way." *Mamm*'s warning was almost a whisper.

"You should heed your *mamm*'s words." *Dat* placed his sandwich on his plate. "I'm the head of this family, and I know what's best for you."

Christiana sat up taller. "Jeff is not a bad man. In fact, he's converted his machine to a power inverter to please you. He's willing to do anything to prove to you that he loves me and wants to be with me."

"How do you know this?" *Dat* asked.

"I spoke to him today after we evacuated the building." Her hands trembled, and she gripped the table to try to steady herself. "I was worried about him, and I wanted to make sure he was okay."

"You were told to stay away from him," *Dat* barked.

"I know, and I have stayed away from him. But you need to trust me. And I wish you would trust Jeff. He's not Aquilla."

Mamm gasped as *Dat*'s eyes widened.

"What did you say to me?" *Dat*'s voice boomed to the ceiling.

"I said he's not Aquilla." Her voice was thin and reedy, but her gaze never left her father's.

"Who's Aquilla?" Phoebe divided a look between Christiana and *Dat.*

"Who told you about him?" *Dat* demanded.

"*Mammi.* She told me at church. She asked me why I was upset, and I told her all about Jeff and how you won't let me see him. She said you're overprotective because you don't want Phoebe and me to wind up like Aquilla."

"Who *is* Aquilla?" Phoebe asked again. "Will someone answer me?"

"Shh," *Mamm* told her.

Dat looked so angry. "She had no right to —"

"Actually, she did." Christiana's voice rose as something inside of her shattered despite her father's anger, and her frustration broke free. "I'm upset that you never told Phoebe or me about your *bruder.* We would have liked to know. I'm sorry that you lost him.

395

I'm certain you miss him all the time. But I'm also sorry that what he did ruined your faith in your own *kinner.*"

"You're out of line," *Dat* said.

"No, I'm not." Christiana shook her head as tears traced down her cheek. "I've never given you a reason to distrust me. I've always been a respectful and dutiful *dochder.* I don't want to leave the church. I love my family and my church district. But I also love Jeff, and I want him in my life. It's not fair that what Aquilla did has jaded you forever."

"You have no right to question my rules," *Dat* said, nearly sputtering. "And you have no idea what it's like to lose a sibling. I pray you never do."

Christiana looked at Phoebe as she sniffed and wiped her eyes with a napkin. "Of course I never want to experience that. I love *mei schweschder.*" Then she turned back to *Dat.* "But Jeff is a *gut,* solid Amish man. He loves me, and we want to be together. Please don't judge Jeff because of your *bruder*'s mistakes. Jeff is not going to leave the church and start using drugs."

"That's it, Christiana!" *Dat* pounded his fist on the table, and Christiana, *Mamm,* and Phoebe all jumped. "You are not going to go back to that market, and you are not to see Jeff again."

"Freeman," *Mamm* began, "let's talk about this. I think you're being too harsh. She does have a point about Jeff. She just said he stopped using electricity. Maybe he deserves another chance."

Stunned, Christiana's eyes rounded as she turned to her mother. *Mamm* had finally defended her!

"Lynn, you are not going to go against me."

Mamm sighed. "Christiana needs to at least go back to the market when it reopens to get her things."

"Fine." Then *Dat* turned his attention back to Christiana. "You may go back to get your supplies and close up your booth. Then you will reopen your stand here and never go to the market again." He picked up his sandwich. "Let's eat."

Christiana looked down at her plate, her appetite dissolved. "I'm not hungry." She stood. "I'm going to my room."

Before her family could respond, she hurried out of the kitchen and up the stairs to her bedroom. After closing the door, she changed into fresh clothes and then dropped onto her bed.

Hugging a pillow to her chest, she stared out her window and began to cry. She'd lost

Jeff for good today, and she felt as if she were spiraling into a nightmare.

She closed her eyes as she replayed her conversation and kiss with Jeff by the trees. She'd told him to try again with her father, but that had been a mistake. She had to let him know it would be a waste of time to talk to her father. *Dat* had made up his mind, and there was nothing she could do to change his decision.

Where are you, God? I was certain to the depth of my bones that you had sent me to minister to Jeff. If that's true, then why can't I be with him? Why would you lead me to Jeff and then take him away? I'm confused, and I'm broken. Help me understand and heal my heart —

A knock on her door pulled her from her prayer. She wiped her eyes as the door opened, revealing *Mamm*. She sat up and leaned back against the pillows.

"May I come in?" *Mamm* asked.

"Of course."

Mamm crossed the room and then sat down on the edge of her bed. "I'm sorry." She took Christiana's hand in hers. "You asked me to talk to your *dat,* and I've tried different ways to suggest that he give Jeff a chance. But each time he told me he wouldn't change his mind. I didn't tell you because I didn't want you to give up hope. I wanted to fix this for you because you've been so *bedauerlich.*"

"It's not your fault." Christiana stared down at the log cabin quilt her father's mother had made for her many years ago. "I thought maybe I could convince him that Jeff is a *gut* man when I told him he'd stopped using electricity. Then when *Dat* insisted he was a bad man, I snapped. I never should have brought up Aquilla, but it was just too much. I couldn't take it anymore. Now I've made the whole situation worse."

"But everything you said was true," *Mamm* told her.

Christiana's eyes snapped to her mother's. "You think so?"

"*Ya,* I do. That's why I tried to tell him he's wrong. I'm sorry I let you down again."

"You didn't let me down." Christiana reached over and hugged her mother. "*Danki* for trying, but now I have to figure out how to let Jeff go."

"Don't give up hope, *mei liewe.* Keep praying and trust that God will somehow find a way for you and Jeff to be together."

Jeff guided his horse up the Kurtzes' driveway later that evening. He'd spent all afternoon working on his father's farm and thinking about Christiana. He couldn't get the kiss they'd shared out of his mind. He needed to see her before he went crazy.

He halted the horse at the top of the driveway and then hurried up the back-porch steps. He knocked on the door and then waited, his pulse tripping as he imagined Christiana's beautiful face.

"Jeff?" Christiana asked when she opened the back door. She looked past him as she stepped out onto the porch. "What are you doing here?"

"I had to see you." He smiled. "I just kept thinking that today is the day to talk to your *dat*. I feel confident that he'll listen to me and give me another chance."

"This isn't a *gut* idea." Her grim expression sent a knife slicing through his chest. "You should leave."

"Why?"

"I told *mei dat* about the fire, and when I said it might have started in your booth, he decided it had because you used electricity. I tried explaining that you've converted from electricity, but he wouldn't listen. He said you're a danger to me" — her voice wobbled — "and now I can't even keep my booth at the market. I have to reopen my bake stand here."

"No." He shook his head. "Tell me that's a cruel joke. It can't be true."

"I wish it wasn't true, but it is. I'm so sorry. I'll miss you more than I can say." She looked past him, and her eyes widened. "You need to go."

"No." Jeff looked over his shoulder as Freeman started walking from the barn to the porch. He turned to face him.

"Freeman." He swallowed against his dry throat. "I came to talk to you. I love your *dochder*. Christiana is everything to me, and I want to build a life with her. Please give me your permission to date her. I'll do whatever it takes to convince you I'm worthy of her."

"You have a lot of nerve coming to *mei haus*." Freeman looked furious as he climbed the steps. "You almost burn down the market and put *mei dochder* in harm's way and then think I'm going to give you permission to date her?"

"No one has proven that fire was my fault," Jeff said. "And if they do prove that it was, I'll pay to repair the damage and take my burnishing machine home."

"You are not welcome here." Freeman nearly spat the words at him.

"You're not listening to me." Jeff's voice scraped from his throat. "I want to prove to

401

you that I'm worthy of Christiana." He walked toward him, his body thrumming with desperation.

"A man who breaks the rules of the church is not worthy. Go." Freeman pointed to Jeff's waiting horse and buggy. "Leave now."

"Jeff." Christiana grabbed his arm. "I'm so sorry." Tears raced down her cheeks, and he longed to wipe them away and pull her into his arms.

"It's not your fault." Jeff narrowed his eyes. "I won't give up on you. I promise I will fight for you."

"Jeff," Freeman growled. "Get off my property now."

Jeff turned to Freeman. "This isn't over."

"*Ya,* it is. Now leave." Freeman pointed to the driveway. "Stay away from *mei dochder.*" He turned to Christiana. "Go inside."

"I love you, Jeff," Christiana said before fleeing into the house.

Jeff marched to his buggy as renewed determination surged through his veins. There was no way he would give up now. He was going to get Christiana back. He just had to figure out how.

Jeff spotted lanterns glowing on his father's back porch when he stepped out of his barn later that evening. He headed toward the lights, his parents' faces coming into focus as he approached.

"Jeff." *Mamm* smiled at him. "Where were you so late tonight?"

"I went to see Christiana and her *daed,* but it didn't go well." Jeff climbed the steps and then leaned back against the railing. "Now her *dat* blames me for the fire even though they haven't proved it was my fault. He said I'm a danger to her." Jeff rubbed his throbbing temples. "All I know is that I love Christiana and want to be with her, but I can't if her *daed* forbids it. Now he's forbidding her from having a booth in the market because of me. I might not ever see her again."

"That's outrageous," *Mamm* said. "Why is he doing this to Christiana? If she loves you, he's just making her miserable. How can he do that to his own *kind*?"

"I don't know." Jeff groaned. He felt as if the floor were falling out from under him. Unless he could find a way to convince Freeman he was wrong about him, he'd lost Christiana for good. How could he go on without at least seeing her beautiful face at the market?

"I don't believe the fire was your fault," *Dat* said. "I don't believe the power inverter

403

caught fire."

"I don't either," Jeff said.

"What if you prove that it wasn't your fault?" *Mamm* said. "Would that convince Freeman you're not a danger to Christiana?"

"Maybe. But, of course, that's not the only thing he has against me."

"What do you remember about the fire?" *Dat* asked.

Jeff looked at his father. "It was all so strange. It was as if flames were coming from the booth next door."

"Christiana's booth?" *Mamm* asked.

"No." Jeff shook his head. "The vacant booth on the other side."

"But if it's vacant, how could it catch fire?" *Mamm* asked.

"That's a very *gut* question." Jeff racked his brain, trying to make sense of everything that had happened today.

"Talk to the fire marshal again as soon as possible," *Dat* said. "If he can prove you didn't start the fire, then Freeman will have to admit you aren't a danger to Christiana at the market. Maybe he'll at least let her keep her booth."

Jeff nodded. "I'll do that. *Gut nacht.*" He descended the porch steps as a tiny seed of hope took root in him.

His father called his name as he started down the path toward his house.

"We believe in you. And Christiana does too. Don't give up hope."

"Danki." Jeff smiled. At least he had his parents. Now he just had to convince Freeman to believe in him too.

27

Jeff's hand trembled as he knocked on Kent Dobson's office door the following Saturday morning. He took a deep breath as he awaited the sound of Kent's voice.

"Come in," Kent called.

Jeff stepped into his office, which was located at the back of the market. "I came as soon as I received your message on my father's business phone. You have something to tell me? I decided to see you in person rather than call you back."

"Oh. I'm glad you came, Jeff. Have a seat." Kent sat down behind his desk and gestured to the chair in front of it.

"Thanks." Jeff sank into the chair and removed his straw hat. "What do you have to tell me?"

"I met with the fire marshal earlier, and he gave me the results of his investigation."

"Okay." Jeff absently twirled the hat in his hands. *This is it. He's going to ask me to clear*

406

out my booth.

"The fire started in the vacant booth beside yours."

Jeff stopped twirling his hat and leaned forward. "I know I told him I thought I saw flames coming from that booth, but how is that possible if no one was in there?"

"Matches."

"Matches?" Jeff shook his head. "I don't understand."

"Did you see three boys running around the market the day of the fire?" Kent asked.

Jeff considered the question and then nodded. "I did."

"Well, they found a pack of matches and thought it would be fun to play with them. You'd think they'd be old enough to know better, have better things to do. But they sneaked into that empty booth, and then one of them came up with the brilliant idea to burn a newspaper left in there. Then poof!" Kent held up his hands. "It went up in flames. They dropped it and ran. Later the boy who did it felt guilty and told his father what happened. The father contacted the fire department, and he's agreed to pay for the damages."

Jeff's shoulders relaxed in relief. "I can't believe I didn't hear the commotion, but I'm so glad the boy told his father the truth."

"I am too."

"We should have all the repairs done next week, and I'm still planning to reopen next Thursday." Kent frowned. "You might want to stop by your booth and see how much damage you have. I'll reimburse you for the expense of replenishing any of your inventory and replacing any equipment."

"Thank you." Jeff stood and shook Kent's hand. "I'm so relieved. I didn't think my power converter had caught on fire, but when I got your message, I thought for sure I was going to be blamed. I was afraid you were going to kick me out of the market."

"Not at all. I'm grateful you weren't hurt. You acted quickly when you grabbed that fire extinguisher. You're one of the reasons the fire didn't spread."

"Thank you again. I'll see you next week, Kent."

Jeff stepped out into the hallway and almost walked right into Salina. "I'm so sorry. I didn't see you there." He looked past her, hoping to see Christiana, but Salina was alone.

"It's okay." Salina glanced at the office door. "Were you talking to Kent? I stopped by to find out how soon we can reopen."

"*Ya,* I was talking to Kent." Jeff jammed his thumb toward the office. "He left a message that he had something to tell me. I was afraid he was going to say the fire was my fault, but he just told me it wasn't."

Her expression brightened. "They found out what caused it?"

"*Ya.*" He explained what Kent told him about the fire and then said, "The market should reopen next Thursday."

"That's *wunderbaar.*" Salina clapped her hands.

"*Ya.*" Jeff's thoughts turned to Christiana. "How is Christiana?"

Salina sighed. "She misses you."

"I miss her."

"She's told me about her *dat.*" Salina folded her arms over her chest. "He's always been strict, but I never imagined he'd behave like this."

"Do you know why?"

Salina's expression grew even more serious. "I do now. Christiana found out her *dat* had an older *bruder* she never knew existed. He left the church and died of a drug overdose."

Jeff took a moment to let that sink in. "So Freeman is afraid if I influence Christiana to leave the faith, she could follow the same path?"

"*Ya,* I believe that's it." Salina sighed.

Jeff leaned back against the wall and let

his head smack the concrete. "I never imagined my burnishing machine would cause me to lose the love of my life and be blamed for a fire. You might not know this yet, but I went to see Freeman the evening of the fire. Not only would he not listen, but he blamed me for the fire. He assumed my burnishing machine was to blame. And, of course, I didn't know at the time that it wasn't."

"Oh no. But none of this is your fault, Jeff. *Onkel* Freeman is just inordinately overprotective because of what he and his parents went through when his *bruder* died."

"So how do I fix this?"

Salina rubbed her chin. "I'm going to Christiana's *haus* today. I want to see her, and while I'm there, I'll talk to *Onkel* Freeman. I'll tell him you didn't cause the fire and that you never put anyone in danger."

"Do you think that will help?"

"Maybe?" She shrugged. "It's worth a try. At least he might let her keep her booth."

"*Danki.*" Jeff straightened and pushed his hat back on his head. "Please tell Christiana I miss her and think of her all the time. And tell her that I love her."

"I will." Salina gave him a weak smile. "I'll

do the best I can."

"That's all I can ask."

Christiana stepped onto the porch just as a van pulled up in the driveway. She walked down the steps, wondering who had come.

"Salina!" Christiana rushed down the path and met her cousin as she climbed out of the vehicle. *"Wie geht's?"*

"I'm well. How are you?" Salina gave her a hug.

"Fine. What brings you here today?" Christiana asked as they walked toward her house together.

"I just wanted to visit."

"Oh. Then come inside, and I'll make us tea."

They entered the kitchen together, and Christiana filled the kettle and set it on a burner before pulling out a container of cookies. When she opened the lid and found macadamia nut cookies, her heart twisted. Oh, how she missed taking Jeff's favorite cookies to him.

Christiana pushed the thought away and set the container on the table. "How are your parents?"

"They're well." Salina set down the mugs she'd taken from a cabinet. "Where are your *mamm* and Phoebe?"

"They're upstairs working on a quilt for a customer." Christiana put the sugar bowl and two tea bags on the table. "*Dat* had to go into his office today. He's supposed to be home in a few hours."

"Oh." Salina sat down at the table.

The kettle whistled, and Christiana filled the mugs. Then she sat down across from Salina. Above them, a sewing machine chattered.

Christiana eyed her cousin with suspicion. "It's rare that you come by on a Saturday. Why don't you tell me why you're really here?"

"Josiah came to see me last night, and he asked me to be his girlfriend." Salina smiled as she picked up a cookie and broke it in half.

"That's great." Christiana touched her hand. "I'm so *froh* for you."

"*Danki.*" Salina's smile faded. "But that's not the only reason I came to see you. I stopped by the market today to see when Kent thought we might reopen, and I ran into Jeff."

Christiana stilled, and her heartbeat thudded. "And . . ."

"He had just met with Kent and found out he didn't cause the fire."

Christiana gasped. "He didn't?"

412

"No. Some *buwe* were playing with matches." Salina told her everything she'd learned from Jeff. "And the market will reopen on Thursday."

"That's *wunderbaar.*" Christiana gripped her mug of tea. "I'm so glad Jeff wasn't held responsible."

"He asked me to give you a message."

Christiana braced herself.

"He said he misses you and thinks of you all the time. And he loves you."

Tears pricked Christiana's eyes at the words. "I can't stop thinking about him either."

"I think you need to tell your *dat* that Jeff isn't guilty." Salina leaned forward. "Maybe then he'll see that he's not a bad man."

"It's no use." Christiana wiped her eyes with a paper napkin and cleared her throat. "*Dat* has made his decision. I can't see Jeff, and I can't keep my booth. I guess I'll clean it out on Thursday."

Salina tapped the table with her finger. "But Jeff did nothing wrong. Won't that make your *dat* see he overreacted and at least let you stay at the market?"

"No." Christiana shook her head. "He'd already formed his opinion about Jeff before the fire even happened, and he confessed he never really wanted me to open the booth.

Why would this news change his mind?"

"Change his mind about what?"

Christiana looked up as *Mamm* walked into the kitchen.

"Hi, *Aenti* Lynn." Salina gave her a little wave.

"How are you, Salina?" *Mamm* asked.

"I'm fine, *danki.*"

Mamm sat down next to Christiana and swiped a cookie from the container. "These are *appeditlich.*" Then she divided a look between Christiana and Salina. "What were you two talking about before I interrupted?"

"Salina stopped by the market today and found out the fire wasn't Jeff's fault." Christiana explained what happened. "The market is going to reopen on Thursday. Salina thinks I should tell *Dat* that Jeff didn't cause the fire. She thinks that will convince him Jeff isn't a danger to me and at least let me keep my booth open."

Mamm seemed to be considering that plan as she bit into her cookie.

"Do you think it might work, *Mamm*?" Christiana wanted to believe it would, but deep down, she was sure her father would never bend.

Mamm stared down at her cookie as she chewed, and Christiana slumped back in the chair.

414

"I've failed you," *Mamm* said.

Christiana angled her body toward her mother. "You said that before, and I told you I don't think you have."

Mamm looked up, but before she could speak, Salina stood. "I'll give you two a few minutes alone." Then she stepped into the mudroom, and they heard the back door click shut.

"No, Christiana, I haven't fought for you as hard as I should have," *Mamm* began. "When you asked me about Aquilla, at first I was upset. But the more I think about it, the more I see that your *dat* has always used his *bruder* as an excuse to keep you and Phoebe close to home. He's always been afraid of losing you both, and I never questioned it because I wanted you close too."

Mamm sighed as she pushed the crumbs on the tablecloth around with her fingertip. "Your *dat* is a *gut* man. But he's not just overprotective; he's hurting you." She met Christiana's gaze, and her blue eyes glistened. "I'm sorry for not defending you better."

Christiana searched her mother's eyes. "What are you saying?"

"I'm saying I'll try harder to convince your *dat* that Jeff isn't the enemy. I'll tell him it's time to let you grow up and choose your mate. Jeff is a hard worker who's faithful to the Amish church. And if he makes you *froh,* we shouldn't stand in your way. It isn't our place to stop you from dating him."

Christiana yelped as she hugged her *mamm.* "*Danki. Danki* so much."

"*Gern gschehne.*" *Mamm* touched Christiana's shoulder. "Just give me a few days. I'll have to use some approach I haven't tried before to help him see my point of view."

"I trust you." Christiana smiled, the first true smile she'd had in weeks.

Christiana stepped onto the front porch Wednesday evening and sank into her favorite rocking chair. She breathed in the warm air and took in the brilliant sunset as thoughts of Jeff filled her mind. Tomorrow she was supposed to clean out her booth at the market and say good-bye. The idea of seeing Jeff for the last time filled her with sadness, but she had hope too. For the past few days she'd prayed fervently, asking God to give her mother the right words and to help her father really listen. There was still time.

The screen door opened and clicked shut behind her as *Mamm* appeared with a tray.

"May I join you?"

"Of course." Christiana smiled as her mother handed her one of two cups of tea and then set the tray on the porch floor. *"Danki."*

"Gern gschehne."

They sipped in silence for a few moments while they both looked out toward the pastures. Christiana wanted to ask her mother if she and *Dat* had talked, but she sensed *Mamm* was about to tell her.

"It's a *schee* night," *Mamm* said.

"It is." Christiana turned toward her mother and took in the way her lips formed a flat line. Something was wrong.

"I need to talk to you," *Mamm* said.

"Oh?" Christiana tried to swallow her growing trepidation.

Mamm's sigh seemed to make her shoulders sag. "I've spoken to your *daed* about Jeff."

"And . . ." Christiana held her breath.

"I'm sorry, Christiana, but he refuses to change his mind. He insists that you can't see Jeff or sell your baked goods at the marketplace." *Mamm* placed her hand on top of Christiana's and gave it a gentle squeeze. "I've been praying and asking God for the right words to help you. I'm so very sorry that I couldn't change his mind. I

417

truly did my best."

Christiana nodded as grief consumed her.

"I can't stand to see you so *bedauerlich.* It's breaking my heart, but I can't seem to fix this." *Mamm*'s voice broke as her eyes filled with tears.

"*Danki* for trying," Christiana whispered as her own tears rolled down warm cheeks.

Mamm cleared her throat and handed Christiana some tissues from her pocket. "Are you going to be okay?"

"*Ya.*" Christiana nodded, but her broken heart said otherwise.

Mamm took a long drink of tea and then stood. "I'm going to go back inside. Are you coming?"

"I think I'll sit out here for a few minutes."

Mamm studied her. "Do you want me to stay?"

"No, I'll be fine. I just need a few minutes alone."

"All right. Remember, I'm here if you want to talk." *Mamm* lifted the tray from the floor and stepped into the house. The door clicked shut behind her.

As soon as Christiana was alone, she heaved a deep breath. Then anguish poured from every cell of her body. Burying her face in her hands, she sobbed. Hopelessness overwhelmed her. She'd lost Jeff forever, and she could do nothing about it.

Somehow she had to accept that the man she loved would no longer be a part of her life. But how would her heart ever heal?

Only God could heal her heart. She closed her eyes and begged him for relief.

28

Jeff stepped into his booth the following morning and froze. Freeman Kurtz was standing at his slightly charred worktable. Worry nearly overwhelmed him as he hurried to the back of his booth and set his lunchbox on a stool that still looked sturdy.

"Did something happen? Is Christiana all right?"

"She's fine." Freeman pointed to a stool beside him. "Please, let's both have a seat. I'd like to speak to you if you have a few moments before the market opens."

"*Ya,* of course." Jeff put his lunchbox on the floor and sat down beside him. "What's going on?"

"Let me start at the beginning. *Mei fraa* has been talking to me this week, and one of the things she's made me realize is that I've been wrong about quite a few things, including you."

When Freeman paused, Jeff opened his

mouth, but he couldn't speak.

Freeman picked at a loose piece of wood on the table. "I had a *bruder* who died when I was fifteen years old. His name was Aquilla, and he was ten years older than me. He left the Amish church and wound up with a bad crowd. He died of a drug overdose at twenty-five."

"I'm so sorry."

"*Danki.* When Aquilla died, everything changed." Freeman kept his eyes focused on the table as he spoke. "My parents were never the same, and neither was I. *Mei dat* would go out to the barn at night to be alone, but I caught him crying many times. *Mei mamm* would retreat to her sewing room, but I heard her sobs. The three of us never got over losing *mei bruder.*"

Jeff nodded.

"Lynn made me realize that I've used Aquilla as an excuse to keep our *kinner* close to home. I didn't want Christiana to have a bake stand because I was afraid an *Englisher* might influence her, but Lynn insisted." Freeman touched his beard. "I also didn't want her to come to the market for the same reason. And then she met you."

Jeff swallowed.

"You were a double threat because Christiana fell in love with you, which meant she could get married and leave us. But also, you're more worldly than we are because you use electricity."

Jeff shook his head and opened his mouth to protest, but Freeman held up an index finger.

"Please," Freeman said. "Just let me finish." He paused and took a breath. "I was afraid you would corrupt Christiana and lead her to a life similar to what Aquilla experienced. When Christiana and you tried to dissuade me, I kept thinking of how broken my parents were when he died."

He sat up straight and faced Jeff. "I say Lynn made me realize these things, but the truth is they didn't sink in until last night when I heard Christiana crying out on the front porch. Lynn told me I was punishing Christiana with my own fears, but I didn't understand it until I could hear the heartbreak in *mei dochder*'s sobs. I don't want to be the cause of *mei kind*'s pain. If I do that, I'm hurting her as much as Aquilla hurt us with the choices he made."

The breath stalled in Jeff's lungs.

"So I'm here today to not only apologize to you but to ask for your forgiveness." Freeman's tone shifted to almost pleading. "Will you forgive me for misjudging you and for blaming you for my own fears?"

"*Ya,* of course." Jeff's body thrummed with a mixture of confusion and excitement.

"And if you're still interested in dating Christiana, I give you my blessing."

Jeff gasped as he sat up. "Are you serious?"

"Of course I am."

"I would be honored. *Danki* so much." Jeff shook Freeman's hand as happiness and excitement filtered through him. "Does she know you're here talking to me?"

"No." Freeman shook his head. "No one knows. My family thinks I just left for work early today. I did go there, but then I had one of my employees' drivers bring me here." He stood. "I'm sorry for all the heartache I've caused both you and Christiana. I hope you can find it in your heart to understand my motives, as misguided as they were."

"I do, and I appreciate your honesty."

"*Gut.*" Freeman gave him a curt nod. "You're a *gut,* Christian man. I should have seen that from the start."

"I promise I will cherish Christiana and take *gut* care of her for as long as she'll allow me to be a part of her life."

"I know you will, *sohn.*" Freeman shook his hand again. "I should get to work, but I'd like to talk to *mei dochder* first. She

423

should be in her booth by now."

"To pack up."

"She thinks she's here to pack up, but I'm going to tell her she can stay."

Jeff's heart soared. "I'm glad you made that decision."

"I am too." Freeman smiled. "Have a *gut* day. I'm sure I'll see you soon."

"*Ya,* you will." Jeff couldn't stop a smile.

"And you're welcome at *mei haus.*"

"*Danki.*" The words were like a hymn to Jeff's ears.

Christiana entered the market's back door with a heavy heart. *Mamm* and Phoebe had offered to help her pack up, but she wanted to do it alone. Besides, she didn't want them to see her after she'd said her final good-bye to Jeff. Her sorrow was already difficult for them to bear.

Christiana blinked as she rounded the corner into her aisle. She was almost certain her father was coming out of Jeff's booth, but she had to be imagining the sight. Why would *Dat* be at the market at all, let alone talking to Jeff? He'd arranged for someone else to come uninstall her oven.

But it *was* her father, and her stomach soured. Had he come to give Jeff another lecture about staying away from her? She hoped not. Her heart couldn't take any more arguments about or criticisms of Jeff.

"Hi." *Dat* held his hat in his hands as he approached her. "May I have a word with you?"

"Ya." She led them into her booth and turned to face him. "Why are you here?"

"I came to apologize to you and Jeff. I just left him."

Her eyes narrowed as she studied him. Perhaps she should have her hearing checked. "Did you just say you want to apologize?"

"Ya." His smile was hesitant. "I did."

"Why?"

"I realized that you and your *mamm* have been right all along. I was using what happened to *mei bruder* as an excuse to be overprotective. I was wrong." He frowned. "I was wrong about Jeff, and I was wrong to keep you away from him. I'm sorry for hurting you. You have my permission to date him and to keep your booth here if you'd like to."

His lower lip trembled. "I just hope you can forgive me for the pain I've caused you."

"Oh, *Dat!*" She launched herself into his arms as elation buzzed through her. "You've made me so *froh.* I can't even tell you how thrilled I am."

Dat laughed, but then he grew serious again. "I'm sorry it took me so long to realize that I was hurting you, not protecting you. Your *mamm* has been talking to me this week. I wouldn't listen, but then everything she'd been trying to tell me clicked into place when I heard you crying your heart out on the porch last night. I realized that while I was trying to protect you, I was ruining your life."

"You didn't ruin my life." Christiana smiled up at him. "You've just made me happier than I've ever been."

"I'm so *froh*." *Dat* touched her cheek. "*Danki* for forgiving me. I've told Jeff that he's welcome to date you. I trust you to abide by my rules and the church's rules."

"Of course."

He glanced around the booth. "I guess you do want to keep your business open since it's been flourishing?"

Christiana nodded. "I do. I love the Bake Shop and being here at the market. It means so much to me to have this space to do what I love — share my baked goods as well as spend time with my cousins."

"*Gut.*" *Dat* smiled. "I need to get to work. Did you tell my driver to wait for you to pack up?"

"*Ya.*"

"I'll let him know that you need thirty minutes so you can talk to Jeff before you go home to bake for tomorrow." He gestured toward the back of the booth. "And I'll cancel the call for the men to move your oven back to the *haus*."

"May I ask Jeff to take me home tonight?" she asked.

"*Ya.* I'll see you then." He turned to leave.

"*Dat,*" she called.

"*Ya?*" His eyebrows rose.

"*Danki.*"

"*Gern gschehne, mei liewe.*" *Dat* waved before disappearing around the corner.

Christiana swallowed a happy screech and then hurried into Jeff's booth.

Jeff looked up from his worktable and blessed her with a dazzling smile. "Hi." He stood.

"Hi." She went to him, her heart threatening to beat out of her chest.

"I guess you just talked to your *dat.*"

"I did." She smiled up at him.

"Will you be my girlfriend?" he asked, his smile wide.

"I'd be honored to be your girlfriend."

He closed his eyes and leaned his head back. "I never thought I'd hear those words come from your lips."

"You just did, and it's not a dream."

"I'm so grateful." His voice was husky. He pulled her into his arms and then leaned down and brushed his lips over hers, sending pure joy roaring through every cell of her body. "I love you, Christy."

"I love you too," she whispered before resting her head on his shoulder.

EPILOGUE

"I can't believe Thanksgiving is next week," Christiana said as she sat between Jeff and Salina at the Coffee Corner. "This year is flying by."

"*Ya,* it is." Jeff winked at her as he lifted his cup of coffee and took a sip.

"*Mammi* is hosting again this year, right?" Leanna asked.

"She always does," Bethany sang out with her usual pep. "I love when we all get together at *Mammi*'s *haus.* It's so much fun. I'm grateful to have such a *wunderbaar* extended family."

"I am too." Christiana smiled as she looked at Jeff again. She had so much to be thankful for this year.

She and Jeff had spent a lot of time together, and she relished every minute with him. Not only were they getting to know each other better, but they were getting to know each other's families as well.

They had fallen into an easy routine. Each week they had supper at one of their parents' houses, and they enjoyed talking, laughing, and playing games with their families.

On market days, Jeff picked her up in his buggy, and then they started their morning at the Coffee Corner, visiting with her cousins before they walked to their booths together.

At lunchtime, they ate together at a picnic table, and they took turns bringing lunch. When it was closing time, Jeff helped her clean up and then gave her a ride home.

Christiana was so happy that most days her cheeks ached from smiling. She was so grateful that her father had finally allowed her to date Jeff.

"Well, Christy," Jeff began as he stood, "it's time to get to work." He waved at her cousins. "We'll see you all later."

The women waved and said good-bye as Christiana and Jeff left. He threaded his fingers with hers as they walked side by side, passing Daisy, who lay in a corner of a cardboard box, napping on her back as customers pointed at her and chuckled.

"I need to ask you a question," he said as they approached his booth.

"What?" She smiled up at him.

"Will you be my date at *mei bruder*'s wedding in two weeks?"

"I'd love to. I thought you'd never ask."

"Great." He pulled her into his booth and then cupped his hand to her cheek. "I want to thank you."

"For what?"

"For making me the happiest man on the planet. I've told you this before, but after Ella left me, I thought I'd spend the rest of my life as a *bedauerlich* and lonely bachelor. I was miserable. Then you showed me it's possible to find love after that kind of loss. In fact, I love you in a way I've never loved before. I've realized that God was with me all along. He led me to you, and you're the greatest blessing in my life."

Jeff leaned down, and her breath hitched in her lungs. When his lips brushed hers, she lost herself in his kiss, feeling as if she were floating on a cloud.

When they parted, she saw an intensity in his eyes. "You're the love of my life, Christy. I love you with my whole heart, and I will do my best to always cherish you and make you *froh.*"

She touched his chin. *"Ich liebe dich."*

As Jeff pulled her close for a hug, Christiana felt overwhelming gratitude. God had led her not only to the Bake Shop but to

Jeff and the chance to fall in love. Now he would guide them into their future together, and she silently thanked him for his loving care.

ACKNOWLEDGMENTS

As always, I'm thankful for my loving family, including my mother, Lola Goebelbecker; my husband, Joe; and my sons, Zac and Matt. I'm blessed to have such an awesome and amazing family that puts up with me when I'm stressed out on a book deadline.

Special thanks to my mother and my dear friend Becky Biddy, who graciously read the draft of this book to check for typos. Your friendship is a blessing!

I'm also grateful to my special Amish friend, who patiently answers my endless stream of questions.

Thank you to my wonderful church family at Morning Star Lutheran in Matthews, North Carolina, for your encouragement, prayers, love, and friendship. You all mean so much to my family and me.

Thank you to Zac Weikal and the fabulous members of my Bakery Bunch! I'm so thankful for your friendship and your excitement about my books. You all are amazing!

To my agent, Natasha Kern — I can't thank you enough for your guidance, advice, and friendship. You are a tremendous blessing in my life.

Thank you to my amazing editor, Jocelyn Bailey, for your friendship and guidance. I appreciate how you push me to dig deeper with each book and improve my writing. I've learned so much from you, and I look forward to our future projects together. I also cherish our fun emails and text messages. You are a delight!

I'm grateful to editor Jean Bloom, who helped me polish and refine the story. Jean, you are a master at connecting the dots and filling in the gaps. I'm so thankful that we can continue to work together!

I'm grateful to each and every person at HarperCollins Christian Publishing who helped make this book a reality.

To my readers — thank you for choosing my novels. My books are a blessing in my life for many reasons, including the special friendships I've formed with my readers. Thank you for your email messages, Facebook notes, and letters.

Thank you most of all to God — for giving me the inspiration and the words to glorify you. I'm grateful and humbled you've chosen this path for me.

DISCUSSION QUESTIONS

1. At the beginning of the story, Jeff is still angry and hurt after his fiancée, Ella, broke up with him on their wedding day more than a year earlier. As the story progresses, he's able to forgive Ella and move on. What do you think helped him overcome his hurt and anger?
2. Christiana enjoys spending time with her three favorite cousins. Do you have a special family member you like to spend time with? If so, who is it and why are you close to him or her?
3. Jeff opened his booth at the market to channel his grief after suffering through a painful breakup. Have you ever been through a tough time? If so, what ways did you find to cope?
4. Freeman refuses to allow Christiana to date Jeff when he learns Jeff uses electricity in his booth. Close to the end of the story, he realizes he made a mistake and

asks for Christiana and Jeff's forgiveness. What do you think finally made him realize he'd been wrong in keeping Christiana and Jeff apart? One thing or a combination of things?

5. Lynn realizes she has enabled Freeman's tendency to be overprotective of his children. What do you think made her realize that she needed to step in and defend Christiana? Do you agree or disagree with how she handled the situation?

6. Christiana's grandmother taught her how to bake and inspired her bakery business. Did you learn a special hobby or trade from a family member? If so, what is it?

7. Jeff is afraid to trust Christiana with his heart. He's afraid she'll leave him just like Ella did. Then he realizes he's ready to love again. What do you think caused him to change his point of view on love?

8. Which character do you identify with the most? Which character do you think carries the most emotional stake in the story? Is it Christiana, Jeff, or someone else?

9. Freeman lost his older brother when he was fifteen years old, and he still grieves the loss. Think of a time when you felt lost and alone. Where did you find strength? What Bible verses helped?

10. What did you know about the Amish

before reading this book? What did you learn?

ABOUT THE AUTHOR

Amy Clipston is the award-winning and bestselling author of the Kauffman Amish Bakery, Hearts of Lancaster Grand Hotel, Amish Heirloom, Amish Homestead, and Amish Marketplace series. Her novels have hit multiple bestseller lists including CBD, CBA, and ECPA. Amy holds a degree in communication from Virginia Wesleyan University and works full-time for the City of Charlotte, NC. Amy lives in North Carolina with her husband, two sons, and four spoiled rotten cats.

Visit her online at AmyClipston.com
Facebook: AmyClipstonBooks
Twitter: @AmyClipston
Instagram: @amy_clipston

The employees of Thorndike Press hope you have enjoyed this Large Print book. All our Thorndike, Wheeler, and Kennebec Large Print titles are designed for easy reading, and all our books are made to last. Other Thorndike Press Large Print books are available at your library, through selected bookstores, or directly from us.

For information about titles, please call:
  (800) 223-1244

or visit our website at:
  gale.com/thorndike

To share your comments, please write:
  Publisher
  Thorndike Press
  10 Water St., Suite 310
  Waterville, ME 04901